W.W. ROWE

Nabokov & others:

PATTERNS IN RUSSIAN LITERATURE

ardis

W.W. Rowe

Nabokov and Others: Patterns in Russian Literature

Copyright©1979 by Ardis

Published by Ardis Publishers,
2901 Heatherway,
Ann Arbor, Michigan, 48104.

Library of Congress Catalog Card No.: 79-51639

ISBN 0-88233-335-6

The publishers gratefully acknowledge the permission of New York University Press
to reprint "Gogol's Descriptive Double Image and Its Use in *Dead Souls*" from W.W.
Rowe's *Through Gogol's Looking Glass* (1976).

For Eleanor

The technical preparation of this book was carried out by

William S. Carson
Anne H. Musselman
Nancy C. Startz

as part of an Interim Project sponsored by Macalester College, St. Paul, Minnesota. Ardis gratefully acknowledges Macalester's contribution.

CONTENTS

Like an ice-skater cutting an intricate figure, a major writer may often be tracing patterns, seemingly random or eccentric, around a single, unwavering pivot. His divagations are in fact a constant return.

— *George Steiner*

The writer's art is his real passport. His identity should be immediately recognized by a special pattern or unique coloration.

—*Vladimir Nabokov*

PREFACE

Both Pushkin and Tolstoi have expressed pleased astonishment that their characters can act quite independently, without auctorial manipulation. Nabokov may have a better perspective: his characters, he has claimed, are galley slaves.

An author must ultimately assume full responsibility for ordering his written world. And the ordering is uniquely his, as close inspection reveals. I admit many influences, including New Criticism and Formalism, on the methods employed below; I also realize that textual analysis is not satisfying for everyone. Still, the methods below have probably been applied much less, and less thoroughly, to Russian literature than to various others, especially English.

But what are patterns in literature? And is it worthwhile, or even defensible, to "find" them? Generally I have tried to avoid Intention, yet it is true that the writers discussed below all seem quite interested in the workings of Fate. Pushkin's and Nabokov's concern with fatidic numbers and dates, Gogol's, Tolstoi's, and Dostoevsky's fondness for prophetic dreams and other types of foreshadowing, Lermontov's interest in "testing one's fate"—these and other factors suggest that many patterns examined below exist not merely in the eye of the beholder.

Plots are often patterned. One episode may seem to echo one or more others—creating, for example, what one critic calls "situation rhyme" in Dostoevsky. One event may seem to reverse another—for instance, the hero-heroine and heroine-hero scenes in Pushkin's *Eugene Onegin*. In many different ways, the future may seem anticipated. Techniques range from characters' explicit predictions to hints discernible only in retrospect. Tolstoi favors what I term "unlikely prophets"; Gogol and Nabokov have numerous characters make "unwitting predictions."

11

By still another method, familiar details reappear at key points in the narration. In Nabokov's Humbert's rather extreme formulation: "We all have such fateful objects—it may be a recurrent landscape in one case, a number in another—carefully chosen by the gods to attract events of special significance for us: here shall John always stumble; there shall Jane's heart always break."

Yet patterns may exist with little or no conspiratorial atmosphere. The repetition, or design, may seem totally uncontrived. Especially then, the writer's style is a contributing factor. Virtually any author, I feel, tends to repeat certain phrases and words so as to suggest a pattern or design. And more: similar situations, and emotions, seem to take similar verbal shape. Ideally, a sensitive reader could identify a familiar author from almost any page not seen before. He could parody many novelists after reading only 50 or 100 pages. In short, I believe that every great writer who uses the same language uses a different one.

Of course, this approach has its weaknesses. Not every pattern is worthwhile (or even pleasant) to detect. In the famous death scene of Turgenev's *Fathers and Sons*, for example, Bazarov ecstatically applies to Odintsova the very same word (*slavnaya*, "marvellous") that Nikolai Kirsanov enthusiastically uses to describe a horse.

Patterns may seem questionably convincing. In Olesha's *Envy*, the doomsday machine Ophelia flies in a "figure eight" pattern above Ivan Babichev just three pages after a bee flies in a "figure eight" pattern above Lilya's aunt. The parallel (and foreshadowing?) is strengthened as the bee proceeds to sting Lilya's aunt, and as Ophelia later impales Ivan with the stinger-like needle protruding from her head.

The limits of a pattern may be difficult to establish. It is surely not fortuitous that in Karamzin's "Poor Liza," the heroine's daydream (of a "shepherd" who "takes her hand") seems reified in Erast: the author explicitly suggests this. But is it patterned that Erast soon begins to call Liza his "shepherdess," that she then obeys him "like a lamb," and that he finally takes her "by the hand" just prior to terminating their relationship? And what of the "young shepherds" who are pictured singing "mournful songs" as the story opens?

Patterns may have quite different effects upon the reader. In Gogol's "Old World Landowners," Pulheria Ivanovna rather oddly insists that her death has been signaled by the return of her "gray cat." She then insists on being buried in her "gray dress," and the pattern seems the more eerie in conjunction with another cat-human parallel in the story. In Chekhov's "The Lady with the Dog," we are somewhat abruptly told that Anna Sergeevna was wearing Gurov's "favorite gray dress"—somewhat abruptly, because this dress has never been mentioned. However, she has gray eyes, and as the story ends, it is emphasized that only when his hair was turning gray did Gurov really experience love. Moreover, when Gurov follows her to St. Petersburg he stays in a room with gray cloth covering the entire floor, a gray blanket on his bed, and a gray inkwell on the table; and he repeatedly notices, and hates, the gray fence in front of her house. Still, Chechov's use of gray does not produce Gogolian eeriness; rather, it serves to promote a Chekhovian atmosphere of vaguely hopeless dreariness.

When Pushkin's Eugene Onegin uses the same word *(blazhenstvo,* "bliss") in his letter to Tatiana in a way that ironically reverses its earlier appearance in his "confession" to her—then (as I attempt to show) these two details become part of a symmetrical pattern of Pushkinian ironic reversal that is central to the entire novel. The parts of a pattern pleasingly reflect the whole. It is my hope that most readers will find some of the patterns discussed below convincing enough to be helpfully revealing of their authors' written worlds.

Chapter One

PUSHKINIAN IMPATIENT EXPECTATION AND ITS FUNCTION IN *EUGENE ONEGIN*

As is well known, Pushkin generally keeps a safe distance from the experiences of his characters.[1] But these characters of course keenly feel what they experience, as the reader vividly realizes. A major factor in this vivifying process, as I will seek to show, is Pushkin's use of impatient expectation. The effects produced are sometimes quite complex, involving the pace at which the reader is allowed to follow the plot and even the symmetrical structuring of a given work.

The Tales of Belkin are laced with impatient expectation. The first story, "The Shot," features Silvio's long wait for an opportunity to terrify his old enemy, the Count. Silvio is insulted: everyone expects a duel, but in vain. Then a description of how people in remote places eagerly await mail leads to Silvio's reaction upon receiving a letter: "he tore away the seal with an aspect of the greatest impatience."[2] Silvio soon tells the narrator that as his duel with the Count began, he awaited him "with indescribable impatience"(92-3). Every day since that duel, he has thirsted for revenge. Finishing his explanation, Silvio walks about the room "like a tiger in his cage."

In Part Two, a description

of how people in the country eagerly await a neighbor's arrival leads to our narrator's expectation regarding the young Countess: "I burned with impatience to see her" (95). As J. Thomas Shaw has observed, this may be considered a "false expectation" because it is the Count who proves to be the center of interest.[3] Shaw also notes that this is symmetrical to the vain expectation of a duel early in Part One.

Admitted to the Count's study, our narrator awaits him "with some kind of trepidation, as a provincial suppliant awaits the minister's appearance." He then hears of the second duel: how the Count urged Silvio to shoot quickly before his bride returned, how he waited with excruciating impatience until Silvio finally declared himself satisfied. The reader of course tends to share all this expectation, and his experience is intensified by a background motif of bullet holes (Silvio's honey-comb-like walls, his shot-through hat, the twice-pierced picture in the Count's study) and details of marksmanship (Silvio's "planting bullet upon bullet" into a playing card [88] anticipates his "planting one on another" into the Count's picutre [97], reinforced by the memory of how he would shoot a fly into the wall [98]).[4]

In "The Blizzard," the reader is twice made to wait impatiently because the narration abruptly shifts focus: when Marya Gavrilovna leaves for the church and when Vladimir arrives there ("What news awaited him!").[5] Of course Vladimir's frantic impatience, when he becomes lost in the blizzard, is described at great length. And his impatience with the slow old peasant adds a humorous touch. The reader's curiosity about Vladimir's "half-crazy letter" (111) is then intensified by Marya Gavrilovna's new neighbors, who await a new hero "with curiosity" (112). When Burmin appears, we join Marya Gavrilovna in wondering "why he is not yet proposing at her feet" (114). Marya Gavrilovna, we are told, "awaited with impatience for the moment of romantic explanation." Meanwhile, all the neighbors confidently anticipate marriage. Then, when Vladimir finally arrives to explain, Marya's mother waits for him at the house, thinking: "perhaps everything will be settled today!" Only after all this is Vladimir's delay explained, whereupon the final words ("and threw himself at her feet") echo and resolve Marya Gavrilovna's earlier impatience ("not yet proposing at her feet").

In "The Coffinmaker" the theme of impatient expectation takes on a darkly humorous twist as it is emphasized that the hero desires to do good business. As we soon learn, Prokhorov, in need of funds, is anxiously awaiting the death of an old merchant's wife. Later, in Prokhorov's nightmare, a certain skeleton is terribly impatient to visit him (127). And when Prokhorov finally awakens, he "waits in silence" to learn the outcome of his nocturnal adventure—only to discover that it was all a dream.

"The Stationmaster" opens with a long description that emphasizes the impatience of travelers in need of fresh horses. This includes even the narrator's own vexation when he does not receive the horses he had rightfully expected. We are thus well prepared for Minsky's impatient rage (in Vyrin's story), assuaged only by Dunya's appearance and attentiveness.

Having urged Dunya to let Minsky take her to the church, Vyrin is soon beseiged by doubts and impatience. Possessed by "anxiety," he is "unable to wait" and goes to the church himself (137). Not finding her, he returns to wait "in excruciating agitation" for the coachman's return. Learning the truth, he visits Minsky early in the morning but is forced to wait until eleven o'clock. That evening, he waits at Dunya's door "in painful expectation" (141) before failing to take her home.

As in "The Shot," background details intensify the reader's expectation as he connects them throughout the story. The pictures of the Prodigal Son on the Stationmaster's wall, repeatedly mentioned, increase our expectation that Dunya may return.[6] This is especially so because, as Carl Proffer has noted, Vyrin himself echoes the Prodigal (bludnyi) Son Motif when he hopes to bring back his "stray (zabludshuiu) lamb" (138) and also because the German inscriptions beneath each picture of the Prodigal Son may be seen to anticipate the fateful conversation in German between Minsky and his German Doctor.[7]

In "Mistress into Maid," we read that Liza "waited with impatience for the whole day" (149) to learn about Alexei from Nastya. And her quick interruptions finally cause Nastya to say: "How impatient you are!" With rather pleasing symmetry, it is then Liza who, upon returning from her masquerade, is hurriedly questioned by an "impatient" Nastya (155).

Prior to their first meeting, Liza waits for Alexei with a "strongly" beating heart (153); Alexei waits "about a half hour" for the second meeting "in unbearable expectation" (156)—a similar Pushkinian symmetry.[8] Finally, Alexei waits to meet and to impress Muromsky's daughter "with impatience" (162).

However, having wasted a pose of supreme indifference upon the unexpectedly appearing Miss Jackson, he is ironically surprised by a newly disguised Liza. And of course the irony intensifies near the end, when the hero cannot marry the heroine because he must marry the heroine—which forms a Pushkinian symmetry with the second Belkin tale, wherein the hero cannot marry the heroine because they are already married.

In *The Captain's Daughter*,Grinev is tortured by curiosity (398) to learn where his father will send him. Then, en route to military service, he urges his driver on "impatiently" (406)—after which he becomes lost in the snow and meets Pugachev.

At Belogorsk, Grinev learns of Shvabrin's slander of Marya Ivanovna and awaits "with impatience" a chance for revenge (435). He also waits "with impatience" (439) for an answer to his letter to his father (requesting his marriage blessing).

As Pugachev closes in on Belogorsk, Grinev feels "an impatient expectation of danger" (459). Imagining himself Masha's knight-protector, he "thirsts" to prove his worth and waits "with impatience" (461) for the opportunity. When Pugachev takes Belogorsk, Grinev is "tortured" most of all by uncertainty as to Masha's fate. He repeatedly asks about her: first "impatiently" and then "with indescribable agitation" (469). At Orenburg, Grinev receives Masha's desperate letter and frantically requests soldiers to take Belogorsk. The Gereral advises him "to have patience" (494). Cries Grinev in desperation: "Have patience!"

Finally, Grinev gains Masha only to be arrested as a traitor. His parents wait "with impatience" (532) for favorable news. Masha then explains her plight to the incognito Empress (in pleasing symmetry to Grinev's earlier openness with the incognito tsar-pretender). En route to the palace, Masha feels that all will be decided: her heart "beats violently" (539). She then returns to Anna Vlasevna, who has been "impatiently" awaiting her, and "somehow" answers a "shower" of questions. As in the second and last of *The Tales of Belkin*, Pushkin's final focus is thus primarily upon the impatient expectations of the young lovers, whose triumphant happiness seems quite superfluous to relate.

Like the four pictures of the Prodigal Son in "The Stationmaster," the four pictures that Grinev sees upon his arrival at Belogrosk may be deemed playfully prophetic. Grinev sees: "The Taking of Kistrin and of Ochakov, also The Choosing of a Bride and The Burial of a Cat" (4l7). If these are seen to anticipate the seiges of Belogorsk and Orenburg,Shvabrin's choice of Masha, and Pugachev's execution, we may note a further similarity to "The Stationmaster." Just as the role of Dunya as a "Prodigal Daughter" is only partially fulfilled (she returns, but too late), so Orenburg, unlike Belogorsk, is not captured, and Shvabrin's "choice" finally becomes Grinev's. Two other wall decorations are not prophetic within the story but form a Pushkinian symmetry: "the diploma of the deceased Commandant, as a sad epitaph of the past" (509) and the framed letter from the Empress (540), as a triumphant pledge of the future.

In *The Gypsies,* Zemfira's father cannot sleep: she has not returned from a late walk. At last Zemfira appears with Aleko, whom she met in the "wilderness" beyond the mound. "He," she declares, "is ready to follow me everywhere" (IV:208).[9] All this anticipates the ending: Aleko , missing Zemfira at night, "impatiently" follows her trail beyond the mound, where he kills her and her lover. His noctunal impatience thus echoes her father's, especially because Zemfira's "unfaithfulness" seems to be a fated replay of her own mother's. Also aptly, the poem ends with repeated mention of the "wilderness" where fateful passions cannot be escaped or avoided. Moreover, when Aleko asks Zemfira's tather why he had not killed her unfaithful mother, he (Aleko) calls the mother "treacherous" *(kovarnoi),* an adjective applied earlier to Fate as the reader was told that fateful passion would soon awaken in Aleko: "just wait!"(212). The reader's expectations are thus associated with Fate itself.

Zemfira's ironically prophetic declaration that Aleko is "ready to follow her everywhere" somewhat resembles the statement by Dunya's father ("the Stationmaster") urging her to drive off with Minski: He's "not a wolf and won't eat you up" (VI:137). A further parallel irony is that Dunya is bound for "church" when she leaves; Zemfira is discovered, and killed, beyond the mound near the "grave." Within *The Gypsies,* of course, a Pushkinian symmetry is formed as Zemfira "finds" Aleko early in the poem in the same place where he finds her near the end.

Quite aptly, Aleko seems fatefully associated with the gypsies' trained bear.[10] The first day after Aleko joins them, we are told that the bear's chains jangle "impatiently." Later, we learn that Aleko has become "free" as the gypsies. This flows into a description of the bear, "a fugitive from his native lair."

(Aleko, of course, is a fugitive from "the law.") We then learn that as the gypsies perform for alms, Aleko leads the bear. This juxtaposition of "free" hero and captive bear is tinged with irony, for Aleko's "freedom" among the gypsies may be seen as a form of captivity. And as the captive bear "gnaws his chains," we may recall the fateful passions that will soon "awaken" in Aleko: "just wait!" Yet the two "fugitives" are even aptly balanced by contrast. The bear, born to be free, is forced to be less so; Aleko, as Zemfira's father announces to him at the end, was not "born for the life of the wild."

Without strong emphasis on fated tragedy, Pushkin repeatedly features in *Eugene Onegin* what may be termed "doomed" impatient expectation. Essential elements of the symmetrical structure of this novel are the anxious expectations of both heroine and hero after their letters to each other. Both expectations, of course, result in rejection. Moreover, Lensky waits "long" and "impatiently" at the site of the duel prior to his death. In effect, the three main characters impatiently await disaster. This pattern is reinforced by other details, for example Napoleon's eager expectation of Moscow's surrender:

> not revelry, not a welcoming gift—
> a conflagration she prepared
> for the impatient hero.[11]

Napoleon's ironic impatience thus reflects Tatiana's, Onegin's and Lensky's. And Napoleon's may be seen as an apt precursor of Onegin's, since it precedes only his in context; since Moscow is feminine in Russian and, also like Tatiana, is "Russian in her soul" (205); and since Napoleon, like Onegin, is termed "hero."

Numerous other instances of impatient expectation, though not always doomed, enrich the central pattern. The novel opens on an appropriately expectant note: "when *will* the devil take you?" This question is resolved for the reader only at the end of Chapter One, when Onegin's uncle dies. Just prior to this, "a greedy host of creditors" (117) after his father dies parallel the hero's own initial expectation.

Early in Chapter One, we read of the crowd's impatience before Istomina dances. Then, as she appears, a hesitant enjambment enhances the breathless beauty of Pushkin's description: "Istomina stands: she,/ while touching..." (103). Somewhat

similarly, an interstrophic enjambment vivifies Tatiana's breathless falling on the garden bench when she realizes that Onegin
has finally appeared to answer her letter (171). As Nabokov has
noted (II:405-6), this apt evocation is echoed in Chapter Eight,
when Onegin finally rushes to Tatiana after she fails to answer
his letters. Here, we may observe that in all three instances, the
verbal rhythm of breathless expectation intensifies a protracted
impatience just prior to its resolution.

Chapters Two and Three develop a double "doomed" anticipation of marriage. Lensky, who believes that a "kindred soul
awaits him daily" (129), is expected to marry Olga; Onegin, Tatiana. Indeed, "all the neighbors" anticipate both weddings with
great confidence (152). And this "gossip" dangerously enflames
Tatiana's imagination: her heart and soul had long "waited—
for somebody." Olga's father, who "destined" her for Lensky,
has already died after wondering: "Shall I be there to see the
day?" (143)—yet another instance of doomed expectation. And
the verb used to express this *(dozhdus')* is soon used to describe
Tatiana's recognition of Onegin as the one for whom her soul
had been waiting (153).

Tatiana now succumbs completely to her intense expectations, thinking both day and night of Onegin. Finally, unable
to sleep,[12] she writes to him: "I'm waiting for you..."(167).
She is destined, of course, to wait much longer than she expects.
Pushkin then adds a gently humorous touch as Tatiana grows
impatient while trying to persuade her "slow-witted" nurse to
have the letter delivered. She then "waits" in anxious agony for
a reply (170), further tortured by Lensky's suggestion that perhaps "the mail" has detained his friend.

At last Onegin arrives, and she rushes breathlessly to the garden: "Tatiana waited with impatience" (173). But even this expectation is at least briefly doomed. As Nabokov puts it, "Tatiana continues in a tremor of apprehension, but Onegin does not
appear" (I:36). And of course when he finally does appear, she
is doomed still more. But for this, Pushkin chooses to make the
reader wait until the next chapter: "some other time I'll tell the
rest." We are thus especially sympathetic to Tatiana's impatience
as we begin Chapter Four. Moreover, Pushkin teasingly terms the
meeting "unlooked-for" *(nezhdanoi)*, a word which combines
"unexpected" quite ironically with its root meaning "una-
waited."[13]

Finally (in the sixth completed stanza of Four), Onegin begins his reply. "I'm not made for bliss" (181), he declares, a notion he will ironically echo in his own desperate letter late in the novel: "to melt in agonies before you,/ grow pale and waste away... that's bliss!" (298). Almost as if to expand the symmetry still further, Pushkin had already associated Tatiana's desire for "bliss" with Onegin with her doom (156). And Onegin himself had adopted a condescending attitude towards the Romantic Lensky's "brief bliss" (132).[14]

Chapter Four ends on the much-professed note of Lensky's apparent happiness. We may thus begin to question the certainty of his much-anticipated "transports" (198) with Olga. In Nabokov's words: "He thinks that only two weeks remain till his wedding. Actually, a little less than that remains till his death" (I:40). Then, in Tatiana's dream, Onegin's treatment of Lensky seems quite obviously prophetic. And as Onegin flirts with Olga at the party, Lensky waits impatiently for the end of the mazurka—only to discover that his expectation was doomed: Olga had already promised Onegin the cotillion as well. Yet the reader is made to wait for the next chapter (as at the end of Three) for further developments, although we are told that "two bullets" will decide Lensky's "fate" (224).

Early in Chapter Six we see Lensky, who has challenged Onegin, waiting for his answer "Boiling with an impatient enmity" (233). And the poem he writes on the eve of the duel continues the theme of expectation: "What has the coming day in store for me?" Then, despite Zaretsky's opinion that "Onegin's sure to be already waiting for us," it is of course Lensky who waits "long" and "impatiently" (239). His impatience prior to his death is thus repeatedly reinforced.[15]

As at the end of Three and Five, the reader is told that the story will continue "But not now" (247). Chapter Seven then shows us a quite different Olga, who seems to expect something rather different from her marriage.[16] We then follow Tatiana, who breathlessly enters Onegin's former residence and greedily examines his old books "with a flutter" (261). Her expectations, however, seem rather typically disappointed, as she is finally moved to wonder if her hero is "a parody."

Chapter Eight focuses Onegin, dazzled by Tatiana, accepting in feverish haste an invitation by her husband. And now it is Onegin who "spends both day and night" (296) in eager expectation, just as Tatiana dreamed impatiently of him "both the days and nights" (153). This leads to his desperate letter: "I must be certain in the morning/ of seeing you during the day" (298). Finally, he rushes to Tatiana and falls at her feet,[17] whereupon she completes the Pushkinian symmetry by crushing his expectations as he had formerly crushed hers. And the symmetry typically includes an ironic balance: Onegin had rejected Tatiana because he would be unable to love her faithfully ("would cease to love at once" [181]); she now rejects him because she must continue to be faithful to her husband.

Pushkinian "doomed" expectation is of course not confined to *Eugene Onegin*. In *The Stone Guest*, Don Carlos, somewhat like Lensky, waits impatiently before his challenge is accepted and he is killed. In *The Bronze Horseman*, Eugene feverishly waits for the waters to subside, only to be driven mad by the death of his Parasha. In "The Queen of Spades," Hermann waits "like a tiger" (VI:336) for his chance to learn the Countess' secret—only to go mad after he does. In "Tazit," a father's triple doomed impatient expectation leads him to disown his son. There is also Ruslan's doomed expectation of finding Liudmila in bed (IV:15-16) and a somewhat similar episode in "Vadim" (IV:161). In Pushkin's short poem "The Water Nymph," a monk sits upon the bank of a lake, anxiously awaiting the return of a beautiful mermaid. The poem then ends with a glimpse of the drowned monk's beard floating in the water (I:364). Still other impatient expectations followed by death occur in "The Brigand Brothers" (IV:173) and "Poltava" (IV:263-4).

In Pushkin's play *The Water Nymph*, his use of impatient expectation is quite complex. As the play opens, a miller's daughter has been waiting eight days for her lover, the prince. When he arrives, she exclaims:

> **Ah, finally you've remembered me!**
> **Aren't you ashamed to torture me so long**
> **With empty cruel expectation? (V:428)**

"Empty cruel" refers of course to the past eight days, but the words soon become ironically true as she learns of his imminent marriage to another girl. He gives her some farewell presents, and she echoes her statement that he has "remembered" *(vspomnil)* her by "remembering" *(vspomnila)* that he has made her pregnant. Then, throwing one present into the river, she follows it and drowns herself.

After his marriage, the prince meets the miller, now demented, who says: "We waited long for you yesterday." And to the question "who waited," he replies: "My daughter, of course" (446). This rather eerie recollection aptly anticipates the ending of the play, as the miller's daughter, now a water nymph, instructs her daughter to tell the prince that she still loves him and is "waiting for him" (451). She then declares that every day she has thought of revenge, which now seems within reach. Finally, as the prince, drawn to the river bank by some "unknown force," meets his own water-nymph daughter, the play seems to end on a note of easily projected Pushkinian symmetry.

Also typically, details reflect and reinforce the plot. The prince gives the miller's daughter three farewell presents: a cloth band, a necklace, and money for her father. As seen above, the girl follows her cloth band into the river. The miller throws the money into the river before telling the prince that his daughter has been waiting for him. He also suggests that the necklace has strangled his daughter. Finally, we may note the prince's indignant statement when his wife sends men to protect him: "Am I a child,/ who cannot take a step without a nurse?" (448). Soon after this, it is his own "wondrous child" who, as the play ends, appears to promote the revenge of her mother, "waiting for" the prince beneath the waters. Somewhat like the use of "church" ("The Stationmaster") and "grave" (The Gypsies) noted above, the prince's mention of "child" adds a touch of Pushkinian irony to his fate.

As we have seen, Pushkin's use of impatient expectation generates a major vivifying force in his writing. The emotion ranges from grim viciousness (Silvio and Hermann wait "like tigers") to the warm hopefulness of heroines who read French novels and are "consequently" in love. In virtually all cases, the characters seem more human, believable. This effect may draw in part upon the familiar intensity of a child's impatience for a birthday or some other holiday. Yet the author's attitude seems neither condescending nor mocking, thanks to Pushkin's balanced, versatile perspective.

Occasionally, a mildly humorous impatience tends to relieve the central, painful one—for example, Vladimir's conversations with the bearded peasant in "The Blizzard" and Tatiana's urging her "slow-witted" nurse to help with the letter. Often, Pushkinian impatient expectation is presented symmetrically, for example the painful hopes of Tatiana and Onegin. Moreover, details typically reflect and enrich the central effect, such as Napoleon's crushed expectations in Chapter Seven. And the reader's expectations, though sometimes quite playfully evoked,[18] frequently blend with the characters', further vivifying their experiences.

Especially in *Eugene Onegin,* Pushkinian impatient expectation often ends in rejection, disappointment, or defeat. A stark plot outline could well seem darkly fateful. Yet as Pushkin presents it, even the cumulative effect of apparently doomed expectation is neither ominous nor gloomy.[19] Indeed, the tone of gentle irony which characterizes the novel is surely one measure of the uncanny balance of Pushkin's art.

NOTES

1. Simon Karlinsky has aptly likened Pushkin to Chekhov and Nabokov in this respect ("Nabokov and Chekhov: the lesser Russian tradition," *TriQuarterly,* No. 17, Winter, 1970, p. 14).

2. A. S. Pushkin, *Polnoe sobranie sochinenii v desiati tomakh* (Moscow, 1962-66), VI, 89.

3. J. Thomas Shaw, "Pushkin's 'The Shot'," *Indiana Slavic Studies* vol. III (The Hague, 1963), p. 118.

4. Shaw (p. 127) ingeniously associates the playing card with the Count.

5. This technique is used quite frequently in *Ruslan and Liudmila.*

6. I am indebted to Carl R. Proffer for noting that this was first pointed out by M. O. Gershenzon. See Proffer, ed., *From Karamzin to Bunin* (Bloomington, 1969), p. 5.

7. See *ibid.,* pp. 5, 49.

8. In *Count Nulin,* Natalya Pavlovna waits most excitedly for the arrival of the Count, whose carriage has overturned (lines 95-103), and then she "waits impatiently" (line 135) for him to appear at dinner. Later that night, it is the Count who, filled with "flaming desire," stealthily and breathlessly makes his way to Natalya Pavlovna's bedchamber (lines 258-266).

9. I am indebted to Walter Arndt for this translation, as well as for several other phrases from *The Gypsies,* in his *Pushkin Threefold* (New York, 1972), pp. 275-313.

10. For other opinions about this bear, see Carl R. Proffer, ed. and trans., *The Critical Prose of Alexander Pushkin* (Bloomington, 1969), p. 110.

11. Vladimir Nabokov, *Eugene Onegin* (Princeton, 1975). I, p. 268. All subsequent references to Pushkin's novel will be to this translation.

12. This aspect of Pushkinian impatient expectation occurs with Tatiana three times (Three, XVII; Six, II; Seven, XLIII).

13. The effect is repeated early in Chapter Six, p. 228.

14. Nabokov has "brief rapture," even though the word *(blazhenstvu)* is the same one used for the other three uses of "bliss"—and despite his "method of 'signal words'" in his revised edition, which does however change his previous "rapture!" in Onegin's Letter to the "bliss!" quoted above.

15. Conversely to the theme of doomed impatient expectation, indifference seems considerably safer in the novel. Onegin, who sleeps a "dead sleep" at duel time, wins. Olga, whose supposed devotion fades suspiciously fast, loves again. And of course when Onegin indifferently relinquishes his father's estate to creditors, he soon receives his uncle's riches.

16. See Nabokov's comment, III, pp. 79-80.

17. Tatiana herself emphasizes his falling at her feet (306), an action frequently performed by Pushkin's heroes, for example Burmin in "The Blizzard."

18. In *Eugene Onegin,* Pushkin elicits his readers' expectations with effects that range from carefully calculated suspense to near flippancy and playfulness. (These last two terms are repeatedly used by Richard Freeborn to characterize the tone of Pushkin's novel in *The Rise of The Russian Novel,* Cambridge, 1973, pp. 10-12.) As we have seen, the reader must wait until the end of Chapter One for the resolution of its opening. And questions raised near the end of Three, Four, Five, and Six are answered only considerably later.

But the reader's expectations are not always satisfied. For instance, Onegin's wit, so highly lauded early in One, is never fully demonstrated, as Nabokov has observed (I:22). And "the art of soft passion," allegedly Onegin's foremost skill (99), ironically leads the reader to expect a seduction of the heroine. He wins her, of course, without this "art," which, when activated, fails.

The lengthy digression in One that favors a woman's feet above all else terminates rather abruptly with the assertion that female feet are "deceptive" (110). Still more playfully, Pushkin toys with our expectations in Four: "(the reader now expects the rhyme 'froze-rose'—/ here you are, take it quick!)" (194). Then, at the end of Five, we must wait while Pushkin indulges in a digression stressing the notion that digressions should be avoided. This playful irony recurs at the close of the penultimate chapter, as Freeborn has noted (11): "though late but there's an introduction" (277).

19. As Freeborn has observed (12), what Pushkin's Onegin stanza achieves "is never somber."

Chapter Two

DUALITY AND SYMMETRY IN LERMONTOV'S *A HERO OF OUR TIME*

Commentators have been justifiably intrigued by the patterning of Lermontov's novel.[1] Despite its five parts and three narrators, however, the work seems most informed by duality as a structural principle. Even individual episodes, actions, descriptions, speeches continually occur in pairs. Moreover, there often seems to be a balancing of these pairs. In several cases, the spacing of this balancing within the novel promotes a remarkable symmetry.

To begin with, the novel easily "divides into two basic parts", as K. Loks has put it,[2] with two corresponding introductions. Loks also sees the novel as comprising two planes. The first one involves Pechorin's relationship to other people; the second, his inner self.[3] Somewhat similarly, Viktor Vinogradov observes that "the image of Pechorin is depicted on two planes"—outside observation and self-disclosure. In his view, this results in a novel of two parts, each with its own inner unity but organically bound to each other by semantic parallelism.[4] Boris Eikhenbaum has used the term "dual composition" to suggest the development of a complex plot in conjunction with a gradual revelation of the hero's inner world.[5]

Much of the duality in the novel relates to the hero. V. G. Belinsky has described the "duality of Pechorin"[6] by paraphrasing what the latter tells Werner: "Within me there are two persons: one of them lives in the full sense of the word, the other cogitates and judges him." (163). Earlier, Pechorin suggests to Princess Mary that his soul split in two early in life: "One half of my soul . . . had died . . . the other half stirred and lived. . ." (127).

This pair of statements seems part of a larger patterning. We encounter two descriptions of Pechorin by the other two narrators and two by himself. First, Maksim Maksimich describes him as "a little odd" (10-11). Pechorin, we learn, is sometimes cowardly, sometimes brave; alternately taciturn and garrulous. The author's "portrait" (56-57) of Pechorin also features contrasts and contradictions. His arms do not swing when he walks, and his eyes do not laugh when he is laughing. This description is framed by two yawns (55, 59), the second of which is said to be feigned.

Pechorin's two descriptions of himself seem calculated to engage the pity of his listener. The first, told to Maksim Maksimich, is of his "unfortunate disposition" (39). The second, told to Princess Mary, is of his becoming "a moral cripple" early in life (127).

Pechorin persuades two women quite similarly. With Bela, he supposes that she may love someone else (25). "Or is it," he continues, that she finds him completely hateful. "Or" does her faith forbid her to return his feelings. Later, Pechorin urges Vera to renew their affair: perhaps she loves her second husband. "Or is he very jealous?" (103). Or perhaps she fears losing his money. After these two speeches, we read vivid descriptions of the two women's eyes: Bela's express "distrust" and Vera's "despair"; but each soon gives in to Pechorin's wishes.

The similarity of these two persuasion scenes and of many other pairs of incidents throughout the novel almost gives one a feeling that destiny is being replayed. As Nabokov has observed of "The Fatalist," the scene of Vulich with the pistol "...curiously echoes that of the duel in 'Princess Mary' (p. 164), and there are other echoes further on (cf. p. 158, 'this is becoming a bore,' and p. 186, 'I became bored with the long procedure')" (210). Earlier, Mr. Nabokov remarks that in "The Fatalist," "...the crucial passage also turns on a pistol being or not being loaded . . . and a kind of duel by proxy is fought between Pechorin and Vulich, with Fate, instead of the smirking dragoon, supervising the lethal arrangements"(x). Another parallel perhaps mentally adduced by

Nabokov: "You are a strange fellow!" (to Pechorin, 164) and "What an odd fellow!" (of Vulich, 184). There is even a discernible echo of Pechorin's feigned awakening by officers immediately after the garden chase (152) in his real awakening by officers after Vulich's death (190)—just as the imaginary nocturnal terrorists of the first scene perhaps correspond to the drunken Efimich and his nocturnal slayings.

Pechorin's experiences seem to come before the reader in twos. He is grazed by two bullets—on the knee by Grushnitsky (169) and on the shoulder by Efimich (193). He overhears two key plots—against Princess Mary (112) and against himself (146). These are to embarrass her at the dance and to humiliate him in a sham duel, both of which he later thwarts. He learns two important secrets from Werner, both times cautioning the latter not to reveal them further. These are Princess Mary's "pleasant delusion" regarding Grushnitsky's rank (94) and the "murderous alteration" to load only Grushnitsky's pistol (157). Pechorin then exploits both secrets quite devastatingly (116, 170).

With varying degrees of irony, Pechorin announces both to Vera (104) and to Grushnitsky (110) that he plans to flirt with, or court, Princess Mary. Later he is informed both by the young Princess (148) and by the old Princess (178) that his rank and "situation" are not serious obstacles. He also performs a rather ironic "bow" before each Princess (178,180). The first follows the mother's suggestion that he is "a gentleman"; the second, her daughter's statement, "I hate you."

Pechorin warns Grushnitsky twice and "tests" him twice. The warnings relate to asking Princess Mary for the mazurka ("Look out, you might be forestalled," 132) and ascending to the duel ground ("Don't fall beforehand," 166). In the "tests," Pechorin twice scrutinizes Grushnitsky. As the Dragoon Captain proposes his plan to humiliate Pechorin: "In a tremor of eagerness, I awaited Grushnitsky's reply . . . If Grushnitsky had refused, I would have thrown myself upon his neck" (147). Then, at the duel: "I decided to give Grushnitsky every advantage; I wished to test him. A spark of magnanimity might awaken in his soul . . . but vanity and weakness of character were to triumph!" (167).

Pechorin squelches the Dragoon Captain twice: "So it was you that I hit so awkwardly on the head?" (155) and "If so, you and I will fight a duel on the same conditions" (170). Both times, the Captain observes a painful, chagrined silence. Pechorin also

29

twice toys with Werner. First, the latter is allowed to believe he has crucially cautioned Pechorin against marriage: "Werner left, fully convinced that he had put me on my guard" (139). Then, prior to the duel, Pechorin suggests to his worried friend that "the expectation of a violent death" is a "genuine illness": "This thought impressed the doctor and he cheered up" (161).

As Nabokov has observed (210), Pechorin notices two corpses near the end of "Princess Mary": Grushnitsky's (171) and that of his own horse (180). He also receives "two notes" (172), one from Werner ("sleep in peace...if you can") and one from Vera ("in none is evil so attractive"). The second seems a direct echo of Pechorin's earlier thoughts of Vera ("What does she love me for so much... Can evil possibly be so attractive?", 120). And this pair of references to "attractive evil" seems paralleled by another pair of "vice" references. Pechorin declared that Vera "is the only woman who has completely understood me with all my petty weaknesses and wicked passions" (120). This tends to recall the author's introductory assertion that Pechorin is "composed of all the vices of our generation in the fullness of their development" (2). Quite rightly, this pair of references suggests that Vera's note (which John Mersereau, Jr. terms "the final verdict on Pechorin"[7]) is more informative than either the pair of descriptions by the two narrators or the pair by Pechorin himself. Thus, the end of Vera's description ("none can be so genuinely unhappy as you, because none tries so hard to convince himself of the contrary") both echoes and explains Pechorin's earlier dilemma: "...I only know that if I am a cause of unhappiness for others, I am no less unhappy myself" (40). This statement, in turn, forms yet another pair with Pechorin's sad suspicion that his "only function on earth is to ruin other people's hopes" (132-33). Finally, this pair seems paralleled by yet another. For in the words of Richard Freeborn, who sees Pechorin as "seducer, or pretender to that role" with Princess Mary and "executioner" to Grushnitsky: "In both cases he tries to mitigate his vengeful role by the private justification that he... 'played the miserable role of executioner or traitor' or, as he puts it on the eve of his duel with Grushnistky: 'how many times I have played the role of an axe in the hands of fate.' "[8]

Pechorin and Grushnitky form an obvious pair.[9] They frequently evince similar intentions leading to opposite results—a balance climaxed by their duel. Pechorin writes that Grushnitksy's "object is to become the hero of a novel" (85). Werner says that for Princess Mary, Pechorin has become "the hero of a novel in the latest fashion" (95). Pechorin playfully twists Grushnitsky's French aphorism by substituting a despising of women (88) for a hatred of men (87). Oddly enough, the two are reversed even in appearance: Pechorin seems no more than twenty-three, though he might be thirty (56); Grushnitsky looks about twenty-five, yet he is hardly twenty-one (84).

In yet another association, Pechorin preempts an imaginary Grushnitsky. For as Nabokov has noted (208), Pechorin utters to Princess Mary (138) the same sort of speech he had earlier imagined Grushnitsky telling her (85). Both speeches are to the effect: "No, you had better not know what is in my soul!"

Perhaps still more ironically, Pechorin's resourceful imagination arranges a victory which seems to be replayed as a defeat. His words to Bela ("Farewell, I am going—where? How should I know? Perchance, I shall not be long running after a bullet or a sword blow: remember me then. . . .", 27) are echoed in Vera's letter ("Farewell, farewell. . . I perish—but what does it matter? If I could be sure that you will always remember me. . . ", 174). Before, Pechorin's victory with Princess Mary echoed the words he had contemptuously assigned to Grushnitsky; now, his loss of Vera is underscored by the echo of his successful words to Bela.

As "Princess Mary" begins, Pechorin opens his window early in the morning: "...my room was filled with the perfume of flowers growing in the modest front garden" (81). Soon after, he first sees Princess Mary: "...there emanated from her that ineffable fragrance which breathes sometimes from a beloved woman's letter (86). This early pair of references to emanating fragrance are reflected in another, crucial pair later on. First, there is Pechorin's famous pronouncement: "...there is boundless delight in the possession of a young, barely unfolded soul! It is like a flower whose best fragrance emanates to meet the first ray of the sun. It should be plucked that very minute and after inhaling one's fill of it, one should throw it away on the road: perchance, someone will pick it up! (123). This rather cruel attitude (a plucked flower soon dies, even if "picked up") presumably suggests Pechorin's treatment of Princess Mary. Soon after this, he tells her: "One half of my soul ...had withered away—while the other half stirred and lived..." (127). Here, Pechorin is explaining how he became "a moral cripple": misunderstood as a young boy, he "learned to hate."

And his eloquence seems most successfully to counter Princess Mary's charge that he is "worse than a murderer": ...she was sorry for me!" In the overall context, however, Pechorin seems to be admitting that his attitude towards Princess Mary is a sort of revenge[10]: the desire to pluck a young soul-flower (above, in his journal) smacks of retaliation for having been driven to cut away half of his own flower-soul.

Still greater irony derives from what may be termed the horse-goat/woman theme. Azamat's double theft (goat, Bela) seems paralleled by Kazbich's song: "Gold can purchase you a foursome of wives,/ But a spirited steed is a priceless possession" (18). This seems especially so because Pechorin simultaneously loses both Vera and his own horse at the end of "Princess Mary." Moreover, losing Karagyoz, Kazbich "fell on the ground and began to sob like a child" (22). Losing Vera, Pechorin "fell on the wet grass and began crying like a child" (175). The irony reaches its climax in the following pair of descriptions. In "Princess Mary" Pechorin had declared: "I love to gallop on a spirited horse through tall grass . . . the soul feels easy . . . There is no feminine gaze that I would not forget. . ."(106). After reading Vera's letter: "Like a madman, I . . . galloped . . . I galloped on, breathless with impatience . . . . I felt that she had become dearer to me than anything in the world . . .!(174-5).

The overall dualistic pattern of *A Hero of Our Time* seems reflected even in Lermontov's use of individual words. Early in "Princess Mary," Pechorin predicts[11] that he and Grushnitsky will "meet on a narrow path, and one of us will fare ill"(85). Later, Pechorin insists that the duel be fought on "a narrow bit of flat nature" (165), so that a light wound will be fatal. Just prior to the duel, Pechorin is struck by the blueness and freshness of the morning: he feels "a kind of delicious languor" and is "in love with nature" (161-02). As "Princess Mary" began, he had also noted the blueness and freshness of the morning, adding: "a kind of joyful feeling permeates all my veins" (81-2). Mersereau connects these two observations, terming the first one "a lyrical overture to the tragedy that is to follow."[12] If one recalls Freeborn's remark that "Princess Mary" is "composed of two relationships" (Pechorin as "seducer" and "executioner"), then both his descriptions of the morning may be seen as ironic overtures.

Just before relating Bela's death, Maksim Maksimich twice employs the words "unlucky day!" (42). The "nonsense" (118) that Vera supposedly tells Pechorin seems echoed by the "non-sense" (137) he almost feels for Princess Mary. The "comedy" (76) he finds just before the undine kisses him seems echoed (as Peace has suggested[13]) by the *"commedia!"* (171) of Grushnit-sky's death. There are others, including two pairs of references to "jests" by Pechorin (11,27; 146,184). As Nabokov noted concerning the word "separating" at the end of "Princess Mary": "It is just like Lermontov and his casual style to let this long and limp word appear twice in the same, final, sentence" (210).

The symmetry of duality in Lermontov's novel becomes most evident if one pictures its five stories in linear arrangement, with "Taman" as the centerpiece. In the inner pair, Pechorin undermines the person named by the title: Maksim Maksimich, Princess Mary. The outer pair relates the deaths of the two people so named.

The first and last stories are also symmetrically balanced by statements about fate. In Nabokov's words: "Maksim Maksimich closes the book with much the same remark as the one he makes about Pechorin at the beginning" (210). These two statements suggest that both Pechorin (11) and Vulich (194) had extraordinary fates "assigned" to them "at their birth." Vinogradov (after emphasizing this parallel) observes that Maksim Maksimich balks before "two metaphysical questions" which are "the two central themes" of the novel. These he sees as "predestination" and "the social genesis of disillusionment as a characteristic psychologcial trait of contemporary man."[14]

The first and last stories also seem balanced by what could be termed knife-blade foreshadowings. The ring of Azamat's dagger against Kazbich's chain-armor (18) anticipates the latter's stabbing of Bela with his dagger (43). Efimich's slashing a pig in two (189) prefigures his cutting Vulich in two (191) with the same sword. Somewhat similarly, Pechorin's success in having Azamat steal the goat (11) seems to suggest the notion of having him steal his sister (20). And Vulich's early success seems to suggest to Pechorin the notion of taking Efimich alive: "It occurred to me to test my fate as Vulich had" (193). In each case, the rather obvious local duality is only a part of the overall dualistic symmetry.

Yet another balance between "Bela" and "The Fatalist" is that both stories have "false endings," as Eikhenbaum has put it.[15] "Bela" ends with the narrator's hope that we respect Maksim Maksimich: "If you admit that, I shall be fully rewarded for my story, which perhaps has been too long" (49). The ending of "The Fatalist," which, Eikhenbaum notes, also features Maksim Maksimich, also seems final—yet the novel's chronological conclusion is of course the ending of "Maksim Maksimich," or perhaps the "Introduction to Pechorin's Journal," wherein we learn of Pechorin's death.

Moving towards the center of the book, we may note a rather unexpected parallel between the very different stories "Maksim Maksimich" and "Princess Mary." Near the end of each, Pechorin parts forever from a friend who has anxiously observed his adventures and attempted quite successfully to offer counsel. (Pechorin learns key information from each,[16] but he counters their suggestions with rather disarming ironies.) In the first parting, Pechorin "...proffered his hand while Maksim Makismich wanted to throw himself on Pechorin's neck" (62).[17] As Pechorin parts from Werner: "He would have liked to shake my hand, and...would have thrown himself on my neck; but I remained cold as stone..." (177). Merssereau observes that these two paralleled episodes emphasize the hero's "essential aloneness."[18]

The central story has its own dualistic symmetry.[19] Just as the entire novel opens and closes with Maksim's similar statements about fate, "Taman" opens and closes with the ironic notion[20] that Pechorin is "on official business" (65, 80). Arriving, Pechorin and his Cossack are led to two huts, which are termed "an evil place" (65). These words are later repeated by a friend of Pechorin's Cossack (71). Pechorin sees the hopeful silhouette of "two ships" (66) outlined against the pale horizon. These two are of course no help; later, however, two other boats prove most unfavorable. (One carries away the hero's belongings; the other carries him to his near death.) Early in the story, Pechorin is greatly disturbed by the blind boy's "two white eyes" (66). Later, as he follows his undine to the boat, there is no moon: "...only two little stars, like two guiding beacons, sparkled in the dark-blue vault" (77).[21]

As Mersereau has noted, "Taman" contains "two allusions to Pechorin's past."[22] It also contains two details which interlock with passages elsewhere in the novel. As Nabokov has put it (203), the "breakers" (68) of the Taman seascape "reappear" in the next story as "breakers" on p. 181. Somewhat similarly, Pechorin's statement about his undine ("breeding in women, as in horses, is a great thing," 73) reflects ironically back into the preceding story upon the portrait of Pechorin himself ("a sign of breeding in man, as a black mane and a black tail in a white horse," 57). Vinogradov has stressed this parallel.[23]

The overall dualistic structure of Lermontov's novel seems especially remarkable if one considers that some of the parts were separately composed and published. Yet as a finished, final product, the work seems ordered by a pleasing, balanced symmetry. As Mersereau has suggested, Lermontov could have planned the entire novel in advance: he was "a literary genius" and "knew what he was doing."[24] Ultimately, the dualistic structure gives us a faintly uneasy feeling that fate is somehow being replayed—that the hero's various adventures form an appropriately patterned prelude to his decision (in Peace's words) "to measure himself against Fate itself"[25] in "The Fatalist". Indeed, the fact that Vulich successfully tests Fate only to die a violent death lends additional persuasiveness to Nabokov's suspicion that Pechorin's death (after *his* successful testing of Fate) "was a violent one" (203). And if it was, Maksim Maksimich's opening and closing suggestions (that Pechorin and Vulich had extraordinary fates "assigned" to them "at their birth") acquire—in relation to the hero—an eerie tinge of unwitting precognition.

NOTES

1. Richard Peace describes the three narrators as "leapfrogging over one another's backs"—each is "built up" only to be "pulled down" ("The Role of *Taman'* in Lermontov's *Geroi nashego vremeni, The Slavonic and East European Review,* January, 1967, p. 13.) Vladimir Nabokov observes that"...the structural trick consists in bringing Pechorin gradually nearer and nearer until he takes over; but by the time he takes over he is dead" (*A Hero of Our Time,* Translated from the Russian by Vladimir Nabokov in collaboration with Dmitri Nabokov, New York, 1958, p.*vii.* All quotations from the novel are taken from this translation.)

The last known episode in Pechorin's life is the second story in the book. We learn of Pechorin's death between this and the third (middle) story, which recounts the earliest part of his life. Thus the novel could be likened to a movie sequence of someone turning a cartwheel, starting however upside down, near the middle of the motion. The sudden ending flows into a beginning, whereupon the movie sequence finally provides the (previously unseen) first part of the cartwheel. To borrow from E.E. Cummings, stories 12345death are presented 45death123.

2. K. Loks, "Proza Lermontova," *Literaturnaia ucheba,* No. 8, August, 1938, p. 13. B. Tomashevskii observes that although the novel, in its first editions, was divided between "Taman" and "Princess Mary", this was done only to keep the two halves approximately equal in length ("Proza Lermontova i zapadno-evropeiskaia literaturnaia traditsiia," *Literaturnoe nasledstvo,* Nos. 43-44, Moscow, 1941, p. 509).

3. Loks, p.11.

4. Viktor Vinogradov, "Stil' prozy Lermontova," *Literaturnoe nasledstvo,* Nos. 43-44, Moscow,1941, p. 565.

5. B.M. Eikhenbaum, *Stat'i o Lermontove* (Leningrad, 1961), p. 249.

6. V.G. Belinskii, *Polnoe sobranie sochinenii* (Moscow, 1953-59), IV, 243. Loks also stresses Pechorin's "duality" (p.11), and Vinogradov finds that Pechorin's inner duality seems to result in a struggle of two voices (pp. 613-4).

7. John Mersereau,Jr., *Mikhail Lermontov* (Carbondale, Ill., 1962), p. 128. Mersereau also discerns the duality in Vera's life: "Twice unhappily married, she twice sacrifices for Pechorin the peace of mind that marriage has secured for her." (p. 128.)

8. Richard Freeborn, *The Rise of the Russian Novel* (London, 1973), p. 65.

9. Freeborn observes that Grushnitsky is "Pechorin's *alter ego* in several senses" (p. 67).

10. Freeborn terms "vengeance" the "theme" of the novel (p. 39).

11. Mersereau associates this prediction with Werner's "foreboding" that Grushnitsky will be Pechorin's "victim" (p. 118).

12. Mersereau, pp. 122, 117.

13. Peace, p. 20.

14. Vinogradov, p. 576.

15. B.M. Eikhenbaum, *Lermontov* (Munich, 1967), p.152.

16. Freeborn notes Maksim Maksimich's *faux pas* in telling Pechorin what he has overheard. He also remarks Maksim Maksimich's *faux pas* in ordering the sentry to fire at Kazbich (p. 49); thus we have yet another instance of duality.

In addition, Freeborn connects two episodes in "Bela" which could be termed Kasbich's dual revenge: on Azamat, by killing his father; on Pechorin, by killing Bela (p. 51).

17. This forms another pair, for Maksim Maksimich also feels inadequately remembered by Bela (47).

18. Mersereau, p. 130.

19. Peace has convincingly argued that the plot of "Taman" reverses the plot of "Bela" (p. 28).

20. Peace discusses the second instance (p. 16).

21. This connection may seem contrived—such is the danger of this type of analysis. Still, it is tempting to relate the ominous quality of the blind boy's eyes to a description (in "Bela") of Kazbich: "...Pechorin was not the only one to admire the pretty young princess: from a corner of the room, there looked at her another pair of eyes, immobile and fiery" (13). Yet surely, not every pair of elements is vitally dualistic : Grushnitsky's two uniforms, the two songs in the novel, Pechorin's dusty velvet jacket "fastened only by the two lower buttons" (56).

22. Mersereau, p. 111.

23. Vinogradov, p. 587.

24. Mersereau, p. 134.

Belinskii has declared that in all the stories there is "one idea", expressed in the hero himself (IV, 199). For a discussion of various sequences in which the tales may have been planned and written, see Eikhenbaum, *Stat'i,* pp. 243-8.

25. Peace, p. 29.

Chapter Three

GOGOL'S DESCRIPTIVE DOUBLE IMAGE AND ITS USE IN *DEAD SOULS*

Andrei Bely has aptly observed that "nothing" in Nikolai Gogol's writing "exists without design." What are rather coyly presented as bothersome trivia, he finds, actually reflect the essence of Gogolian reality.[1] Carl Proffer has demonstrated that even in widely separated passages, Gogol makes use of "interlocking detail."[2] The present essay seeks to show that a Gogolian pair of similar episodes or details sometimes serves to reinforce, or even to modify, a third. Such pairs may thus be called descriptive double images. The effect occurs most often in *Dead Souls,* where Vladimir Nabokov's suggestion that in Gogol's world "two and two make five"[3] seems especially appropriate.

Gogol employed descriptive double images even in his early works, such as *Evenings on a Farm Near Dikanka.* In "St. John's Eve," we read that "poor Petrus owned nothing more than one grey jacket, which had more holes in it than a Jew has gold coins in his pocket."[4] Then, after making a deal with the devil to obtain money, Petrus finds that: "His memory was like the pocket of an old miser, out of which you cannot wheedle a penny" (146). This repeated image of a pocket filled with seemingly inaccessible coins proves quite appropriate. For although Petrus now discovers his sacks of devil's gold, he loses them at the end. In Bely's terms, two apparently trivial details reflect the essence of Gogolian reality. Taken together, they form a double image that tends to modify, or reinforce, the story's ending.

In "May Night, or The Drowned Maiden" we are told that the Village Head is a widower who lives with his "sister-in-law." As she is described, however, it seems clear that "mistress" is a more appropriate term (161). Later, when she is twice wrongly presumed to be someone else, the resulting double image of mistaken identity aptly reflects her "sister-in-law" role. This same story features some furtive nocturnal kissing, subtly reinforced by two apparently casual details. First, we read that "the night wind, having stolen up momentarily, kisses" the "virginal groves" of cherry trees (159). Later, drowned maidens are likened to "a riverside reed, touched at the quiet hour of twilight by the airy lips of the wind" (176).

In Part Two of *Evenings,* the effect assumes a rather grotesque twist. Ivan Shponka, terrified at the prospect of marriage, has a nightmare in which he discovers a wife in his ear (307). Earlier in the story, Storchenko had twice described how a cockroach crawled into his ear at night. This unpleasant double image thus anticipates and reflects Shponka's nightmare.

What is perhaps Gogol's most complex use of the effect occurs in his Petersburg tale "Nevsky Prospect." At the very end, we are casually told that "two fat men have stopped" to discuss "how strangely two crows are sitting, each facing the other" (III:45-6). As I have developed elsewhere, this final double image (of silhouette-like shapes, both facing each other) may be seen to echo and reflect a complex sequence of "two halves, precariously joined together" throughout the story. These strangely related shapes are: butterflies, small-waisted dresses, a champagne glass, the pairs of adjacent fat men and crows, and even the two symmetrical halves of the story itself.[5]

Gogol frequently employed descriptive double images in *Dead Souls.* Ultimately, the effect may be seen as essential in shaping the narration and structure of the entire completed volume of this novel. To begin with, the two main meanings of the title (dead souls and dead serfs) seem quite appropriate in describing the living inhabitants. "Who is dead?" asks Bely. "The peasants who have died? Their owners?"[6] Actually, two of the character's souls are described as effectively dead: Sobakevich's (VI:101) and the Prosecutor's (210). The apt ambiguity of the title is thus reinforced by another double image. Moreover, even the meaning "serf" seems appropriate to describe "owners" who are enslaved by their passions and limitations.

Early in the novel, as Chichikov leaves Korobochka's estate: "roads kept crawling off in all directions like a catch of crayfish shaken out of a sack"(60). The scattered, squirming crayfish aptly suggest a lost traveler's unsettling bewilderment. But the crooked appendages of each individual crayfish also serve to evoke the roads. In odd sideways motion, both the crawling crayfish bodies and each one's appendages form a double image that helps to evoke the unknown roads.

Another such image utilizes both bodies and eyes. As Chichikov first observes Plyushkin, we are told that the latter's tiny eyes "...ran out from under his bushy brows like mice, when, having poked their keen little snouts out of dark holes, ears alert and whiskers twitching, they peer out to see if a cat or prankish brat is lurking about, and suspiciously sniff the very air" (116). Here, both the motion of the mice's bodies and the expression of their presumably inquisitive eyes combine to describe Plyushkin's eyes. Yet most readers will probably not consciously realize that this suggestive description involves a subtle double image of surprisingly disparate components. And all this seems to support Proffer's contention that Plyushkin "*is* like a mouse who has stuck his head...from his dark, dank, death-infested house."[7]

When Chichikov enters the district court to legalize his purchase deeds, he hears a vigorous scratching of pens: "The sound of the quills was loud and resembled several cartloads of brushwood being driven through a forest over at least six inches of heaped-up dried leaves" (142). The jostling loads of brushwood suggest a multilayered noise by themselves, but the crackling leaves below enrich it. The hyperbole is thus doubled, adding a humorous depth to the sound of energetic paper-copying.

This compounded phonetic effect resembles an earlier one. Preparing to strike, Korobochka's clock emits "a strange hissing" that sounds "as if the entire room was filled with snakes" (45). The striking of the clock is then said to resemble someone "banging a cracked pot with a stick, after which the pendulum started peacefully ticking right and left again." Caught in abrupt Gogolian focus, both stick and striking snake faintly resemble the vivid pendulum.

When Manilov praises the Governor to Chichikov, we read that he "squinted his eyes almost completely closed from pleasure like a tomcat lightly tickled behind the ears with a finger" (28). Manilov's flattering words of course caress his own ears, completing a double image of humorous satisfaction. But Chichikov is also busy making similar statements, and the cat's purring pleasure tends to flavor his posture as well. As Proffer has noted, Chichikov is likened to a cat late in the novel.[8] Proffer also persuasively suggests, with reference to the description of Plyushkin's eyes discussed above, that Plyushkin is a mouse who fears the cat Chichikov.[9]

Inasmuch as he is a man, however, Chichikov is a performer. And his humorous proficiency in swindling is frequently reinforced by suggestions of legerdemain. Our first two glimpses of Chichikov's hands in action:

> **The gentleman tossed off his cap and unwound from his neck a woolen rainbow-colored scarf...(9)**

> **In the gestures of this gentleman there was something quite solid, and he blew his nose exceedingly loudly. (10)**

This second description is partly from the inn servant's point of view: he feels great respect for the trumpet-like sound of Chichikov's nose-blowing. Chichikov's initial manipulations of handkerchief and rainbow-colored scarf form a double image that introduces a long series of magician-like flourishes. For example, he soon wipes his face "from all sides" with a towel (13), and he continually wipes his brow during difficult negotiations. While exploring the town, he tears down a poster, which disappears into the magician's main receptacle: Chichikov's famous "box, in which he had the habit of storing whatever things he came across" (12).

When Chichikov arrives at Manilov's, host and guest walk to the living room, while Gogol digresses to describe Manilov. Nearly four pages later, we find the two friends standing at the living room door, engaged in a profusion of "after-you" amenities, humorously reinforced by the reader's own retarded progress. Gogol's digression, moreover, contains a double image of comic procrastination. The master of the house, we read, had a book in his study lying open at "the fourteenth page, which he had been reading constantly for two years already" (25). In the next sentence, we learn that Manilov has been warning his guests "for several years" not to sit in two unfinished chairs: "they're not ready yet." This double image of perpetual near-accomplishment serves to intensify the length of time then taken by Manilov and Chichikov to pass through the living room door. When Gogol at last returns to them, we are told that they have been standing there "for several minutes already"(26), each imploring the other to go in first.

Gogol's depiction of the Manilovs' kissing functions similarly. "Exceedingly often," we read, Manilov "having abondoned his pipe," the couple would affix to each other's lips "such a long and languid kiss that in its duration one could easily have smoked through a small straw cigar" (26). Both the abondoned pipe and the intrusive cigar evoke an oral pleasure that blends uneasily with that of the Manilovs' lips. Smoking doubly flavors the kissing. And there is more: two pages earlier, Manilov's pipe-smoking repeatedly attends the fading of his ambitions. Then, after the kiss description, we see "pretty little rows" of ashes knocked from his pipe and hear him tell Chichikov of a "most excellent" man who "never released his pipe from his mouth, not only at the table but even, if I may say so, in all other places"(32). The picture of kissing is thus tainted by two concentric frames of double smoking images.

The ending of Chapter Seven, which Nabokov has dubbed the "Rhapsody of the Boots,"[10] stands in vivid contrast to an earlier double image of humorous bootlessness. First, Korobochka's girl has her bare feet so caked with mud that she appears to be wearing boots (58-9). Next we read of Plyushkin's peasants leaping barefoot across the yard on frosty mornings to don a single pair of indoor communal boots (124). Later, when the lieutenant from Ryazan gloats fondly over his five pairs of boots (153), his pleasure seems even richer by dint of following this double bootlessness.

Gogol uses portraits to form a highly complex descriptive double image in the novel. Manilov is the first to encounter Chichikov's unusual business proposal, whereupon:

> **The two friends...remained motionless, staring into each other's eyes like those portraits that used to hang opposite each other**

in the old days...(34).

In sharp contrast, Sobakevich receives the proposal "without the slightest surprise" (101) and even embarks on a vigorous encomium of his own dead souls. The last words of this are uttered:

> ...addressing the portraits of Bagration and Kolokotronis that were hanging on the wall, as often happens during a conversation when one person suddenly, for no good reason, addresses...a third person who happens to be there...from whom he expects no answer, opinion, or confirmation but at whom, however, he stares so fixedly as if to request his mediation...(103).

Chichikov and Sobakevich then differ so greatly on price that their negotiations come to a standstill:

> The silence lasted for about two minutes. Eagle-nosed Bagration gazed from the wall upon the transaction with intense interest (105).

The ironic humor of the word "transaction" is amplified by a Gogolian life and death reversal:[11] the portrait seems somehow more alive than the two silent people it observes. Less obviously, this two-minute scene is intensified by the previous double image juxtaposed above. The first turned people into portraits; the second, portraits into people. With both processes occurring during the "transaction," the enhanced composite reversal at last becomes complete.

Sheer narrative space tends to disguise such effects. The story of Kifa Mokevich and Moky Kifovich, which Gogol inserts with such triumphant irrelevance near the end, is actually the final part of a descriptive construction that spans the entire novel. This story terminates with the claim that Kifa and Moky have "looked out" of the end of the book "as out of a window" to help answer accusations that Chichikov is not a sufficiently patriotic hero (245). These two sudden heads in the window are actually remote descendants of the two samovars (one of which has a beard and is human) that look out of a shop window in Chichikov's hotel (8) and of the two Sobakevich faces which appear together in the window, only to vanish almost immediately (94). This strange double image of two faces in a window (first half

42

alive, then evanescent) perhaps suggests that the final pair will be of humorously little "help in answering accusations," as indeed they are.

Another double image is widely separated from what it tends to modify. Chichikov's room at the inn where he first stops is said to be of the sort found in most provincial hotels:

> ...a quiet room with cockroaches peeking like plums out of all the corners and with a door, always blocked by a dresser, leading to the adjoining room, where one's neighbor is settled: a silent, unobtrusive person but exceedingly curious and anxious to learn every possible detail about the newcomer. (8)

Note the parallel description: "quiet...peeking" (room with roaches)—"silent...curious" (room with neighbor). The soundless expectancy of each reinforces the other. Much later, after Nozdryov has exposed the nature and scope of Chichikov's dealings, the latter retreats to his room. There,

> with a door blocked by a dresser and cockroaches sometimes peeking out of the corners, his spirits and thoughts were just as restless and uneasy as the armchair in which he was sitting. (174)

Chichikov is now oppressed by the intense curiosity of an entire town. The town has replaced the inquisitive neighbor. Thus, Gogol subtly draws upon the earlier double image of silent expectancy to evoke a suggestive background for his hero's feelings.

When at last the town's ladies react to Chichikov's dealings, rumor emphasizes his alleged plans to abduct the Governor's daughter. Chichikov supposedly "had a wife he'd deserted," who "had written a very moving letter to the Governor" (191). There immediately follows a version that denies the existence of Chichikov's wife. As this version is developed, the "wife" gradually disappears, remaining in the reader's memory as a vague, mostly erased image. But all this has happened before. A greedy and joyous Plyushkin first presumes the existence of Chichikov's wife by showering blessings on his children(123). Later, Plyushkin considers giving Chichikov his silver pocket watch "to impress his fiancée" (130). Chichikov's "wife" has thus been presumed and then denied in two separate instances before he finally becomes ill and stays in his hotel room for two or three days "so as not to end his life, God forbid, without descendants" (211). His personal projection of a presumed wife into the future is thus uneasily tinged by the double disappearance of his two previous ones.

All this is followed by yet another double denial of Chichikov's "wife." Chichikov, we learn, had previously obtained a promotion by almost promising to marry an official's daughter. The promotion, of course, killed the proposal (230). After this, we read that just before the novel began Chichikov "had been thinking of much that was pleasant, of a woman, of a nursery, and a smile would follow such thoughts" (234). Then, in his attempts to rationalize dealing in dead souls, he repeatedly wonders what his children will say if he leaves them no fortune (238). But by this point in the narration his scheme has already been detected; the hypothetical family for which he supposedly undertook it therefore quite typically tends to fade away.

Bely has noted that the oddly sideways motion of Chichikov's carriage throughout the novel corresponds to the hero's arrivals at unintended destinations.[12] The exposure of Chichikov's ghostly estate largely results from the pronouncements of Nozdryov and Korobochka. Earlier, Nozdryov had gambled away his own carriage but managed to transfer himself to Chichikov's vehicle. The gambled-away carriage thus retards the progress of Chichikov's own Plyushkin-bound one. Korobochka's fairy-tale-like "mellon" coach later brings her to town with news that helps to ruin Chichikov (176-77). As Nabokov had phrased it, this carriage finally arrives "in a comparatively tangible world."[13] A blending of unpresent and intangible carriages thus strangely hinders the picaresque progress of Chichikov's own, prosperously rolling one.

Bely has termed the entire plot of Volume One of *Dead Souls* "a closed circle, whirling on its axle, blurring the spokes."[14] His interpretation stresses four details: the wheel discussed on page one, the wheel that delays Chichikov's final escape, and the names of two dead serfs ("The Wheel" and "Drive-to-where-you-won't-get"[15]). As Bely notes, it is significant that the name "Wheel" impresses Chichikov.[16] This double image of dead-people-as-wheels forms a faint, strange symmetry with the almost personified wheel on page one. When Chichikov's escape is finally delayed by presumably the same wheel, it also blends into a double image, and its motion contributes to the Russia-as-troika finale.

But as Bely imaginatively suggests, this motion also applies to Chichikov himself: "At the beginning Chichikov is not a person, but some sort of full-bodied wheel . . . ."[17] Bely goes on to imply that even the peasants' conversation as the novel opens (Will the wheel reach Kazan?) can also apply to Chichikov himself. Actually, the wording which precedes this conversation subtly confirms Bely's inspiration. Chichikov's arrival, we were told,

> caused no commotion and was not accompanied by anything unusual; only two Russian muzhiks standing at the door of a tavern opposite the inn made certain remarks which referred, however, more to the carriage than to the person seated therein. (7)

Since the peasants only discuss a wheel on the carriage, the effect is one of humorous Gogolian anti-climax. Yet their quaint speculations (Will the wheel reach Kazan?) tend to obscure an apparent contradiction: their remarks were said to refer *"more to* the carriage *than to* the person seated therein."[18] Perhaps, then, the peasants' words do refer at least partially, and of course, unwittingly, to Chichikov himself. As Proffer has shown, the wheel is frequently, and fatefully, associated with Chichikov later in the novel.[19] Thus, as Bely seems to have suspected, the projected uncertainty of the wheel on page one may be associated with Chichikov's own uncertain course throughout. Finally, the wheel's breakdown coincides with the failure of Chichikov's dead soul scheme, and the repair of the wheel makes possible his escape.[20] Then, at the very end, the double real wheel image (uneasily reflected by the double dead-serf-as-wheel image) tends to help characterize Chichikov himself as a wheel in the troika that is Russia, both of them rolling headlong into the future, rushing mysteriously into the temporal-spacial unknown.

NOTES

1. Andrei Belyi, *Masterstvo Gogolia* (Munich, 1969), p. 44.
2. Carl R. Proffer, *The Simile and Gogol's "Dead Souls,"* (The Hague, 1967), pp. 82, 172.

3. Vladimir Nabokov, *Nikolai Gogol* (New York, 1961), p. 145.

4. N. V. Gogol, *Polnoe sobranie sochinenii* (Moscow, 1937-52), I, 141. Subsequent references to Gogol's works will be to this edition.

5. See my *Through Gogol's Looking Glass* (New York, 1976), pp. 95-99.

6. Belyi, p. 103.

7. Proffer, p. 86.

8. *Ibid.*, p. 86.

9. *Ibid.*, p. 86.

10. Nabokov, p. 83.

11. As Proffer has noted, it is appropriate that Sobakevich "turns to *inanimate* people (the portraits) to present his dead souls as apparently alive" (p. 89).

12. Belyi, pp. 95-96.

13. Nabokov, p. 94.

14. Belyi, p. 102. (Nabokov has noted this, p. 76.) This image occurs in the final troika passage (247).

15. This translation is Nabokov's (p. 101). The Russian is *Doezhai-ne-doedesh'* (137).

16. Belyi, p. 98.

17. *Ibid.*, p. 24.

18. Strategic placement of "however" *(vprochem)* further conceals the apparent contradiction.

19. For example, after Nozdryov exposes him, Chichikov is likened to "a crooked wheel" (Proffer, pp. 132-33; Gogol, p. 173).

20. The repair of the wheel may even be seen to anticipate the moral recovery that Gogol intended for his hero.

Chapter Four

**SOME FATEFUL
PATTERNS IN TOLSTOI**

Although Leo Tolstoi is famous for his treatment of historical causation and predetermination in *War and Peace*, a variety of fateful patterns can be discerned in many of his works. These patterns include recurrent images, numbers, words and phrases, and a series of what may be termed unlikely prophets.

In *Childhood, Boyhood, and Youth* the question is raised: Will the "predictions" of the holy fool Grisha prove true? Nicholas Irtenev's mother, at least, declares that she has "good reason" to believe such predictions: "Kiryusha foretold the exact day and hour of death for deceased papa."[1] The apparently meaningless mutterings of a holy fool afford a rich opportunity for unexpected predictions: the mental deformity of such a person renders the accuracy of his predictions quite ironic.

In *War and Peace*, the one-eyed Kutuzov (who is often called "blind") sees considerably farther than many others. In *The Cossacks*, Lukashka's dumb sister tells him by hand signals that he must kill another Chechen (III: 216). Later, a Chechen whom Lukashka is trying to capture alive critically wounds him.

One would scarcely expect Dolly Oblonsky, deceived by her husband in *Anna Karenina*, to be an expert forecaster of marriages. Yet as Oblonsky himself tells

Levin, Dolly has "the gift of prophecy," especially concerning marriages (VIII: 48). Then, having cited an example of Dolly's accuracy, he reveals her prediction that Kitty will be Levin's wife "for sure." At this point, of course, the marriage is by no means "sure"—and soon appears still less so.

Mary Bolkonsky, in *War and Peace*, also seems an unlikely marriage forecaster, yet she correctly predicts that Andrew will not marry again, especially Natasha (V: 244). Somewhat similarly, Natasha's "prediction" about Dolokhov's hope to marry Sonya "proves true" (49). Moreover, Natasha correctly prophesies that Nicholas will not marry Sonya (52). "God knows why I know," she remarks. The accuracy of Natasha's humble, unselfish predictions seems especially appropriate in *War and Peace*, where smug, selfish predictions often prove false. Early in the novel, there is also the oddly prophetic question (*"vous trouvez que l'assassinat est grandeur d'ame?"*) put by Lise to Pierre when he is discussing Napoleon (V: 28). Of course, this strange interconnection with Pierre's eventual decision to assassinate Napoleon seems quite natural in context. Yet the very naturalness of Lise's motivation tends to render her words more unexpectedly prophetic.

Tolstoi's most remarkable unlikely prophets not only lack logical insight but even reveal motivation tending to belie accuracy. As *Childhood, Boyhood, and Youth* opens, for example, Nicholas Irtenev invents a reason for crying: he pretends that he has just dreamed of his mother's death. The "dream" of course soon proves true. In *War and Peace*, Petya Rostov says that Natasha "was in love with that fat one with the glasses" (IV: 299)—presumably for no other reason than that Natasha has just called Petya a fool. Clearly, Natasha realizes this "love" (for Pierre) only very much later. And when Sonya makes her famous predictions before the candles and mirrors, she merely feigns to see the future (V: 302-03). "Why shouldn't I say that I saw something?" she wonders. "Others really do see!" As is well known, she unwittingly predicts not only Andrew's death (including the expression on his face?) but also Pierre's marriage to Natasha. After describing Andrew lying down, Sonya feigns to see "something blue and red," and Natasha had already told her mother that Pierre was "dark blue with red" (203).

Early in *Anna Karenina* (VIII: 85-86), Kitty enthusiastically persuades Anna to come to the ball. Anna repeatedly likens Kitty's own expectations of the ball to a blissful "fog" (*tuman*).

Then, at the very moment when Kitty, in anguish, perceives the intense feeling between Anna and Vronsky, we are told that the entire ball was covered by a "fog [*tumanom*] in Kitty's soul" (95).

Later in the novel, Dolly manages to comfort Kitty, who is suffering because of her previous passion for Vronsky. Kitty then says that she will visit Dolly to help cure her children of scarlet fever: "I have had scarlet fever," she declares (143). Soon after this, an ambassador's wife likens passion to scarlet fever in conversation with Vronsky (155). "One must pass through it," she says. Sidney Schultze[2] has connected the passion simile with little Tanya's scarlet fever.

A fateful image pattern common to both of Tolstoi's major novels involves suggestions of childhood and fairy-tale-like pleasure. Early in *War and Peace*, Pierre is compared to "a child in a toy shop" (IV: 17). He later plays at being Napoleon, piercing an invisible enemy with his sword (70). Natasha, age thirteen, runs in with her doll (52-53), and she hides in the conservatory "as if under a cap of invisibility" (58), a Russian fairy-tale image. Such descriptions tend to unite Natasha and Pierre long before it is clear that they will marry each other.

Somewhat similarly, Levin is struck at the skating rink by Kitty's expression "of childish clarity and goodness" and by the "childishness of her face" (VIII: 38). Her smile, we are told, always carried him off to "an enchanted world where he experienced tender, soft feelings like those he recalled from rare days of his early childhood." He is also reminded of how he used to associate Kitty with an English fairy tale (40). Levin himself is compared, early in the novel, to a "boy" (27), a "twelve-year-old girl" (28), and a "child" (43). These similar introductory descriptions tend to unite Kitty and Levin even though she soon refuses his first proposal of marriage. In a vague, suggestive dimension, the two remain subtly associated until they are in fact united.

The Cossacks affords an early example of Tolstoian fateful patterning. In this story, after drinking wine with Olenin, Uncle Eroshka watches moths flying into the candle flame. "Fool, fool!" he says. "You're destroying your own self, and I pity you" (III: 208). At the end of the story they again drink, and Olenin leaves, saying: "Farewell, Uncle!" Eroshka replies: "Is that any way to say goodbye? Fool! fool! . . . You see, I love you, I pity you so!" (299). The parallel wording may be seen to suggest that

Olenin has been "destroying his own self" like a "piteous" moth, flying blindly into the passion of his love for Maryanka.

The famous description of Anna Karenina's suicide as a dying candle flame (IX: 369) may be traced from the warm shining expression that she cannot "extinguish" upon meeting Vronsky (VIII: 73), which grows stronger as she dances with him (94), to the metaphorical light at the train station as he follows her to Petersburg: "a red fire blinded her eyes" (116), and finally, to the question she asks just two pages before the description of her death as an extinguished flame: "Why not put out the candle?"

This association of fire with Anna could cause us to wonder about the other three main characters and elements. Levin, who constantly works in the fields, can easily be associated with earth. Kitty, who is advised "to drink the waters" (VIII: 136), regains her health at "the little German waters" (238). But is it possible to associate Vronsky, the fourth main character, with the fourth element, air? When Anna is on board the train to return to Petersburg, we may recall, she finds it "very hot" and goes out onto the platform "to get some air" (VIII: 117). There she finds that: "'The wind seemed to have been just waiting for her; it joyfully whistled and wanted to seize her and carry her off. . . .'" Anna breathes deeply of the cold air and looks around. She then takes "another deep breath in order to get her fill of the air"—and meets Vronsky. Why is he following her? He must be with her and "cannot do otherwise," he declares.

> At that moment the wind, as if overcoming an obstacle, scattered snow from the carriage roofs and rattled some kind of torn-off sheet of iron, and the hollow whistle of the steam engine roared mournfully and gloomily in front. All the terror of the storm seemed still more beautiful to her now. He had said what her soul desired but her reason feared.

Twice here the air seems associated with Vronsky, especially since the wind is twice appropriately personified. First, Anna feels that she needs air; the wind, waiting for her, wants to carry her off. Then, just as Vronsky says that he must be with her, the wind is said to have overcome an obstacle: he has clearly declared his intentions. And of course Anna's view of the storm as "beautiful terror" aptly suggests her attitude towards an affair with Vronsky.

These proposed elemental associations seem supported by several other factors in the novel. First, we may note that the primary elements are Anna and Levin: fire and earth are fed by air and water, respectively. And surely, Anna and Levin are the main characters; Schultze (42-47) has demonstrated that the entire novel may be seen as thirty-four segments, seventeen alternately devoted to Anna and to Levin. Even on the most general level, our attention shifts back and forth, focusing on their twin arrivals in Part One, following their twin loves throughout, and merging, intensified, when they finally meet in Part Seven.

More specifically, we may note that just as fire needs air, Anna needed air when she met Vronsky on the station platform. And as earth needs water, Levin seems to need water when he works in the fields, vainly attempting to forget Kitty. Mowing with his peasants, Levin enjoys a drink of water from the river more than any drink he has ever had (VIII: 280). And the rain unexpectedly gives him "a pleasant sensation" as he "joyously" feels it upon his shoulders (279). Elsewhere, as Schultze has observed (229), Levin is described as "a fish on land." Moreover, he finds new love for Kitty and their son in the rain, when he discovers that they have not been hit by lightning (IX: 416). The two main love relationships in the novel thus seem intensified by the elemental force of storms; Anna-Vronsky, by a winter snowstorm, Levin-Kitty by a spring thunderstorm.[3]

Even the elemental incompatibility between fire and water seems consistent with the initial rivalry between Kitty and Anna for Vronsky's love. And although Anna prevails (air being more compatible with fire than with water), she feels guilty; subsequently, water is associated with disaster for her. She unwisely reveals her feeling for Vronsky when he causes the death of Frou-Frou (who has frequently been seen to suggest Anna) at "a ditch with water" (VIII: 222). Later, when Anna thinks of what she has done to Karenin, she is likened to someone in danger of drowning (IX: 35-36). Finally, she kills herself like a bather "going into the water" (IX: 368)—a vestige of Tolstoi's earlier plan to have Anna drown herself in the Neva River.[4] Elementally, the water image is highly appropriate, suggesting an end both to Anna's fiery passion and to the flame of her life. Earlier, moreover, after Anna's display of emotion at the horse race, Karenin is likened to "a person who had vainly tried to extinguish a fire" (VIII: 224).

In what may be termed yet another elemental dimension of *Anna Karenina*, fire-related images may be associated with each of the four main characters. Besides Anna's image, the flame of a candle, we may note the following. When Levin arrives at the skating rink to find Kitty, she is repeatedly likened to the sun (VIII: 37-39). Levin himself is strongly associated with the stars. In Part Two, various stars (and especially Venus) seem to inspire Levin to ask Oblonsky about Kitty (184-85).[5] Later, "having gazed at the stars" (305), Levin sees Kitty in a passing carriage and realizes that he loves *"her."* Finally as the novel ends, Levin gazes at the stars and they seem to help him find direction and meaning in his life. And Vronsky? As Schultze has demonstrated, electricity is associated with Vronksy throughout the novel (220).

As with the four elements, these fire-related images have several appropriate associations. Electricity is a dangerous force, especially in water—which, we recall, was Kitty's element. And as noted above, Levin fears that lightning has killed Kitty. Lightning, of course, travels through air, Vronsky's element. The sun (Kitty) warms and gives life, which aptly relates to Levin's element, earth. Finally, the flame obviously coincides with Anna's element, fire.

Yet another appropriate aspect of these images may be seen by grouping them as Kitty-Levin and Anna-Vronsky. The former images (sun-stars) suggest permanence compared to the latter (flame-electricity). This aptness even seems to include the four characters' relationships to suicide. Anna commits suicide; Vronsky attempts it, and he can be seen to be trying to kill himself at the end of the novel. Kitty despairs, and Levin apparently comes close to suicide; but their permanence endures, and they survive.

If such patterns exist in *War and Peace*, they are not as consistent. Pierre seems associated with fire: he himself relates the brilliant comet of 1812 to the condition of his soul (V: 389). He also makes his famous declaration about the futility of holding his "immortal soul" captive against a quite fiery background: the "fire-like" haze of the rising moon and "the red fires of campfires" (VII: 114-15). Moreover, Pierre remains in the burning city of Moscow and saves a child in a flaming building (VI: 411). However, water is suggested by the "globe of droplets" that Pierre sees when Platon Karataev dies (VII: 170). This "liquid" globe seems to inspire Pierre's vision of himself sinking "somewhere into the water, so that the water closed over his head" (171). In addition, Natasha sees Pierre as having emerged from a Russian bath (*banya*) near the end of the novel (VII: 237). Perhaps both Pierre and Anna Karenina may be seen as moving from association with fire to submersion in water, with the difference that Pierre emerges, and then is further cleansed by the *banya*.

Volume Three, part one of *War and Peace* opens to focus on the question: What caused the War of 1812? After arguing that there were an incalculable number of causes, Tolstoi concludes that the war had no single, exceptional cause: " . . . the event had to occur only because it had to occur" (VI: 9). His point, as he finally puts it, is that no matter how much control we seem (from our perspective) to have over our actions, they are nevertheless, in terms of historical causation, "determined from eternity" (*opredeleno predvechno*). This phrase is later combined with the above notion "had to occur" *(dolzhno bylo sovershit'sya)* at a key point in Pierre's life. Having decided that his own name, like Napoleon's, has the fateful numerological value 666, Pierre concludes that his role (as Napoleon's killer) is "determined from eternity" and therefore, that he must not undertake anything (such as joining the army) but rather wait for what "has to occur" (VI: 87).

Pierre's calculations are based upon a prophecy taken from the Revelation of St. John. According to the Apocalypse, "the beast" is a man whose number is 666. With very flexible figuring, Pierre manages to match both his own name and Napoleon's to the number 666. He thus deems it his lot to kill "the beast," and he lists what he feels are the fateful forces in his life: his love for Natasha, Antichrist, Napoleon's invasion, the comet, 666, and the two names with this numerological value.[6]

This emphasis upon fateful sixes may cause us to wonder if there are others. The following examples seem to suggest that in *War and Peace*, and perhaps even elsewhere, Tolstoi sometimes associates the number six with a nearness to—and an escape from—death. Pierre of course does not succeed in carrying out his 666-inspired plan to kill Napoleon.

As many have noted, we are quite pointedly told that Pierre's father has his "sixth stroke" while the "sixth anglaise" is being played (IV: 90). These "sixth's" seem quite ominously juxtaposed, yet Pierre's father dies only after one more stroke (102), so the pattern of six-related escape from death seems to hold.

Pierre himself is close to death twice. Late in the novel, as the French execute prisoners, we are told that Pierre was "the sixth" in line to be shot (VII: 46). The prisoners are then executed *in pairs* until the fifth, a young factory worker, is shot alone: Pierre unexpectedly survives. Earlier at the duel with Dolokhov, Pierre, "having walked about six steps" (V: 30), had somehow managed to wound his adversary, who then fired with great effort and missed.[7] Not only does this "six" typically attend an unlikely escape from death (Pierre has never before held a pistol in his hand), Tolstoi clearly suggests that the outcome of the duel was fated (see below).

Early in *Resurrection*, we learn that Katyusha was the daughter of an unmarried serf woman whose first five children had been allowed to die of starvation.

> The sixth child, fathered by a gypsy tramp, was a girl, and her fate would have been the very same, but it happened that one of the two older ladies . . . gave milk and money to the mother, and the little girl remained alive. And so the older ladies called her "the saved one." (XI: 11)

In the overall context of Tolstoi's world, it seems quite appropriate that this "sixth" child comes so close to death and yet survives. Note also the reference to Katyusha's "fate."

As a kind of corollary to the notion that Tolstoian sixes may be associated with escape from death, the number seven (perhaps one step further?) sometimes seems related to death itself. For example, the old Count Bezukhov does in fact die soon after his seventh stroke (IV: 102). Moreover, on the page following the ominous juxtaposition of sixth's ("stroke" and "anglaise"), we find a juxtaposition of sevens. The old Count is said to be in his "seventh decade," and this is immediately followed by a reference to someone who received the sacrament "seven times" before dying (91). The crowd that kills Vereshchagin is likened to the "seventh and last wave that shatters a ship" (VI: 361). The Freemasons whom Pierre joins have a list of "seven virtues," and number seven is "The love of death" (V: 84).

In *Sebastopol in May*, the fatally wounded Parskukhin decides to count soldiers. He reaches a total of seven before he dies (II: 136-37). In *War and Peace*, it is repeatedly noted that General Schmidt was killed "at seven o'clock" (IV: 205). Curiously enough, Anna Pirogova, the model for Anna Karenina, arrived at the railroad station "at seven o'clock" and threw herself under "train number seven."[8] In the novel itself, Vronsky is given "number seven" for the race in which he causes Frou-Frou's death (VIII: 217).

54

Seeking out Levin at his hotel, Oblonsky says: "Levin—number seven, eh?" (413). Finding "number seven," Oblonsky enters and exclaims: "Ah! Killed it?" This refers to the bear that Levin has recently killed. The two friends then discuss "death" at some length, and Levin declares that death haunts him.

Returning to *War and Peace*, we may note that if Nicholas's disastrous loss to Dolokhov at cards may be considered a symbolic death, it is the "seven of hearts" that does him in (V: 58-59). Tolstoi repeatedly stresses the fateful seven: Nicholas's decision to stake on it, his agonizing wait for a seven to appear, and his refusal to believe that "a stupid chance" would cause "the seven" to ruin him. There is even what could be termed a "life review" of past experiences that flashes before Nicholas immediately prior to his "death" by the seven.

> **At that minute his home life—little jokes with Petya, conversations with Sonya, duets with Natasha, piquet with his father and even his peaceful bed in the Povarsky house—appeared to him with such force, clarity and charm that it all seemed a long-past, lost and unappreciated happiness.**

By what seems a coincidence,[9] Tolstoi uses the word "seven" *(semyorka)* seven times in describing this fateful episode.

As R.F. Christian has demonstrated, various kinds of repetition are a major distinguishing feature of Tolstoi's style.[10] Tolstoian repetitions sometimes form parts of fateful patterns. In *Anna Karenina*, when Levin finally meets Anna, he notices something special about her: "Besides intelligence, grace, and beauty, she also had truthfulness" (IX: 294). The Russian word *pravdivost'*, here rendered "truthfulness," also has connotations of sincerity and uprightness. Levin feels "truthfulness" deeply; in fact, it is a dominant characteristic of his beloved Kitty. Kitty's "truthful [*pravdivie*] eyes" are frequently mentioned, for example both times Levin proposes to her (VIII: 59, 437). An especially significant reference occurs in Part Three of the novel, when Levin gazes at the sky just before dawn, pondering the changes in his views of life. A carriage passes by, and two "truthful eyes" look out at him (VIII: 307). We are told that this was Kitty only five lines later, but by the adjective *pravdivie*, one could have guessed. "There were no other eyes like those in the world. There was only one being in the world capable of focusing for him the entire world and meaning of life." Truthfulness is thus developed as a crucial quality for Levin, and it seems quite significant that he singles out this quality in Anna, especially so late in the novel.

After Kitty passes by in the carriage, Levin decides that a "mysterious [*tainstvennaya*] change" in the clouds confirms a great change in his own life (VIII: 307). Then, just prior to Levin's successful proposal, we are told that he and Kitty had "not a conversation, but some sort of mysterious [*tainstvennoe*] communication" (429). Very early in the novel, this same word had been continually applied (30-32) to Levin's impressions of Kitty, her family, and love.

Schultze has demonstrated that the influence of strange forces upon the characters in *Anna Karenina* is frequently suggested by the repetition of various words and phrases.[11] Perhaps most strikingly, a person is said to act "involuntarily" or "against his will." As the novel opens, we are told twice in one sentence that Oblonsky smiled "entirely involuntarily" (VIII:9) when exposed in his affair with the French governess. And when his sister Anna first meets Vronsky, her face displays an immediate, vital attraction that shines out "against her will" and "despite her will" (73). In *War and Peace*, as Pierre begins the duel (discussed above) that he quite miraculously wins against Dolokhov, we are told that the affair was taking place "independent of the will of people" (V: 30).

While such wordings, as Schultze observes, may suggest either positive or negative forces, Tolstoi also employs three other phrases which consistently seem to fit a patterned evaluation. Two are positive; one is negative. In *War and Peace*, Nicholas is told by the Governor's wife that he should marry Princess Mary. Thinking of Sonya, he answers: "Still, *ma tante*, this cannot be" (VII: 26). Later, as he begins to read Sonya's letter: " . . . his eyes fearfully and joyfully opened wide. 'No, this cannot be!' he said aloud" (34). Near the end of the novel, Pierre has difficulty recognizing Natasha: "But no, this cannot be," he thinks. "This cannot be she" (VII: 299). He then realizes that he loves her: " . . . and still more strongly an agitation of joy and fear seized his soul."

With both Nicholas and Pierre, a mixture of "joy and fear" and the feeling that "this cannot be" precede a happy marriage that seems somewhat unlikely. This pattern holds in *Anna Karenina*. When Levin arrives at the skating rink, seeking Kitty: "He knew she was there by the joy and fear that seized his heart"

(VIII: 37). Then, when he proposes, she answers: "This cannot be . . . forgive me. . ." (59). Later, Levin intensely recalls these words (300). Finally, when he sees Kitty at the Oblonskys', he feels "such joy and together such fear, that it took his breath away" (421). Soon they both have "a feeling of joyful fear" (429), and Levin proposes again, this time successfully. With only the first letter of each word, he asks Kitty the fateful question: "When you answered me 'this cannot be,' did it mean never, or then?" (437).

Her reply ("Then I could not answer otherwise") echoes yet another patterned Tolstoian phrase, one that is temporarily negative. When Levin's first proposal is refused, he answers: "This could not be otherwise." These words, in Tolstoian reality, sometimes appear when a positive, flexible character resigns himself to a temporary setback by a current of fate. In *War and Peace*, Pierre feels "that Helene not only could, but must be his wife, that this could not be otherwise" (IV: 262). Then, when the old Prince Kuragin cleverly congratulates the pair, Pierre thinks: "All this must be so and could not be otherwise" (272). Since Pierre is ultimately destined for Natasha, the repeated phrase "this could not be otherwise" attends a fateful setback similar to Levin's unsuccessful first proposal.

To summarize: the Tolstoian phrases "This cannot be" (*èto-go ne mozhet byt'*) and "joy and fear" (*radost' i strakh*[12]) tend to signal that two positive characters will ultimately be united. The words "This could not be otherwise" (*èto ne moglo byt' inache*) typically suggest that a positive, flexible character is resigning himself to a temporary setback by a current of fate. The idea of resignation to such a setback is of course central to *War and Peace*. On the largest scale, Russia temporarily and painfully concedes Moscow to the French—only to win in the end. Quite similarly, both Pierre and Natasha give in, temporarily and painfully, to Helene and Anatole—only to find each other at the end. The pattern extends even to the use of the French language at these two key points in the novel. Pierre, resigned to marrying Helene, awkwardly declares *"Je vous aime!"* (IV: 272). Anatole, beginning his conquest of Natasha, announces: *"Mais charmante!"* (V:340). Yet Pierre's and Natasha's Russianness seems fated to triumph eventually.

As we have seen, Tolstoi's works contain a variety of fateful patterns. He favors characters who may be termed unlikely prophets, whose unexpected insights suggest that the future can sometimes be discerned. Other fateful patterns include images of childhood and fairy-tale-like pleasure (which anticipate the union of positive characters), various elemental images, survival- and death-related sixes and sevens, and recurrent words and phrases. As employed by Tolstoi, one of these phrases ("It could not be otherwise") may be seen to suggest that positive, flexible characters are ultimately rewarded for not resisting a temporary setback by a current of Fate.

NOTES

1. L.N. Tolstoi, *Sobranie sochinenii v dvenadtsati tomakh* (Moscow, 1958), I, 26. Subsequent references to Tolstoi's works will be to this edition.

2. Sidney Patterson Schultze, *Anna Karenina: A Structural Analysis*, Doctoral Dissertation, Indiana University, 1974, p. 240. Subsequent references to Schultze will be in parentheses in the text.

3. For a discussion of the role of the four seasons in *Anna Karenina* see Schultze, pp. 52-56.

4. Schultze links drowning with the Anna-Vronsky story (231).

5. Schultze suggests (222-23) that Venus "is Kitty" and develops several parallels between this episode and the skating rink scene.

6. A recent (1976) television show parodied the movie *The Omen* by noting that 666 is "the devil's area code," but Leskov was there first. In his story "Night Owls" (*Polunoshchniki*), the Antichrist's cabman, who "knows the road to the devil," is said to have the number 666. (N.S. Leskov, *Sobranie sochinenii v odinnadtsati tomakh*, Moscow, 1956-58, IX, 139.) The number 666 is sometimes said to represent an unholy trinity: Devil, Antichrist, False Prophet.

7. As still another part of the pattern, it may be noted that after both these six-related escapes from death the "orphan" Pierre, extremely dejected, meets the "paternal" Bazdeev and the "maternal" Platon Karataev, both of whom help him find new meaning in life. Bazdeev is twice termed "fatherly" (V: 74, 76), and Platon is twice described as "feminine" (VII: 51, 55).

8. News item in *Tula Province News*, 1872. See George Gibian, ed., *Anna Karenina* (Norton Critical Edition; New York, 1970), p. 745.

9. There is even the fact that Nicholas loses 43,000 rubles—a sum chosen by Dolokhov as the sum of his and Sonya's ages but which also may suggest a seven. At the end, Nicholas wins a paltry twenty-one rubles when pressured by Dolokhov to bet only the amount his debt exceeded 43,000. However, Nicholas had intended to bet 6,000 which, though not quite an "escape from death," would have decreased his debt considerably.

10. R.F. Christian, *Tolstoy's "War and Peace"* (London: Oxford University, 1962), pp. 148-66.

11. Schultze, pp. 166-72.

12. The only variation of this pattern in all of the above examples is the word

ispuganno ("fearfully"), instead of *strakh* ("fear"), applied to Nicholas when he reads Sonya's letter.

Chapter Five

DOSTOEVSKIAN PATTERNED ANTINOMY AND ITS FUNCTION IN *CRIME AND PUNISHMENT*

Antinomy, which may be briefly defined as a contradiction between two apparently correct ideas, is an essential characteristic of Dostoevsky's world. Indeed, Viacheslav Ivanov has seen it as vital to the Dostoevskian "novel-tragedy": "In its whole plan, every novel by Dostoevsky is directed towards a tragic catastrophe...At each moment we are confronted... with tragedy raised, so to speak, to a higher power. It is as if we saw...in its cell-structure a repetition and emphasis of the same principle of antinomy that informs the whole organism."[1] Here we shall attempt to go one step further and show that Dostoevskian antinomy frequently predicates a highly specialized patterning. This patterning pervades both the "cell-structure" and plot structure of *Crime and Punishment.*

Surprisingly often, Dostoevsky creates antinomic effects by means of a three-stage formulation which may be likened to the swinging of a pendulum from one side to the other and then at least partially back. This final swing tends to reconcile the two extremes, and Dostoevsky's reader is led to accept a (muted) contradiction. Deep in *The Brother's Karamazov,* for example, Smerdiakov tells Ivan (at their "third and

final meeting"): "Go home; *it was not you who killed him*."[2]
Ivan seizes him by the throat, crying, "Tell everything, you reptile!"[3] "Well then, it *was* you who killed him, if that's the way
it is," Smerdiakov viciously whispers. Thus, Dostoevsky quickly shifts from one extreme to the other: Ivan did not kill the
old man—he did. Smerdiakov soon declares: "You killed him,
you are the main killer. I was only your accomplice." (X:l45).
His strange logic sends the pendulum partially back to its point
of departure: Ivan himself did not commit the murder, yet he
did kill his father using Smerdiakov as his instrument. This patterned contradiction realistically mutes the question of patri-
cidal guilt, a major concern of the novel.

Before examining the function of patterned antinomy
in *Crime and Punishment*, we should note two intensifying factors. First, many of the characters in this novel are antinomic
mixtures. In his notebooks, Dostoevsky develops the characterization of Sonia by having Marmeladov call her a saint, to which
she replies: "I am a great sinner."[4] In addition to Sonia the saint-
ly sinner, we can discern Porfiry the compassionate pursuer,
Marmeladov the perceptive drunkard, Svidrigailov the vile lover
of children,   Luzhin the respectable villain, and Raskolnikov
the reluctant murderer, reluctant confessor, and reluctant repen-
ter. Razumikhin even asserts that in Raskolnikov "two opposite
characters take turns" (V:222).[5]

Yet another factor intensifying the antinomic patterning
in *Crime and Punishment* is its method of narration. As Leonid
Grossman has explained, "the relating of events almost always
from the subjective position of the main hero (a vestige, in the
final version, of the original first-person narration) transforms the
entire novel into a peculiar internal monologue of Raskolnikov,
which gives the whole history of his crime an exceptional whole-
ness, tenseness, and fascination."[6] Constantly offered Raskolnikov's perceptions in the guise of objective narration, the reader
senses a slight tension between what he is told and what may
in fact be happening.[7] From the very beginning, he is both outside and yet partially inside Raskolnikov.

As the novel opens, we are told that Raskolnikov always
experienced "some kind of sickly and cowardly sensation" while
passing his landlady's door on the stairs. He was heavily in debt
to her and was afraid of meeting her. "Not that he was so cowardly or downtrodden, quite the contrary; but for some time now

he had been in a tense and irritable condition resembling hypo-
chondria" (V:5). Raskolnikov's sickly cowardice is denied; its
opposite affirmed. His state of nervousness and near hypochon-
dria then tends to reconcile the two extremes. The reader may
even sense here Raskolnikov's mental attempt to justify his own
apparent cowardice. This effect soon becomes more obvious:
"Actually, he was not afraid of any landlady at all, no matter
what this one happened to be plotting against him. But to stop
on the stairs and listen to all sorts of nonsense about all those
commonplace, trivial things..." (V:6). By this time the reader
has been subtly introduced to Raskolnikov's inner feelings through
his own point of view. He may be afraid, we feel, but his defen-
sive posture seems generalized ("Actually, he was not afraid of
any landlady at all..."). We almost anticipate the revelation of
a greater fear, one that renders the landlady insignificant by contrast. But such a fear, if it exists, is immediately rationalized as
mundane impatience or irritation ("But to stop on the stairs
..."). As before, the pendulum then swings back towards its point
of departure: "When he reached the street, however, his fear of
meeting his creditor shocked even him" (V:6).

Dostoevsky thus repeats the patterning. Raskolnikov's apparent fear is once again denied and then reaffirmed, realistically
suggesting his inner vacillations and doubts. These two passages
establish a tone, an atmosphere of uncertainty that is maintained
by subsequent patterned antinomies. And the reader's suspicion
that Raskolnikov fears more than just his landlady seems strangely
confirmed by a final impression of intense but inadequately jus-
tified fright ("his fear...shocked even him."). A patterned antinomy in the narration thus enables the reader to share Raskolnikov's inner feelings and thoughts. "In *Crime and Punishment*,"
George Gibian has suggested, "the reader, as well as Raskolnikov,
must struggle to draw his own conclusions from a work which
mirrors the refractory and contradictory materials of life itself
...."[8] This process has two main advantages. Purportedly objective narration subtly reflects Raskolnikov's own contradictory
perceptions, feelings, thoughts. And the reader, in struggling
to resolve these contradictions, vividly shares in the hero's own
experience.

We see other people partially through the eyes of Raskolnikov. At Raskolnikov's first glimpse of him (in the tavern),
Marmeladov is described as "a man...with a face puffy from

continual drunkenness and swollen eyelids from under which shone tiny, slitlike but animated reddish eyes.... In his gaze there seemed to shine even a kind of triumph—apparently there was both sense and intelligence there—but also the gleam of something like madness" (V:15). Marmeladov thus seems a drunkard dulled by drink; but one who has flashes of perception; but whose perceptions seem mixed with something like madness. This patterning subtly previews his tragic story: drunken irresponsibility, flashes of guilt and remorse, and finally a masochistic satisfaction approaching drunken madness.

Our first glimpse of Porfiry Petrovich also seems focused through Raskolnikov: "His round, puffy and slightly snub-nosed face was of a sickly dark yellow color, but quite alert and even derisive. It might even have seemed kindly, except for the expression of his eyes, which shone with a liquid, watery glaze, partly covered by his nearly white eyelashes that blinked as if winking to someone. The look of these eyes was somehow in strange disharmony with the rest of his figure, which had something almost womanish about it, and endowed it with a much more serious air than one at first glance might have expected of it." (V:259) Essentially, this passage blends several opposites: sickliness, alertness; benevolence, derision; feminine passiveness, serious control. The last sentence is itself a three-stage pattern: Porfiry's sly, ironic expression literally surrounds the description of his strangely disharmonious figure. And just as Marmeladov's appearance subtly prefigured his story, so Porfiry's apparently winking eyes serve as a preview of the ensuing psychological duel.

Porfiry tells Raskolnikov to submit a short statement about his pawned belongings. "On ordinary paper?" Raskolnikov inquires. " 'Oh, as ordinary as can be!' and suddenly Porfiry Petrovich looked at him with a kind of obvious mockery, screwing up his eyes as if winking at him. This however may only have seemed so to Raskolnikov, because it lasted only a moment. At least there had been something like that. Raskolnikov could have sworn he had winked at him, the devil only knew why. 'He knows!' flashed through him like lightning" (V:260). Here, both reader and Raskolnikov are led to believe that Porfiry (1) seemed to wink, (2) may not have, and (3) probably did. Our haunting suspicion that he definitely did wink, however, is doubly intensified since Raskolnikov wonders why he winked and even deduces from the wink that Porfiry knows of his crime. Porfiry later asks Raskolnikov if he himself, according to his theory, might be able to go beyond the law: " 'Oh, for instance, kill and steal?' And once again he somehow suddenly winked at him with his left eye, laughing inaudibly—just exactly as he had before " (V:275). This implicit reaffirmation of our previous suspicion (that Porfiry did wink) subtly re-establishes the reader's position inside Raskolnikov's mind at a key point in the encounter.

To provoke Raskolnilov, Porfiry offers a capsulized version of his theory about extraordinary people who supposedly have the right to commit crimes. Raskolnikov reacts wth typical antinomic patterning. " 'That's not exactly the way I had it,' he began.... 'However, I admit you have stated it almost fairly, even, if you like, completely fairly.... The only difference is that...' " (V:269).[9] Porfiry thus seems (1) wrong, (2) right, (3) slightly wrong. Raskolnikov's objection, which he develops at great length, is that extraordinary people are by no means obliged to commit crimes. Porfiry, of course, has said nothing of the sort, but few readers will stop to realize this. Suspense increases the pace. Finally, Raskolnikov qualifies his argument as follows: while furthering the general good, extraordinary people inevitably work some destruction; we must therefore compare the scope of their idea with its destructive effects. The (protracted) patterning is thus (1) extraordinary people are not obliged to commit crimes, but (2) such people, rather, must commit crimes because great actions inevitably cause some destruction; but (3) insofar as they are obliged to work for good, they nevertheless are indirectly obliged to commit certain crimes. The third step is easily inferable but never explicitly stated, yet it symmetrically develops and completes the meaning of Raskolnikov's initial reaction to Porfiry's capsulized version of his theory.

Raskolnikov later awakes from a nightmare echoing the murders to find a visitor staring at him in silence. For about ten minutes he feigns sleep, wondering if he is still dreaming. At last Svidrigailov introduces himself and says he has been bored recently, that he is delighted to have found Raskolnikov. "Do not be angry, Rodion Romanovich, but you yourself seem for some reason terribly strange. Whatever you say, there is something like that in you; and right now—that is, not exactly at this minute, but right now in general..." (V:294). Here the muted contradiction between "right now" and "now in general" tends to distract from Svidrigailov's implication that he understands Raskolnikov because the two of them are similarly strange. Two pages later, Svidrigailov mentions that Marfa Petrovna's ghost comes to visit him, and Raskolnikov exclaims that he suspected as much. " 'Oh-ho? You thought so?' Svidrigailov asked in surprise. 'Did you really? Well, didn't I say that we had a little something in common, eh?' 'You never said that!' Raskolnikov blurted out sharply and heatedly" (V:297). As we have seen, Svidrigailov did not say this but presumably did imply it. The conversation about ghosts continues, Raskolnikov finally asserting, "I do not believe in a future life" (V:299). This statement contradicts his claim to Porfiry about believing literally in the resurrection of Lazarus (V:271). Later, when he insistently asks Sonia to read this part of the Gospels, the contradiction becomes muted: if he does not believe, he is perhaps desperately trying to believe. And this entire protracted three-stage pattern can be seen to preview the final mention of Lazarus in the Epilogue.

Svidrigailov then offers his famous vision of Eternity as a little room with spiders, stressing that his idea may be entirely just. Raskolnikov apparently seems so upset that Svidrigailov remarks: "Well, wasn't I right in saying we were berries from the same field?" (V:300). Just as Porfiry's wink seemed more and more to have happened, so, here, Svidrigailov's earlier hint now seems to have been more explicit. And before he leaves, Svidrigailov stresses the point still more: "I still feel you have something in you that's very much like me" (V:303). It is tempting to view these statements as suggesting Dostoevsky's preoccupation with the double theme. By virtue of antinomic patterning, however, even Svidrigailov has not explicitly stated the Dostoevskian idea to which he so persuasively and repeatedly refers.

F.I. Evnin posits six stages of oscillation that occur in Raskolnikov before the murders.[10] In the present context, these six stages may be grouped, chronologically, as two separate and similar three-stage patternings. The first comprises Raskolnikov's initial rejection of his plan ("no, this is nonsense, this is absurd"); his adducing the Marmeladovs' tragic circumstances as evidence corroborating his theory; and the letter from his mother, which Evnin terms "the third peripeteia" and interprets as inducing Raskolnikov to feel renewed responsibility for the fate of his own family. Next, Raskolnikov sees the girl on the bench, potentially foreshadowing his sister's future and thus forcing him back towards action; but his nightmare about the horse, in Evnin's phrase, "cancels the decision made"; and finally, his accidental encounter with Lizaveta on Haymarket Square points up the decisive opportunity for his crime.

As we have seen, two additional antinomic patterns reflect the murderer's vacillation between reaffirmation of his theory and repentance. The first concerns Raskolnikov's theory as interpreted by Profiry and twice redefined by its inventor. The second turns on Raskolnikov's belief in the resurrection of Lazarus as professed to Porfiry, denied to Svidrigailov, and inferentially reaffirmed with Sonia. Similarly, Raskolnikov tells Porfiry he believes in God (V:271), later taunts Sonia with the thought that God may not exist (V:334), and then earnestly tells her, "Children are the image of Christ: 'Theirs is the kingdom of heaven' " (V:342).

After he finally arrives to admit his guilt, Raskolnikov suddenly leaves, only to return and confess (V: 555-56). This three-stage action may be seen to preview a final protracted patterning, of which it is but the first step. The second step occurs in the Epilogue, where the killer still seems, in A.L. Bem's phrase, "under the spell" of his theory.[11] "Only in this sense did he acknowledge his crime: merely that he had not carried it through, and had turned himself in and confessed" (V:568). At another point he even decides: "My conscience is clear" (V:567). The last scene, however, where we read that "love resurrected" Raskolnikov and Sonia, completes a final patterning by reaffirming the idea of confession, symbolized by the fact that Raskolnikov opens the Gospel, "the very one from which she had read to him about the resurrection of Lazarus" (V:574). Yet the effect is typically blurred and perhaps even purposely unconvincing. That is, we sense a familiar tension in this closing sequence of confession, denial, and precipitous reaffirmation. By virtue of patterned antinomy, our final impression is rather that Raskolnikov has still not fully repented, yet he seems at last to be irrevocably headed in this direction.[12]

Though less systematically than in *Crime and Punishment*, patterned antinomy is employed throughout Dostoevsky's works. Indeed, it often seems that the novelist's very perception of "reality" involved this process. Philip Rahv has called Dostoevsky "the first novelist to have fully accepted and dramatized the principle of uncertainty or indeterminacy in the presentation of character."[13] In *The Idiot,* where Dostoevsky labored so extensively over the creation of a "positively good man," Aglaya says to Prince Myshkin: "I consider you a most honest and most truthful person, more honest and truthful than everyone; and if they say about you that your mind...that is, that sometimes your mind is sick, then that's unfair;...although your mind really is sick...but your main mind is better than all those other people's... because there are two minds: the main one and the lesser one. Isn't that so?" (VI, 486-7). The patterning is typical: (1) Myshkin's mind is not sick, (2) it is sick, and (3) his "main mind" *(glavnyi um)* is not sick, even if the lesser one is. Three-stage antinomy thus contributes to the roundness of this "positively good" character. And the strange logic of the "main mind" seems strikingly similar to Smerdiakov's rationalization (above) that Ivan is the "main killer." More important, this descriptive "cell," to use Ivanov's term, reflects and reinforces the antinomic patterning of the entire organism. For the final scene, wherein Myshkin strokes Rogozhin beside the body of Nastasia Filipovna, leaves us with the impression that the hero has at least partially returned to his afflicted condition which preceded the novel proper.

Besides furthering roundness in characterization, Dostoevskian patterned antinomy effectively depicts emotional ambivalence. The Underground Man affords a quintessential example. "I am a spiteful person," he tells us at the very outset (IV, 133). Then, after repeated affirmations of his "spitefulness," we read: "I was lying recently when I called myself a spiteful person. I lied out of spite" (IV,134). A typical pattern: (1) spiteful, (2) not spiteful, (3) outburst of spite. The ironic twist is reinforced by numerous further references. More important, this initial patterning reflects the protagonist's three-stage attitude towards Liza: his initial spitefulness, subsequent (albeit condescending) kindness, and final, spitefully masochistic hostility.

In *The Brothers Karamazov,* Fyodor Pavlovich's attitude towards his second wife displays yet another Dostoevskian ambivalence. Fyodor Pavlovich, we recall, took no dowry but rather "was enticed only by the remarkable beauty of the innocent young girl and, the main thing, her innocent appearance, which especially struck him, a voluptuary and heretofore a sinful admirer only of vulgar female beauty. 'Those innocent little eyes of hers slashed my soul like a razor,' he used to say afterwards, snickering in his vile way. For a depraved person, however, that too could be only a lustful attraction" (IX, 19). This last remark by the narrator completes a rather subtle patterning. First, innocence seems to replace depravity as the foremost attraction. The two are then blended with typically vivifying tension. Ironically, it is the innocence that inspires the evil, aptly suggested by a razor pleasantly slashing the soul.

Fyodor Pavlovich's alleged reaction to the death of his first wife is reported by means of a more obvious patterning. Some people said he shouted for joy, raising his hands towards the sky; others claimed he cried and sobbed like a child. "Very possibly," continues the narrator, "both one and the other occurred; that is, he both rejoiced at his emancipation and wept for his emancipator—all together" (IX, 15).

A third function of Dostoevskian patterned antinomy is the creation of a tenuous relationship between illusion and reality. In "The Dream of a Ridiculous Man," for example, the protagonist remarks: "Dreams, it appears, are directed not by reason but by desire, not by the head, but by the heart; and yet what complex, crafty things are sometimes fashioned in dreams by my reason! Still, things happen to it when I am asleep that are quite inconceivable" (X, 427). To oversimplify: dreams are (1) emotional, (2) rational, (3) craftily irrational. This patterned uncertainty reflects and reinforces a question repeatedly raised throughout the story: "What difference does it make whether it was a dream or not if this dream proclaimed to me the Truth?" (X, 427). Further on, the protagonist even declares: "You know, I'll tell you a secret: Perhaps all that was not a dream at all!" (X, 436).

If we examine the Russian wording of Dostoevskian patterned antinomy, three repetitions emerge. Most obvious is the combination "Not that...quite the contrary...but..." ("Ne to chtob ...sovsem dazhe naprotiv...no..."), used to describe Raskolnikov's apparent cowardice.[14] Another typical combination is used to suggest Porfiry's diabolically probable wink: "This however may only have seemed so to Raskolnikov, because it lasted only a moment." ("Vprochem, èto, mozhet byt', tol'ko tak pokazalos' Raskolnikovu, potomu chto prodolzhalos' odno mgnovenie.")[15] As with Porfiry's wink, a "flashing" impression typically abets the effect.[16] Other frequently occurring words closely correspond to "that is," "however," and "but" (to-est', vprochem, a), for example, in Lebeziatnikov's description of Katerina Ivanovna's hysterical begging with her children and Sonia's frantic reaction: "Prosto v isstuplenii. To est ne Sofia Semyonovna v isstuplenii a Katerina Ivanonva; a vprochem, i Sofia Semyonovna v isstuplenii. A Katerina Ivanovna sovsem v isstuplenii" (V, 446). The words *to-est, vprochem,* and *a* resist smooth and above all consistent translation into English.

Still other essential words are "almost" *(pochti)* and especially "even" *(dazhe)*. As used to present Dostoevskian antinomy, this last word is neither the playfully ironic *dazhe* of Pushkin ("and even an honest man,"of Zaretsky in *Eugene Onegin*, canto 6, stanza 4) not the humorously reversed *dazhe* of Gogol' ("some even read nothing at all," *Dead Souls*, Ch. 8).[17] Rather, Dostoevsky frequently uses *dazhe* to soften the abruptness of his antinomic patterning, for example, of Raskolnikov's apparent cowardice: "sovsem dazhe naprotiv."[18]

One is tempted to relate antinomy, as an essential characteristic of Dostoevsky's world, to many of what are often considered his favorite themes and devices. And while more space would be needed to do so in detail, we may briefly mention the following. Prolepsis (which anticipates an opposing point of view), pedophilia (which mixes love and victimization), masochism and *zloradstvo* (including such details as unpleasant, even tortured smiles and statements stressing man's supposedly undeniable tiny particle of delight at his neighbor's misfortunes), the blending of illusion and reality (especially through dreams, hallucinations, strange psychic states, and even the feigning of sleep)—all these vividly combine apparent opposites.

As shown above, a highly specialized three-stage patterning leads the reader to accept the (muted) contradiction of Dostoevskian antinomy. Generally, the device promotes roundness in characterization, emotional ambivalence, and a tenous relationship between illusion and reality. And the pattern often reinforces, to use Ivanov's term, the antinomy of the entire organism. The parts reflect the whole, and vice versa.

Finally, the especially systematic antinomic patterning of *Crime and Punishment* is intensified by its numerous antinomic characters and unique narrative method: Dostoevsky blends objective and subjective reality by presenting the story partially through Raskolnikov's eyes. As we have seen, three pairs of key events are presented by antinomic patterning: the hero's oscillations prior to the murders; the re-examination of his theory afterwards; and the uncertainty of his confession. Several three-stage patternings, moreover, seem to prefigure others. Raskolnikov's twice muted initial fright foreshadows his fear and hesitations before killing. Marmeladov's appearance subtly previews his story; Porfiry's appearance, his probable wink. And Raskolnikov's patterned vacillation regarding his belief in the resurrection of Lazarus and the existence of God seems to preview the ending of the Epilogue, which also seems prefigured, by his hesitant confession, as the final stage of confession, regret, and apparent regeneration.

NOTES

1. Vyacheslav Ivanov, *Freedom and the Tragic Life.* Norman Cameron (New York: Noonday Press, 1960), 11.

2. F. M. Dostoevsky, *Sobranie sochinenii* (10 vols; M.: GIXL, 1956-58), X, 144. Dostoevsky's italics. Subsequent references to Dostoevsky's works will be to this edition. Unless otherwise specified, all translations are my own.

3. Incidentally, Ivan's use of the word "reptile" echoes his much earlier statement to Alyosha about Mitia and their father, "One reptile will devour the other" (IX, 179), and thus subtly reflects Ivan's fast-rising suspicions about Smerdiakov, who has not yet explicitly revealed his crime.

4. *The Notebooks for Crime and Punishment,* ed. and tr. Edward Wasiolek (Chicago: Univ. of Chicago Press, 1967); *Iz arkhiva F. M. Dostoevskogo, Prestuplenie i nakazanie: Neizdannye materialy,* ed. I. I. Glivenko (M:GIXL, 1931), 68.

5. Though less systematically, this technique is of course employed elsewhere; for example, Rakitin's view of Alyosha Karamazov as a voluptuous saint: "By your father, a voluptuary; by your mother, a holy fool" (IX, 103).

6. "The Construction of the Novel," in Fyodor Dostoevsky, *Crime and Punishment: The Coulson Translation, Backgrounds and Sources, Essays in Criticism,* ed. George Gibian (New York: W. W. Norton, 1964), 671.

7. Consider especially the allegedly successful role of casualness so desparately played by Raskolnikov when he first meets Porfiry Petrovich (V, 257-9).

8. "Traditional Symbolism in *Crime and Punishment,*" in *Dostoevsky, Crime and Punishment,* 577.

9. This three-stage pattern of reaction is typical; consider also Razumikhin's earlier statement: "I did not say that; however, perhaps you are right, only..."(V, 223).

10. "Plot Structure and Raskolnikov's Oscillations," in *Dostoevsky, Crime and Punishment,* 680-81.

11. "The Problem of Guilt in Dostoevsky's Fiction," in *Dostoevsky, Crime and Punishment,* 659.

12. As George Gibian has suggested (p. 589), the water imagery of the final scene aptly reinforces Raskolnikov's apparent "rebirth," echoing his earlier daydream about drinking from a babbling stream in Egypt.

13. Philip Rahv, "Dostoevsky in *Crime and Punishment*," in *Dostoevsky: A Collection of Critical Essays*, ed. Rene Wellek (Englewood Cliffs, N. J.: Prentice Hall, 1962), 21. "For Dostoevsky," Ivanov has claimed (p. 54), "the personality has a natural antinomy."

14. Other examples in *The Brothers Karamazov* are Katerina Ivanovna's statement to Ivan about his plan to leave for Moscow (IX, 239) and the description of Smerdiakov's sudden "speaking up," compared to that of Balaam's ass (IX, 158).

15. Other examples are the description of Luzhin in Raskolnikov's mother's letter (V, 39) and, in *Netochka Nazvanova*, the little heroine's fanciful conviction that her stepfather has promised to take her away to a house with red curtains (II, 93).

16. See, for example, Ivan's evanescent impression of Smerdiakov's antinomic "timidness" at their "first meeting" (X, 122).

17. Dmitry Chizhevsky has written extensively on Gogol's often astonishing usage of *dazhe*. See his "O 'Shineli' Gogolia," *Sovremennye zapiski*, 67 (Paris, 1938), 173-4, 178-84. See also my "Gogolesque Perception-Expanding Reversals in Nabokov," *Slavic Review*, 30 (1971), 110-20.

18. Consider also Razumikhin's description of Raskolnikov's deceased fiancée: "Krome togo, govoriat, nevesta byla soboi dazhe ne khorosha, to est, govorait, dazhe durna..." (V, 224). The word *pochti* similarly softens the abruptness of a sudden descriptive shift; when Raskolnikov arrives to commit murder: "On chuvstvoval, chto teriaetsia, chto emu pochti strashno, do togo strashno, chto, kazhetsia, smotri on tak . . . eshche s polminuty, to on by ubezhal ot nee" (V, 82).

Chapter Six

CRIME AND PUNISHMENT
AND *THE BROTHERS*
KARAMAZOV:
SOME COMPARATIVE
OBSERVATIONS

Murder and suicide recur almost obsessively in Dostoevsky's works. His first and last major novels, however, seem most extensively concerned with murder and the question of guilt. Indeed, *Crime and Punishment* and *The Brothers Karamazov* are strikingly similar in many ways, as I will seek to demonstrate. Despite a basic shift in emphasis, Dostoevsky may even be seen, in numerous respects, to have come full circle in the writing of these two admittedly quite different works.

While writing *The Brothers Karamazov* Dostoevsky said (in a letter to L. V. Grigoriev dated March 27, 1878) that during the winter he completely reread *Crime and Punishment.* "More than two thirds of the novel," he claimed, struck him as "something entirely new, unfamiliar."[1] This reading may possibly have awakened old patterns and problems; it may even have urged more satisfactory resolutions.

To begin with, we may note a similarity between the murders of the old misers, Alyona Ivanovna and Fyodor Pavlovich. Both are bashed on the head soon after 7:30 in the evening.[2] Both victims open their doors to the murderer, who (presumably, in the case of Fyodor Pavlovich) has convinced them it is safe. After this, there is much ado in each novel about the door being left open.[3] Money is stolen from both victims, from under Alyona Ivanovna's bed (V: 85) and either from under Fyodor Pavlovich's mattress (IX, 154) or from behind his ikons (IX, 152). Both murders (by bashing on the head) are prefigured—Alyona's, by the mare in Raskolnikov's dream, beaten on the face; Fyodor's by Mitya's kicking him in the face.[4] Near the time of each murder another person unexpectedly appears and is also bashed on the head until blood gushes. Lizaveta, whom Raskolnikov bashes on the head, had previously aided him (by mending his shirt, V, 141) and Lizaveta's holy book *(The New Testament)* appears with him at the end of the novel when he is sent to Siberia. Grigory, whom Mitya bashes on the head, had previously aided him (in childhood—stressed at the trial) and Grigory's holy book *(Holy Sayings of Saint Isaac)* turns up in Smerdyakov's room late in the novel,[5] when he confesses to the murder.

Of course, these parallels are not quite exact. To complete this last correspondence, the convicted and presumable murderers (Mitya and Smerdyakov) must be combined. Still, these and numerous other striking and complex parallels suggest that Dostoevsky was thinking along similar lines while creating the two novels, even though parallel situations involve quite disparate characters.

For example, the very different Alyosha and Raskolnikov are both about twenty and are associated with betrothal to a cripple. Both are said to be composed of two opposite characters (by Rakitin, IX, 103-4; and by Razumikhin, V, 222). Moreover, both Alyosha and Raskolnikov are concerned about and often try to help children; and they both envision innocent child victims as especially deserving the Kingdom of Heaven (V, 342; X, 338). Both young men succeed in giving money to suffering families (Alyosha conveys Katerina's; Raskolnikov, his own)—families which are themselves paralleled by suffering children, a mother who is or becomes insane, and a father who drinks from a painful awareness of his own inadequacy. Furthermore, Khokhlakova's eavesdropping on Alyosha's conversation with Lise may be seen to parallel Svidrigailov's eavesdropping on Raskolnikov's confession to Sonya. Even the big stone under which Raskolnikov conceals his stolen money and pledges may bring to mind the big stone near which Alyosha first attempts to transmit Katerina's money to Snegiryov, who tramples the money on the ground.

A further parallel suggests itself between Fyodor Pavlovich

and Svidrigailov. Both are older men who seem to have sent a wife to the grave. Both display an abnormal interest in the innocence of young girls. Svidrigailov finds that the shy, innocent tears of a sixteen-year-old girl are "better than beauty" (V, 501); Fyodor Pavlovich was especially enticed by the "innocent eyes" of his sixteen-year-old second wife (IX, 19). In fact, both men seem to view sex as one of the few important values in life. Svidrigailov stresses that a young girl's innocence is "worth something" (V, 502), that in depravity there is "something permanent, even based on nature" (V, 491). Fyodor Pavlovich emphasizes the "talent" for finding something enticing in any woman whatsoever (IX, 173). More specifically, Fyodor's doomed passion for Grushenka seems to parallel Svidrigailov's for Dunya. And we may note a correspondence between Fyodor's two victimized young wives and Svidrigailov's two girl victims, especially since one of these hangs herself, and the other drowns herself—and drowning is mentioned in connection with each of Fyodor's wives.[6] Prior to their deaths, both men evince an uneasy fascination for the afterworld. Fyodor tells his idea of "devils' hooks" to Alyosha (IX, 34) and Svidrigailov tells his idea of a "little room with spiders" to Raskolnikov (V, 299-300). Both Fyodor and Svidrigailov, moreover, express the feeling that their ominous notions may be fair or just.[7]

Despite their obvious differences, Mitya and Raskolnikov also suggest several parallels. Indeed, Mochulsky finds that the preliminary investigation of Mitya "grows out of" the struggle between Raskolnikov and Porfiry Petrovich.[8] Both Mitya and Raskolnikov contemplate suicide. Both are convicted as murderers and sentenced to labor in Siberia at the end of the novel. Both engage in sewing in order to hide something inside their clothes before the murders (Raskolnikov's axe, Mitya's money). For this purpose, Raskolnikov employs a rag torn from one of his old shirts (V, 74); the Prosecutor suggests that Mitya may have torn his rag from "a shirt, perhaps" (IX, 616), although Mitya proceeds to recall that he used his landlady's hat. Both men are given a complete change of clothes after the murders occur. Moreover, the old hat of each is significantly focused: Raskolnikov's, as possibly identifying him, Mitya's as possibly containing money stolen from the murder victim.

Parallels may also be drawn between Raskolnikov and Ivan Karamazov. "In his nonacceptance of the world," writes Kirpotin,

"Raskolnikov is the precursor of Ivan Karamazov. . . Both Raskolnikov and Ivan Karamazov are seekers of the new Jerusalem."[9] Raskolnikov's fate, asserts Mochulsky, "determines" the fate of Ivan.[10] In Jan Meijer's view, both Ivan and Raskolnikov may be said to possess a "theoretically irritated heart" and both display a similar "conflict between word and deed."[11] A more specific parallel may be seen in the controversial "articles" that both have written, as well as in their mutual notion that "all is permitted," which presumably conduces to murder in each novel.[12] But here a further similarity suggests itself between Raskolnikov and Smerdyakov. For if one believes the latter, these two men both commit murder while strongly influenced by the idea that "all is permitted," as Meijer has noted.[13] The details of these murders, as we have seen, are remarkably similar (more on this below). Afterwards, both men escape detection on a staircase (one by hiding, the other by feigning an epileptic fit). Summoned to the police station, Raskolnikov is horrified by his blood-stained "left sock" (V, 96). Ivan Karamazov is horrified when Smerdyakov produces 3,000 rubles from his left sock (X, 146).

Thus, despite the many differences between the novels, it seems that Dostoevsky's experience of rereading *Crime and Punishment* while composing *The Brothers Karamazov* considerably affected the latter. In fact, Fetyukovich relates at Mitya's trial an incident which suggests Raskolnikov's murder scene. "Recently in Petersburg," he says, a young man of eighteen entered "a money changer's shop" with "an axe" and killed and robbed its owner. Later the young man confessed (X, 283).[14] Also common to both novels is the strong suggestion that a slow-witted Lizaveta is sexually abused.

Both novels contain three instances of what may be termed unsuccessful or incomplete seduction. Early in *Crime and Punishment,* a man tries to take advantage of a young girl in the park but is thwarted by Raskolnikov. After Zosima's death Rakitin brings Alyosha to Grushenka's, but her intention to seduce him also comes to naught. Late in *Crime and Punishment* Svidrigailov dreams of a five-year-old girl whose shameless "harlot-like" expression horrifies him (V, 533). Late in *The Brothers* Ivan horrifies Alyosha by saying that the young girl Lise is offering herself "like a harlot" (X, 116). In yet another pair of instances, seduction is staged only in the mind. By implying that he will help Raskolnikov, Svidrigailov persuades Dunya to come to his apartment. Then, after a violent inner struggle, he releases her. By suggesting that he will help her father, Mitya pressures Katerina into coming to his apartment. Then, after a vivid consideration of cruel options, he releases her.

Perhaps most strikingly however, both novels feature triplicity throughout—well in excess of Dostoevsky's customary fondness for tripartite patterning.[15] Indeed, the number three seems almost a mystical key to the construction of both works. Mochulsky finds a "tripartite principle of composition" in *Crime and Punishment* and refers to the "triple structure" of *The Brothers Karamazov*.[16] And as Meijer has observed, each novel contains three crucial discussions leading to the discovery of the murderer: Raskolnikov's three encounters with Porfiry Petrovich and Ivan Karamazov's three meetings with Smerdyakov.[17] (In Richard Peace's view the latter three meetings reveal to Ivan that he is guilty on three counts: for the idea that all is permitted, for secretly desiring his father's death and for lack of action at a crucial time.[18]) Moreover, Smerdyakov's left eye seems to wink at Ivan three times (IX, 336; X, 122, 133). And Porfiry's left eye seems to wink three times at Raskolnikov (V, 259, 260, 275)—though this requires some inference on the reader's part.[19] In both cases, the left-eye winker is apparently suggesting to a man he presumes to be a murderer[20] that they both "know."

The scope of triplicity in both novels seems to justify a separate, systematic examination of each. In addition to Raskolnikov's three conversations with Porfiry (at the latter's apartment, the police station, and Raskolnikov's room), we may note the following. Raskolnikov visits the police station three times (concerning his debt, to see Porfiry, and to confess). He also visits Sonya's apartment three times (the reading about Lazarus, his confession and prior to giving himself up). He visits Alyona Ivanovna three times (to pledge a ring, to pledge a watch, and to kill her). He also has three sleeping dreams and three daydreams, as Sidney Monas has noted.[21] He confesses three times (mockingly, to Zamyotov; to Sonya; at the police station). And he even has three conversations in taverns (with Marmeladov, Zamyotov, and Svidrigailov). There are also three descriptions of Raskolnikov's theory (by Porfiry, by Raskolnikov, and by Svidrigailov).

Raskolnikov has been said to have three motives (by Maurice Beebe, who terms Raskolnikov "tripartite" and suggests reading the novel "in terms of 'triples' rather than 'doubles' "[22]). Lizaveta's *New Testament,* from which Sonya reads to Raskolnikov, serves to connect these same three people (dead victim, living victim, and murderer), as even their three expressions confirm.[23] The gun that kills Svidrigailov is a three-shot pistol; he is its third possessor (after Marfa and Dunya), and he kills himself with the third shot (V, 521). In addition, Raskolnikov and Svidrigailov are each closely involved with three deaths (Alyona, Lizaveta, Marmeladov; Marfa Petrovna, the girl who hanged herself, the girl who drowned herself).

Raskolnikov envisions "three possibilities" for Sonya (suicide, depravity, and madness, V, 296). He also threatens three people (the stranger who accuses him, Luzhin, and Svidrigailov), as Kirpotin has noted.[24] Svidrigailov, who explicitly suggests three times that he and Raskolnikov are alike (V, 297, 300, 303) claims that Marfa Petrovna's ghost has visited him "three times" (V, 296). He was awake, he insists, "all three times." The driver who killed Marmeladov shouted to warn him "three times" (this is said three times, by three different people, V, 184). There are numerous other instances of triplicity, including three mentions of female drowning, three separate allusions to Lazarus, and even three attentions to the meaning of Razumikhin's name (Vrazumikhin, Rasudkin, Razum).[25] (Somewhat similarly, the word *kara* is used three times in connection with Dmitry Karamazov, which suggests that he is "punishment-daubed," as Peace has noted.[26])

Turning to *The Brothers Karamazov,* we find that triplicity also permeates its basic structure and patina of detail. Fyodor Pavlovich has three lawful sons, the three heroes of the novel, often seen as representing three aspects of man (Ivan, mind; Mitya, body; Alyosha, spirit). And as Matlaw has observed, Ivan's three meetings with Smerdyakov parallel Mitya's three ordeals.[27] In Belknap's words, "The *nadryv* appears in three successive chapters; Mitya's experiences come before the reader in threes..."[28] (He goes on to mention three "confessions of a passionate heart," three attempts to obtain money, and three "ordeals.") Belknap notes that "Mitya . . . enumerates carefully his three possible courses when Katerina Ivanovna came to beg him to cover her father's embezzlement."[29] These are: taking advantage, coldly refusing, aiding her—and Belknap aptly stresses the "impact on the reader" of all three. He has also observed that the book contains "three versions" of the murder: Mitya did it, Smerdyakov did it, and Grigory did it.[30] In Peace's view, three "fathers" suffer at Dmitry's hands: Fyodor Pavlovich, Grigory (who has been like a father to Dmitry), and Snegiryov (Ilyusha's father). Peace also notes that the three chapters following Alyosha's arrival at the inn (where he finds Ivan) "stand in parallel to the three chapters in which Dmitry had unburdened his soul to Alyosha: they are Ivan's 'confession'."[31] He also finds that "the three chapters of 'The Russian Monk' are to be taken as a pendant to the three chapters of Ivan's 'confessions': they are its refutation."[32]

With slight variation, the Epigraph of the novel (the "corn of wheat" passage from John, XII, 24) is given three times (IX, 5, 357, 387). The Grand Inquisitor stresses Christ's "three temptations" in the desert (IX, 316). He also insists that Christ rejected "the three forces, the only three forces" by which man can be ruled and given happiness: miracle, mystery, and authority (IX, 320-21).[33] Dmitry asks Alyosha three times not to forget to convey to Katerina his "good-bye" message, as Wasiolek has noted.[34]

Besides three lawful sons, Fyodor Pavlovich has three servants. At Mitya's trial, there are three judges (X, 191) and three medical experts (X, 206). Also at the trial there are three important references to Gogol's famous troika. The first is by the Prosecutor, who substitutes three of Gogol's heroes (Sobakevich, Nozdryov, Chichikov) for the three horses of the troika (X, 237). He proceeds to discuss the Karamazovs as "contemporary" horses in Russia's troika. Second, the Prosecutor eloquently re-evokes the "fateful *(rokovaia)* troika" (X, 273); third, Fetyukovich alludes to the troika at the climax of his defense speech (X, 305). In addition, Ronald Hingley has found that the novel contains "three main suspense-hooks" (When will Fyodor be murdered; who did it; will Dmitry be convicted).[35] (Hingley has also observed that *Crime and Punishment* contains "two trios" of characters, a virtuous trio—Dunya, her mother, and Razumikhin—and an evil trio—Svidrigailov, Luzhin, and Lebezyatnikov.[36])

Given the frequent references to "3,000 rubles" throughout *The Brothers,* it seems little wonder that this sum is also termed "fateful" *(rokovaia)* during the trial (X, 281). Indeed, the fateful troika and fateful 3,000 rubles are felt, ultimately, to be an integral part of the basic patterning of triplicity in the novel. The famous 3,000 rubles kept by Fyodor in an envelope for Grushenka are desperately needed by Mitya to repay the 3,000 rubles he has taken from Katerina. (Mitya has decided that his father owes him at least 3,000 more of his inheritance.) There is also Mitya's desperate quest of 3,000 rubles prior to the murder.[37] Fyodor sends Ivan to save 3,000 rubles in a business deal, repeatedly emphasizing his need for the 3,000 (IX, 349). And at both wild celebrations with Grushenka, Mitya is supposed to display 3,000 rubles. He also repeatedly offers Mussyalovich 3,000 rubles if both Poles will leave (IX, 533). In addition, Mitya's lawyer is hired for 3,000 rubles (X, 76). Finally, Smerdyakov produces 3,000 rubles in "three bundles" of bills (X, 146) at his "third meeting" with Ivan, who soon accepts "three bundles" (X, 157).

In *Crime and Punishment* the murder is also linked with 3,000 rubles: Svidrigailov tells Dunya that Raskolnikov had hoped to take 3,000 rubles from Alyona (V, 513). He repeats this hypothetical figure, and Raskolnikov himself later confirms that he had hoped to steal "at least 3,000 rubles" (V, 558-59). Framing Sonya, Luzhin claims he had cashed bonds worth 3,000 rubles, leaving "three" hundred-ruble bills on the table; Sonya, he says, hurried to leave the room "three times" (V, 409). In addition, Marfa Petrovna leaves Dunya 3,000 rubles when she dies (V, 304, 322); and Svidrigailov gives Sonya three bonds totaling 3,000 rubles (V, 523).[38]

Perhaps most fatefully of all, triplicity informs the descriptions of murder in both novels. At his "third meeting" with Ivan, Smerdyakov describes the murder in *The Brothers.* He hit Fyodor Pavlovich three times, he claims, with a paperweight weighing about three pounds. The third blow broke the latter's skull and he collapsed (X, 152), whereupon Smerdyakov took the 3,000 rubles from an envelope closed by "three large red wax seals" (IX, 566).

Raskolnikov, who has pawned with Alyona a ring "with three red stones" (V, 69), gains entrance in response to his "third" ring at his third visit to Alyona's (V, 81), after which he hits her three times (hoping to steal 3,000 rubles). As with Smerdyakov, his third and last blow breaks the skull (V, 84). Dostoevsky seems intrigued by this "third-of-three death patterning": in *The Brothers,* Father Ferapont claims to have killed a devil by making the sign of the cross three times (IX, 212); in *Crime and Punishment,* as noted above, Svidrigailov kills himself with the third shot of a three-shot pistol.

Similarly, the parallel death-associated redness ("three red stones" and "three red seals") has further reinforcement in both novels. In *The Brothers,* as Matlaw has put it, "A plethora of red colors appears during and after Mitya's vigil under Fyodor Pavlovich's window, and is clearly designed to emphasize blood spilling."[39] Under this window, Mitya strangely ("not knowing

80

why") whispers, of some berries: "...how red!" (IX, 487). Inside, his father awaits Grushenka in a room divided by a "red screen" with a "red bandage" around his head (IX, 487-88). Earlier, he had adjusted a "red handkerchief" on his forehead, remarking "sententiously" to Alyosha: "Red is better—in white it's too much like a hospital" (IX, 216).

In *Crime and Punishment* Raskolnikov finds under Alyona's bed a trunk covered in "red leather" (V, 85). Opening it, he discovers a coat with a "red lining," beneath which are the pledges he steals. His first reaction, however, is to wipe his "blood-stained hands" on the "red lining." His mind, like Mitya's, strangely focuses redness: " 'Red—well, on red, blood is less noticeable,' he started to decide, then suddenly remembered himself: 'Lord! Am I going crazy, or what?' "

Additional instances of triplicity abound in each novel, yet the phenomenon seems to grade off—such is the weakness of this type of analysis—into a series of rather inconsequential details.[40] No doubt more revealing of common authorial inspiration and intent are the parallel themes, incidents, and ideas in the two novels, such as "all is permitted" (treated above). In addition to those already mentioned, parallels include: the notion that "all are guilty for all," that psychology is a "stick with two ends," and that people are visited by ghosts or spirits. Other mutual details are kissing the earth, a mare beaten across the eyes,[41] and a bitten finger (Lizaveta's V, 71; Alyosha's, IX, 225). Both novels also contain an important early death, not a murder (Marmeladov, Zosima; a late suicide (Svidrigailov, Smerdyakov); and an ending on a note of resurrection. Moreover, both focus on the themes of "Sodom" and "Madonna," feature unpleasant Poles at a party, and contain a late emphasis upon a trip to America. Finally, parallels may be found between the questions of whether or not Raskolnikov and Mitya have "stolen" what they have not spent or used; rationalized notions that the murder victims are less than human; and the final dedications of Sonya and Grushenka, both determined to follow the convicted murderers to Siberia if necessary.

As we have seen, Dostoevsky's first and last major novels are similar in many ways, from dominant themes to minute details. In juxtaposition, the two works not infrequently produce what Meijer has termed a "sensation of *deja lu.*"[42] However, parallel circumstances and problems seem treated quite differently, and resolved differently. We may note a significant symmetrical difference. In

Crime and Punishment the murder scene is vividly focused, whereas in *The Brothers* what seems to be the murder is screened by an ellipsis: the dots stretch entirely across the page (IX, 490).[43] Concerning the question of guilt, however, the reverse seems true. In *The Brothers* at least four persons explicitly acknowledge some responsibility for the murder of Fyodor.[44] In *Crime and Punishment* the guilt is muted by patterned antinomy.[45] Perhaps we could say that guilt is relatively unfocused in Dostoevsky's first novel, while in the last it is the factual crime which remains obscured. As Peace has put it, there is a shift in emphasis from "crime" to "punishment."[46] In the earlier novel factual guilt tends to overcome (even an extraordinary man's) moral non-guilt: in the last, moral guilt tends to outweigh factual non-guilt. This shift in emphasis (from "crime" clarity to "guilt" clarity) seems reflected in a corresponding shift in priority from "all is permitted" to "all are guilty for all."[47] And perhaps this helps to explain why the two structures, though built with many of the same distinctive bricks, seem so very different.

NOTES

1. F. M. Dostoevskii, *Pis'ma.* Ed. A. Dolinin (M. 1959), IV, 14. In July 1878, however, Dostoevsky declared that epilepsy had caused him to forget "all the plots and details" of his novels. (See *Pis'ma*, IV, 30.)

2. Approaching Alyona's apartment, Raskolnikov is horrified to hear a clock strike 7:30. It is "about 7:30" when Mitya rings the bell at the Khokhlakovs' (whence he rushes to Grushenka's and then to his father's). F. M. Dostoevsky, *Sobranie sochinenii v 10 tomakh* (M. 1956-58), V, 80 and IX, 478. Subsequent references will be to this edition.

3. Grigory's "open door" testimony, effectively stressed by the Prosecutor, is earlier explained by Smerdyakov as the fancy of a stubborn old man (IX, 153). See also Dostoevsky's comment, "The open door," which in the drafts directly follows the Prosecutor's pronouncement about "the psychology of Russian crime." F. Dostoevsky, *The Notebooks for The Brothers Karamazov,* ed. Ed. Wasiolek (Chicago, 1971), 257.

For an intriguing interpretation of the "open door" motif in the murder scene and elsewhere in *Crime and Punishment,* see Richard Peace, *Dostoevsky: An Examination of the Major Novels* (London, 1971), 39, 41-42.

4. Mitya's earlier brutality with Grigory may also be seen to prefigure his bashing of Grigory's skull, and the mocking conversation about Lizaveta overheard by Raskolnikov may even be seen to anticipate her victimization.

5. This connection regarding Grigory's book is made in Ralph Matlaw, *The Brothers Karamazov: Novelistic Technique* (The Hague, 1957), 28.

6. These two references to female drowning (in connection with the wives of Fyodor Pavlovich, IX, 12, 19) seem even more suggestive of Svidrigailov and his drowned victim (V, 531) if one considers that in the *Notebooks* Svidrigailov was to tell Raskolnikov that two women had recently drowned themselves. F. Dostoevsky, *The Notebooks*

for *Crime and Punishment,* ed. Ed. Wasiolek (Chicago, 1967), 244.

7. Dostoevskii, IX, 34 and V, 300. "The voluptuary," writes Mochulsky, "condemns himself and thirsts for justice." *Dostoevskii: zhizn' i tvorchestvo* (Paris, 1947), p. 501.

8. Mochul'skii, 490.

9. V. Ia. Kirpotin, *Razocharovanie i krushenie Rodiona Raskol'nikova* (M. 1970), 78.

10. Mochul'skii, 490.

11. Jan M. Meijer, "Some Notes on Dostoevskij and Russian Realism," *Russian Literature,* No. 4 (1973), 13.

12. In Peace's view, Ivan's article "has the same germinal significance for *The Brothers Karamazov* as Raskolnikov's article has for *Crime and Punishment.* Peace, 265.

13. Meijer, 13.

14. The evidence against him, however, is much stronger than that against Raskolnikov.

15. Describing what he deems the main characteristic of Dostoevsky's "structural system," Leonid Grossman notes a tendency in the novels to reveal a tragic situation gradually "in three meetings or three conversations of the heroes." This conduces, he observes, to a careful thematic development "in a little trilogy," a "concise three-act drama" with increasing suspense, horror, and revelation. As examples he cites Raskolnikov's three meetings with Sonya, his three meetings with Porfiry, Myshkin's three meetings with Rogozhin in *The Idiot,* and Ivan's three conversations with Smerdyakov. L. Grossman, "Dostoevskii-khudozhnik," *Tvorchestvo F. M. Dostoevskogo,* ed. N. L. Stepanov (M. 1959), 350-51.

See also my "Dostoevskian Patterned Antinomy and Its Function in *Crime and Punishment,*" above.

16. Mochul'skii, 245, 491.

17. Meijer, 13.

18. Peace, 229.

19. The first time we see Porfiry's general ("as if winking at someone") appearance, but tinged by Raskolnikov's point of view. Second, the latter wonders if Porfiry has "winked at him," strongly suspecting that he had. Finally, we are told that Porfiry "again winked at him with his left eye . . . exactly as before."

20. Smerdyakov tells Ivan that he, Ivan, was the main killer. Although Smerdyakov's first wink precedes the murder, the implied alliance of "knowing" is the same.

21. Sidney Monas, trans. *Crime and Punishment* (NY, 1968), 536.

22. Maurice Beebe, "The Three Motives of Raskolnikov: A Reinterpretation of *Crime and Punishment,*" in: *Crime and Punishment,* Norton Critical Edition (New York, 1964), 632.

23. See my *Dostoevsky: Child and Man in His Works* (NY, 1968), 176.

24. Kirpotin, 423.

25. The list could be made much longer. Raskolnikov has what may be termed three "staircase dramas" (slipping past his landlady as the novel opens; hiding after the murders; and struggling with himself before confessing at the end). His room has three chairs: Sonya's has three windows. Razumikhin even mentions that there was a scandal in room Number Three of the hotel where Dunya and her mother stay (V, 210) and refers to the three fishes which support the world (V, 217).

26. Peace, 281-82, 328.

27. Matlaw, 42.

28. Robert Belknap, *The Structure of The Brothers Karamazov* (The Hague, 1967), 55.

29. Belknap, 112.

30. Belknap, 99-100.

31. Peace, 225.

32. Peace, 227.

33. Edward Wasiolek has observed that "many critics" have confused these three words with the three temptations. *Dostoevsky: The Major Fiction* (Cambridge, Mass., 1964), 167.

34. Wasiolek, 158.

35. *The Undiscovered Dostoevsky* (London, 1962), 198.

36. *The Undiscovered Dostoevsky*, 92.

37. Wasiolek has found that Fyodor hopes to steal the woman Mitya loves with, symbolically, the 3,000 rubles of Mitya's foolish quest (p. 180).

38. The parallel focus even includes the sum of 1,500 rubles. Raskolnikov failed to find 1,500 rubles in the top drawer of Alyona's bureau (V, 158). Mitya, of course, repeatedly claims to have used only 1,500 rubles for each wild celebration.

39. Matlaw, 30.

40. After the murders, for example, Raskolnikov is delirious for "three days" (V, 151). Porfiry tries to trap him by asking if he remembers the painters near Alyona's apartment, but Razumikhin exclaims that Raskolnikov was there "three days" before that (V, 277). Svidrigailov refers three times to his "third day" in Petersburg (V, 254, 295).

In *The Brothers,* as Belknap has noted (pp. 83, 87), three days are covered in detail before Mitya's trial. Prior to the murder of Fyodor, Ivan is intensely aroused by Smerdyakov's insinuation that he may soon have a "three-day" epileptic fit (IX, 338). Much later, Ivan decides to help Mitya escape (X, 141). Ivan's plan, about which he and Katerina argue "for three days," is for Mitya to escape "on the third lap" (X, 314) of the trip to Siberia and to spend "three years" (X, 323) in America. (Each of these last three numbers is repeated.)

41. Matlaw has connected the "mare" descriptions (p. 15).

42. J. M. Meijer, "Situation Rhyme in a Novel of Dostoevskij," *Dutch Contributions to the Fourth International Congress of Slavicists* (The Hague, 1958), 116.

43. In *Crime and Punishment,* a similar elipsis occurs while Raskolnikov is considering murder (V, 72).

44. These are Smerdyakov, Ivan, Dmitry, and Grushenka. According to S. I. Gessen, "Alyosha's guilt consists of forgetting about his brother at the crucial moment." "Tragediia dobra v 'Brat'iakh Karamazovykh' Dostoevskogo," in *O Dostoevskom: stat'i* (Providence, 1966), 217.

45. See my "Dostoevskian Patterned Antinomy," above, 67.

46. Peace, 265.

47. Still another aspect of this symmetrical shift may be seen in the evidence relating to each murder case: of the corresponding late suicides mentioned above, Svidrigailov's may be seen as the death of a threat to convicting Raskolnikov; Smerdyakov's suicide, as the death of a hope for acquiting Mitya.

Chapter Seven

NABOKOV:
THE HOUNDS OF FATE

Ivan Turgenev (who insisted that dogs can smile, and smile very pleasantly) wrote a story, "The Dog," which contains suggestions of supernatural forces. Nikolai Gogol and Kurt Vonnegut, Jr. have written stories wherein dogs seem to conceal from humans a very high intelligence. Vladimir Nabokov persistently associates dogs in his works with human destiny and death. He also frequently associates them with life after death and with supernatural forces.

Rather like Quilty's hidden appearances throughout *Lolita,* or the series of faintly uncanny squirrels in *Pnin,* these dogs are easily unnoticed, yet they regularly appear at fateful moments. However, like Nabokovian clusters of subtly prophetic details, fateful hounds appear in book after book. Thus they may be seen as Nabokovian agents of Fate, or of the author, unobtrusively presiding over, and sometimes promoting, fateful episodes in his characters' lives. Some are quite playful. Some seem almost eerie. All may be considered the faintly suspicious assistants of an authorial conjuror and miracle worker. Here I have traced Nabokov's protean fateful hounds (including even artificial dogs, imaginary dogs, and people described as dog-like) in his seventeen novels, *Speak, Memory,* and numerous other works.[1]

Dogs are ominously associated with death in *Despair.* Sleeping near Felix, whom he has planned to murder, Hermann dreams: "First there was a small dog; but not simply a small dog; a small mock dog, very small, with the minute black eyes of a beetle's larva; it was white through and through...A cold-blooded being, which Nature had twisted into the likeness of a small dog..." (106). Hermann wakes up and sees, on Felix's bed, "like a swooned white larva, that very same dreadful little pseudo dog." Then he awakens from his second dream to discern on Felix's bed the same horror: "small, tallowish-white, with its little black button eyes." Finally he wakes up "for good."

Soon after this, Hermann attempts to prove "the nonexistence of God" (111). He is "ready," he admits, "to accept all, come what may; the burly executioner in his top hat, and then the hollow hum of blank eternity; but I refuse to undergo the tortures of everlasting life, I do not want those cold white little dogs" (113). After murdering Felix, Hermann hides in a hotel room "cursing the barking dogs" (219). He discussed his impending execution, which leads to: "The dogs are barking. I am cold."

These and other ominous dog references[2] may lead one to suspect a hidden seriousness behind Hermann's facetious question: "How do God and Devil combine to form a live dog?" (56). As shown below, a similar reverse spelling turns dog into god in *Ada.* And Hermann's attempt to prove the nonexistence of God, we may recall, led to "those cold white little dogs."

Joseph Campbell has traced a fateful little dog from an eighth-century Arabic text through the Tristan legend to a long passage early in James Joyce's *Ulysses.*[3] He also observes that Joyce, later in the novel, "holding his devil's mirror to nature, reveals the word 'Dog' in reverse to be 'God.' "[4] Nabokov has deemed *Ulysses* the greatest masterpiece of twentieth century prose.[5]

The original Russian version of *Despair* contains all of the above dogs except Hermann's question about the words "live dog." There is, however, the playful suggestion that the word veterinary *(veterinar)* contains a Soviet wind *(sovetskii veter)* (46). Both versions contain a "white-bellied pup" (76; in Russian, 64) which ostensibly promotes Hermann's triple dream. Not present in the Russian is a suggestion that mad Hermann is "going to the dogs" (136).

Dogs are also associated with death and the afterlife—less repulsively than in *Despair,* but perhaps still more intensely—in *Bend Sinister.* This novel generates much of its power from Krug's love for his little boy David. In fact, Nabokov has declared that "...it is for the sake of the pages about David and his father that the book was written and should be read" (xiv). The boy's kindergarten contains "a live shaggy dog called Basso" (142) and a playmate who brings Basso a bone and tells David that his mother is dead. (Krug has not yet told his son the terrible news.) Krug explains to David that the playmate's remark was "stupid":

> "Because even *if* she were dead she would not be dead for you or me."
> "Yes, but she isn't, is she?"
> "Not in our sense. A bone is nothing to you or me but it means a lot to Basso."
> "Daddy, he *growled* over it. He just lay there and growled with his paw on it. Miss Zee said we must not touch him or talk to him while he had it." (143-44)

This delicate, moving passage anticipates Krug's first glimpse of David, brutally murdered, near the end of the novel.

> What looked like a fluffy piebald toy dog was prettily placed at the foot of the bed. Before rushing out of the ward, Krug knocked this thing off the blanket, whereupon the creature, coming to life, gave a snarl of pain and its jaws snapped, norrowly missing his hand. (201)

As this passage echoes and amplifies David's conversation with his father, we may recognize an eerie justification of Miss Zee's warning not to touch the dog who has a bone. And when the toy dog comes angrily to life as in a hideous dream, we begin to realize that this glimpse of David has driven Krug insane. In some sort of nightmare reality (perhaps akin to the earlier dream one in which David's mother cannot die), the toy dog now seems almost to have become Death, and David, its bone.[6]

In *King, Queen, Knave* the Dreyers' Alsatian Tom is a central figure, and his relationships with the three main characters seem closely related to what befalls them. Dreyer and Tom are good friends, and Tom repeatedly interrupts Martha's and Franz's plans to kill Dreyer (163,181). Still later, Martha goes to a desk to obtain a revolver to kill Dreyer: "But at that instant Tom entered the room with a bold buoyant step" (196). Franz says: "I can't do anything with that dog here." He and Martha then expel Tom, who leaves, "with a hurt expression," after which the revolver turns out to be a trick cigar lighter.

The murder plan thus suffers a set-back when Tom is insulted. Somewhat similarly, Martha's murder of Tom is followed by a fatal reversal in her plan to kill Dreyer. While walking Tom, Dreyer nearly discovers his wife's affair with Franz. When they arrive at Franz's apartment building, Tom rushes upstairs and barks loudly at Franz's door. Martha, desperately holding the door shut, resolves: "He shall be destroyed tomorrow." She then has the gardener kill Tom. Finally, Martha's plan to drown Dreyer leads to her own fatal chill. Dying, her very last words are: "Frieda, why is the dog here again? He was killed. He can't be here any more" (271). Nabokov then adds: "And the fools say second sight does not exist."[7]

In *Lolita*, Charlotte is killed by a car which swerves to avoid a dog. As Carl Proffer puts it, "For want of that dog, Lo would have been lost."[8] (Proffer also shows that the dog's role was carefully, and casually, prefigured.) The driver of the car is Fred Beale, whom Humbert terms "the agent of fate" (105). Fred is: "Stodgy and solemn, looking like a kind of assistant executioner, with his bulldog jowls, small black eyes..." (104). As will be shown, there are several other bulldog-faced people in Nabokov's world who seem to be "agents of fate." Most often, such people are males and "executioners."

As will also be shown, the appearance of a lady with a dog in Nabokovian reality often seems to portend tragedy. When Humbert and Lolita first arrive at The Enchanted Hunters, the lobby contains a lady with her dog. Lo, we read, "sank down on her haunches to caress a pale-faced, blue-freckled, black-eared cocker spaniel swooning on the floral carpet under her hand" (119). Then, as they are shown to their room (where she will soon caress a swooning Humbert), Lolita is described as "leaving the dog as she would leave me some day" (120).

Later in the novel, Humbert finds Lolita near a hotel swimming pool: "There she was playing with a damned dog, not me. The animal, a terrier of sorts, was losing and snapping up again and adjusting between his jaws a wet little red ball..." (238).

Alfred Appel has observed that the red ball is "rolled by Quilty, who reappears on p. 239."[9] As before ("leaving the dog as she would leave me some day"), Humbert now ("playing with a damned dog, not me") fails to see the pattern in his own narration. Similarly, Humbert's remark (when Lolita ignores "the ball that the terrier placed before her") applies rather ominously to him: "Who can say what heart-breaks are caused in a dog by our discontinuing a romp?" (240)

When Humbert visits Lolita (Mrs. Schiller) late in the novel, he is loudly greeted by the Schillers' dog. After many "woofs," the dog's voice blends with the sound of the Schillers' door: "woosh-woof." Lolita invites Humbert into the house, abruptly adding: "No, you stay out" (272). For misled readers, Humbert adds "to the dog" in parentheses. As usual, the association is prophetic—Humbert will soon be shown out forever.

Finally, we read: "She and the dog saw me off" (282). Humbert offers to pay Lolita $500 for the car, which news she shares with "the ecstatic dog." After this, the dog chases Humbert's car as he drives off to kill Quilty—which may remind us that another dog had chased his car just prior to Charlotte's death (97).

Humbert tells us that he "loathes" dogs (75), which seems at least partially ironic since the fateful Junk dog facilitates his possession of Lolita. And helpful Fred Beale, with his "bulldog jowls," seems strangely paralleled by helpful Gaston Godin— Humbert relies on his friendship with this homosexual for casting a "spell of absolute security" (183)—who emits "a slow old-dog woof" which causes his jowls to wabble (184). Still, Humbert is chased by a dog as he leaves Lolita forever and proceeds, indirectly, towards his own death. Moreover, Humbert's intense dislike of dogs seems quite in keeping with the apparent conspiracy against him.

Indeed, dogs repeatedly appear when Humbert is being deceived. Rushing after Lolita, he almost knocks over "Miss Fabian's dropsical dackel" (208). He then finds Lolita, who informs him that "a great decision has been made." (She has just called Quilty and planned to deceive Humbert across all America.) Near Kasbeam, Humbert sees "a dog, a bit too large proportionately" (214). He then walks to town, meeting "a huge St. Bernard" on the way. Returning, he sees a red car and "the familiar St. Bernard dog" (215). Lolita has just deceived him with Quilty.

Late in the novel, Lolita goes to the Elphinstone Hospital, where Humbert is "dreadfully rude" to a nurse whose father is "a trainer of sheep dogs" (243). This nurse conspires with Lolita to deceive Humbert in various ways, concealing a letter from Quilty and calling to make sure that Humbert will not interrupt Lolita's escape. The next day, Humbert learns that Quilty, posing as Lolita's uncle, "called for her with a cocker spaniel pup and a smile for everyone" (248).[10]

Another pup may be indirectly associated with Lolita's affair with Charlie Holmes. When Humbert phones Lo at camp, saying he plans to marry her mother: " 'When is the wedding? Hold on a sec, the pup—that pup here has got hold of my sock. Listen—' and she added she guessed she was going to have loads of fun...' " (74). As I have demonstrated elsewhere, "loads of fun" ironically anticipates Lolita's sex with Charlie,[11] who, Humbert is relieved to observe, prevents him from being the girl's first lover.

Among other references to dogs in *Lolita*,[12] one other pattern stands out: dogs seem associated with Humbert's fateful desire for nymphets. While introducing this concept, he fondly refers to the "soft brown puppybodies" (21) of "pre-nubile Nile daughters." Later, as Lolita sits on Humbert's lap, he attains a level of excitement whereon orgasm seems both inevitable and prolongable: "I had ceased to be Humbert the Hound, the sad eyed degenerate cur clasping the boot that would presently kick him away" (62). Here, Humbert's facial expression resembles his later description of himself and other nympholepts as "dog-eyed" (90). As if acknowledging the importance of this echo, Humbert explains:

> ...every once in a while I have to remind the reader of my appearance much as a professional novelist, who has given a character of his some mannerism or a dog, has to go on producing that dog or that mannerism every time the character crops up in the course of the book. There may be more to it in the present case. My gloomy good looks should be kept in the mind's eye if my story is to be properly understood. (106)

What "more to it" is there? Although Humbert the Hound (to use his words) must presumably remain unaware of the fateful influence of dogs in his life, including his intense desire—as a dog-eyed nympholept--for Lolita, he seems to sense that his plight is influenced by mysterious forces: "I have but followed nature. I am nature's faithful hound. Why then this horror that I cannot shake off?" (137).

Like Humbert's, Pnin's actions also seem paralleled by those of dogs. Seeking lodging early in the novel, Pnin "optimistically" rings at the door of the wrong house: "The old Scotty stood beside him in much the same candid attitude as he"(33). After this, the two candid beings achieve their goals: "Miss Dingwall came out with a mop, let the slowpoke, dignified dog in, and directed Pnin to the Clements' clapboard residence."

Another dog may be associated with the end of Pnin's teaching career in the novel. This is "an obese dog" which he had found asleep on his office rug after a summer of teaching in Washington (69). Owned by a colleague, the dog was part of a disappointing rearrangement of Pnin's "lovingly Pninized" office. When Pnin enters the office on one of his three fateful birthdays, the dog is dead (70).

Late in the novel, Pnin befriends "a mangy little white dog" for whom he saves food even when he, Pnin seems to have lost everything: "there was no reason a human's misfortune should interfere with a canine's pleasure" (171). It is this dog who appears with Pnin in his car as the novel ends: "there was simply no saying what miracle might happen"(191). The "miracle," of course, is that Pnin, accompanied by the dog he has helped, travels to safety and success in *Pale Fire.*[13]

Early in *The Real Life of Sebastian Knight,* the narrator examines his deceased brother's study. V. is looking in vain for a picture of Sebastian's female Russian correspondent when he sees two photographs above the bookshelves. He glanced too, he tells us, at the books: the titles on one shelf "seemed to form a vague musical phrase, oddly familiar" (41).

As Anthony Olcott has demonstrated, these book titles are a Nabokovian cluster of seemingly casual details which actually refer to many other parts of the book.[14] Olcott connects one title, *The Lady with the Dog,* rather incidentally with another Chekhov story which later figures in Nabokov's novel. A more direct connection may be seen in V.'s second meeting with Nina (Sebastian's female Russian correspondent), who then has with her a repeatedly mentioned "black bulldog" (154-8). Both Nina and the heroine of *The Lady with the Dog* are married women who have rather unhappy love affairs that begin at health resorts. Moreover, Sebastian himself has a black bull-terrier (103) as Olcott observes. Both the bulldog and the bull-terrier, we may note, are described in connection with practical jokes.

Nina's practical joke, as she appears with her dog, is to confide teasing little details of her own affair (with Sebastian) to V., while pretending that they were confided to her by another woman. "She" (she confides) "thought it would be rather good fun to have him make love to her—because, you see, he looked so very intellectual, and it is always entertaining to see that kind of refined, distant, brainy fellow suddenly go on all fours and wag his tail" (158-9). However, she admits, "...*he* did not turn into a sentimental pup, as she had expected" (159).

Returning to the two photographs which V. "glanced at" just prior to the book titles in Sebastian's study, we find: "One was an enlarged snap-shot of a Chinese stripped to the waist, in the act of being vigourously beheaded, the other was a banal photographic study of a curly child playing with a pup. The taste of their juxtaposition seemed to me questionable, but probably Sebastian had his own reasons for keeping and hanging them so." The first picture anticipates Nina's friend Anatole, an executioner who seems to have saved her life (145-6). The second picture, through "juxtaposition," typically associates a dog with human destiny and death.[15] In *Despair,* as seen above, Hermann mentions a "burly executioner" in conjunction with his "cold white little dogs."

Late in the novel V., trying unsuccessfully to telephone the dying Sebastian's doctor, argues with an "old man with a bulldog face" (197). After their quarrel, V. successfully places his call, but fails to reach Sebastian in time, although he is temporarily deceived into thinking that he has. Just prior to arguing with the bulldog-faced man, V. wonders: "Why was I so unlucky?"

In *Speak, Memory* Nabokov creates a juxtaposition which may remind one of Sebastian Knight's Nina (the lady with the dog) and her friend Anatole (the executioner): "Every other day, on the white Yalta pier (where, as you remember, the lady of Chekhov's 'Lady with the Lapdog' lost her lorgnette among the vacational crowd), various harmless people had, in advance, weights attached to their feet and then were shot by tough Bolshevik sailors imported from Sebastopol for the purpose" (245).[16]

In *Glory* Màrtin Edelweiss, who has just been reminded of his father's death, decides to read himself to sleep. "Martin began to read, choosing the story he knew, loved, could read through one hundred times in a row: 'The Lady with the Little Dog.' Ah, how nicely she lost that lorgnette in the crowd on the pier in Yalta! And here, without any apparent reason, he realized what it was that disturbed him so. Only a year before, in this room, Nelly had slept, and now she was dead" (91).

In *Transparent Things* the image of a "lady with a dog" is persistently associated with death. Late in the novel, Hugh Person refuses to heed a premonition that he should leave the Ascot Hotel. Hugh, we are told, could still have had "a few years of animal pleasure...but after all it was for him to decide, for him to die, if he wished" (98-99). At this point, Hugh learns that he can stay (after all) in the room he had so desired because: "The lady with the little dog was leaving before dinner." That night, Hugh burns to death in this room.

The ostensible reason for the lady and dog's departure was that the dog's owner wanted it back sooner than had been planned. However, this happens immediately after Hugh "decides to die." Just before Hugh's death, the lady and dog drive away in a car (101).

Earlier, when Hugh remembers that 313 is the room he wants, he learns that it is occupied: "A dog yapped on the inside of the door..." (95). This was carefully anticipated as the novel opened, when Hugh arrived at the Ascot on his fourth, and fatal, visit to Switzerland and had to stay on the fourth floor. Hugh closes the lavatory "...door after him but like a stupid pet it whined and immediately followed him into the room" (5).

Transparent Things contains yet another "lady with a dog" who seem fatefully connected with Hugh's death.[17] When Hugh first pursues Armande, he becomes lost but is directed by a female fruitseller, whereupon: "An overaffectionate large white dog started to frisk unpleasantly in his wake and was called back by the woman" (37). Not long before his death, Hugh asks the same woman for directions to the same place: "As she spoke, a large, white, shivering dog crawled from behind a crate and with a shock of futile recognition Hugh remembered that eight years ago he had stopped right here and had noticed that dog, which was pretty old even then and had braved fabulous age only to serve his blind memory" (87). Presumably, Hugh's "shock of recognition" is "futile" because he fails to interpret the dog's fatidic presence and thus, to avert his own death. And this is perhaps why his memory, which sees so much in retrospect, is termed "blind."[18]

Early in the novel, a Nabokovian cluster of prophetic details is introduced as follows: "Hugh examined the items in a souvenir store" (13). The first item, which he finds "rather fetching," is a "green figurine of a female skier." This previews Armande, whom he meets ten years later. The "souvenir," we are told, was "carved and colored in the Grumbei jail by a homosexual convict, rugged Armande Rave, who had strangled his boyfriend's incestuous sister." Hugh, of course, later strangles Armande.

Another "souvenir" is described as follows: "Cute little wrist watch, with picture of doggy adorning its face, for only twenty-two francs. Or should one buy (for one's college roommate) that wooden plate with a central white cross surrounded by all twenty-two cantons? Hugh, too, was twenty-two and had always been harrowed by coincident symbols." The (Swiss) plate, with its white cross and 22 cantons, may hint at Hugh's death: he dies 22 chapters later. More obviously, the 22 cantons link Hugh, age 22, to the 22-franc watch with its "doggy face." And this (as a sort of "coincident symbol" of Hugh's "death time") may allude to the fateful dog who leaves the hotel room when it is time for Hugh to die there.

Finally, the doggy-faced watch seems related to the writer R., who has more than a little in common with Nabokov and greatly influences Hugh's life. R. was "a bulldog mouth" (30). Just before he dies, R. writes: "The entire solar system is but a reflection in the crystal of my (or your) wrist watch" (84). In 1972, Nabokov declared: "...it is no other than a discarnate, but still rather grotesque, Mr. R. who greets newly-dead Hugh in the last line of the book."[19]

We have thus far noted three fateful Nabokovian humans with bulldog faces: R. (with his "bulldog mouth"), the old man (with a "bulldog face" who delays V.'s attempt to reach the dying Sebastian), and "assistant executioner" Fred Beale ("with his bulldog jowls"). M'sieur Pierre, the executioner assigned to kill Cincinnatus in *Invitation to a Beheading*, has "bulldog teeth" (118) with a bulldog grip" (116). En route to the execution, M'sieur Pierre's hands rest "on the bulldog head of his cane" (215).[20]

Sentenced to be executed, Cincinnatus is put in a jail where a guard with a "doglike mask" stands in the corridor (13). When Cincinnatus is finally led out to the carriage which will take him to his place of execution, he is attended by soldiers in "canine masks" (212). Unable to walk, he is supported by M'sieur Pierre and a soldier "with the face of a borzoi" (212-3). Nearing the place of execution, Cincinnatus' carriage is chased by "spotted dogs (216). Finally, as Cincinnatus walks to the scaffold, we read: "Somewhere in the crowd a dog barked" (219).

The novel contains three other potential fateful dog references. Cincinnatus' lawyer is likened to a dog (35). Marthe's son Diomedon has "bulldog jowls" (101) which are said to be not Marthe's, but "someone else's." Diomedes was a cuckolded King of Argos. The "bulldog-executioner" theme, which includes vicious practical jokes, may thus also include cuckolding. Finally, M'sieur Pierre, digging the tunnel to Cincinnatus' cell, is likened to "a hound tunneling his way to a badger" (140). All of the above references are present in the Russian original, except the first mention of M'sieur Pierre's bulldog dentures.[21]

In *The Eye,* Smurov describes Vanya's sister Evgenia as "...a young woman with a nice squarish face that made you think of an amiable and quite handsome bulldog" (39). She is later asked to give her opinion of Smurov. Evgenia smiles, looking like "a cute bulldog" (65), and offers a "rather pale and not very attractive"portrait. If she "executes" Smurov (as one could expect from her bulldog features), it is of course only figuratively: Evgenia reveals to Smurov the crushing news that Vanya loves not him but Mukhin (78). Moreover, bulldog-faced Evgenia deals two other blows to Smurov and his serial selves: she discovers the stolen articles in the maid's room and determines that the maid's lover is not a fireman (85).

Actually, Smurov's love for Vanya, in Nabokov's world, may anyway be considered doomed because of Vanya's resemblance to her sister Evgenia: "The two sisters resembled each other; the frank bulldogish heaviness of the elder's features was just perceptible in Vanya, but in a different way that lent significance and originality to the beauty of her face" (40).

Early in *The Gift,* Fyodor is the victim of a vicious practical joke. Promised a rave review of his poems, he glows with the feeling that he is "...already noticed. Noticed! Thank you, my land, for this remotest..." (41). He reaches the street-car stop: "Shaking her bobbed hair a girl entered the shelter with a small, wheezing, toadlike bulldog. Now this is odd: 'remotest' and 'noticed' are together again and a certain combination is ringing persistently" (42). Fyodor then goes to the Chernyshevskis', where he learns that the rave review was an April Fool's joke. Fyodor's near insight into his own fate ("noticed" was indeed "remotest")—though faintly detectable as an "odd" result of his noticing the bulldog—is thus disguised by poetic inspiration.

Arriving at the Chernyshevskis', he follows another guest up the stairs: "Fyodor had to zigzag behind her at a reduced pace, as you sometimes see a dog do, weaving and shoving its nose past its master's heel now on the right, now on the left" (44). Within a few lines of being likened to a dog, he learns of the cruel joke.

Soon after this, we meet Rudolf, a student who enters into a strange suicide pact with Olya G. and Yasha Chernyshevski: "...swift in his movements and handsome—in a hard, sinewy way, remindful of a gundog" (54). Rudolf (whose soul Yasha loves) loves Olya, who loves Yasha. They decide to terminate their "threefold torture" by shooting themselves. The revolver belongs to Rudolf (57), which may relate to his "gundog" appearance. The three students find "a convenient lonely spot" near a lake "on whose vast shore there was not a soul except for a little man who was tossing a stick into the water at the request of his dog" (59). Yasha shoots himself. Olya and Rudolf then call for help: "...but nobody came: architect Ferdinand Stockschmeisser had long since left with his wet setter" (60).

Late in the novel, the reader is invited to "go into the forest" (343) to an area near the spot where "Yasha Chernyshevski had shot himself" (345). Here, we are told, two people had recently died in a plane crash: "but no one could see the imprint of a daring death beneath the pines, one of which had been shaved from top to bottom by a wing, and the architect Stockschmeisser walking his dog was explaining to a nurse and child what had happened" (343). For the reader who recalls the fateful dog background for Yasha's suicide, the words "explaining what had happened" may acquire a rather eerie tinge.

Near the end of the novel, Fyodor reviews fate's attempts to bring him and Zina together: first, through Lorentz's wife, then through document translation, and finally, by having Fyodor become a boarder at Zina's (375). Just before this, they had seen

Lorentz's wife "with a goggle-eyed, trembling little dog under her arm" (373). Much earlier, during fate's first attempt, Fyodor had said that "Lorentz's pug-faced wife" did not "interest" him "in any way" (71).

When Fyodor's father, who presumably perishes somewhere in Asia, bids his family a "last farewell" (143), one of their dogs reacts quite violently: "the fox terrier choked with barking as it squirmed wildly in Tanya's arms, turning over onto its back and twisting its head over her shoulder" (144). Earlier, "throwing a tennis ball for the fox terriers" (107), Fyodor's father had discovered a queer trick of fate: a rare moth he had found far away appears before him at home. A few other dogs in *The Gift* may seem teasingly fateful—for example, the "agitated" Alsatian who appears just before Fyodor, obviously anticipating making love with Zina that evening, visits her room for the first time (368).

Anna Maria Salehar has noted the regular appearance of certain images in the poem that are subtly woven into the narration of *The Gift:* "The linden, symbolizing Zina, the star representing his father, the darkness, and a light haunt Fyodor to the end."[22] In two of these prose-poetry passages, there are references to dogs (168, 378), which may acknowledge their presence in fate's overall pattern. Dogs even seem associated with blue, which is the novel's predominant color[23]: "(runny ink, blue runaway dog)" (16); "a yawning dog's mouth with 'its bluish palate...' " (84).

The Russian original of *The Gift* contains all of the above dogs, except that the "gundog" used to describe Rudolf is *lyagavoi* (50) and that Lorentz's "pug-faced" wife is *ploskolitsaya* (69).

Nabokov has explained that his story "The Circle," which contains various characters from *The Gift,* is "a small satellite" which "separated itself from the main body of the novel and started to revolve around it" (254). In this story, the two Godunov-Cherdyntsev fox terriers are associated with Innokentiy's doomed passion for Tanya. He first glimpses her with a fox terrier (258). Then, against a background of the Count playing with one fox terrier, Innokentiy sees: "...a second fox terrier, and above all, above all, those eyes gliding through shine and shade, those features still indistinct but already threatening him with fatal fascination, the face of Tanya whose birthday was being fêted: (263). The fascination, if not literally fatal, is quite futile, for Innokentiy is a schoolmaster's son, not allowed to play with Tanya and her friends: "...and, good God, how he hated them all, her boy cousins, her girl friends, the frolicsome dogs" (265). The Russian original contains all of this.

Fateful hounds in *Ada* are concentrated in three partly overlapping areas: love affairs, deaths, and Van Veen's actions. The pattern is further complicated by cross referencing; for example, the Russian phrase "to hell's hounds" attends Ada and Van's first meeting (151), Demon's discovery of their affair (438), and Aqua's insanity prior to her suicide (23).

Somewhat like Humbert Humbert, Van dislikes dogs and yet seems to re-enact, or emulate, their actions without realizing it. When we first see the heroine, she is "preceded by a fluid dackel" (37). Van, we are told, "secretely [sic] disliked dogs, especially at meals, and especially that smallish longish freak with a gamey breath" (61).

Disliked Dack thus appears with Ada prior to her affair with Van. Soon after this, Van notices that Ada has left him and is now at the window "with the slim-waisted dog on a chair peering over splayed front paws out into the garden too" (39). At this point, Marina says: "You can see the Barn from the library window." Later, it is the library window through which Ada and Van both look (the Night of the Burning Barn) just before making love together for the first time.

As the Burning Barn episode draws to a close, we read: "...all the dogs returned well pleased with the night treat...and our two naked children,...giving the couch a parting pat, pattered back with their candlesticks to their innocent bedrooms" (121-2). The dogs, of course, are "well pleased" with the excitement of the fire; the "children," with their lovemaking.

Earlier, when Ada showed Van the house "and all those nooks in it where they were to make love so soon," we read (of the roof): "even the dog had once gone there" (59). Subsequently we are told twice of lovemaking by Ada and Van on the roof (129, 212).

Later in the novel, there is much ado about chasing Dack, who has a "sizable wad of blood-soaked cotton-wool" in his mouth. he is pursued by several females, including Ada, who finally overtakes and tackles him in the garden (68-9). Still later, Van leaves the swimming pool and walks off into the garden; he is pursued, and overtaken, by both Ada and Lucette, who then kiss and fondle him as he lies on the ground. Both girls, we are told, crammed a crushed flower under the rubber belt of his bathing trunks (205). Earlier, we had seen Ada on the grass in the garden "trying to make an anadem of marguerites for the dog while Lucette looked on" (89). As shown below, this anticipates Lucette's death.

When Van is wounded in his duel with The Captain, he is rushed by limousine to a hospital on "the ancient and filthy macintosh on which a decrepit dear dog had once died on the way to the veterinary" (311). Van of course does not die, but his emulation of the dog is typical.

Deep in the novel, Van sees Cordula petting "two unhappy poodlets" (456). He quotes to her an ingenious play on some famous (Terra) lines by John Collins Bossidy ("And this is good old Boston,/ The home of the bean and the cod,/ Where the Lowells talk to the Cabots/ And the Cabots talk only to God.") In Van's version: "The Veens speak only to Tobaks/ But Tobaks speak only to dogs." Carl Proffer has noted that in Russian, "with the Tobaks" would rhyme with "with dogs."[24] Also of significance in the present context, the last word in each line reverses: Tobaks, as Cabots; dogs, as gods.[25] Moreover, Van proceeds to persuade Cordula (she is now Mrs. Tobak, and Lucette will jump to her death from the Tobakoff) to have sex with him: *"C'est bizarre,* an exciting little girl like you who can be so tender with poodles and yet turns down a poor paunchy stiff old Veen" (457). Despite her reply ("The Veens are much too gay as dogs go"), Cordula agrees to make love.

Not long before Lucette commits suicide, she tells Van, "You're mine tonight. Mine, mine, mine!" We then read: "She was quoting Kipling—the same phrase that Ada used to address to Dack" (487). Even here Van is preceded, without realizing it, by the dog he so dislikes.

Dogs in *Ada* are associated with the possibility that the brother-sister affair will be discovered. First, Marina seems suspicious, and Van denies guilt. Marina explains that she is worried by Van's intimacy with little Lucette, not Ada. After this, we read: "The dog came in, turned up a brimming brown eye Vanward..." (223). Van says: "I could never stand that breed. Dackelophobia." Apparently still worried, Marina asks: "But girls—do you like girls, Van, do you have many girls?"

When Ada and Van live together in Manhattan, they take great precautions to avoid being discovered. The "only time" they are careless, they are seen together by "...old Mrs. Arfour who happened to be passing by their front door with her tiny tan-and-gray long-silked Yorkshire terrier" (432). After this, Demon, summoned unexpectedly to Manhattan, notices "Mrs. Arfour, advancing toward him, with her toy terrier." A vegetable cart passes by, and the two do not converse. "But precisely in regard to such a contingency," we read, "Fate had prepared an alternate continuation." Here, as the fateful "lady and dog" do not quite reveal the lovers, it occurs to Demon that Van may be living in Cordula's apartment (which he is doing, but with Ada). Demon goes there and discovers all. Everything, we are told, went "to the hell curs, *k chertyam sobachim*" (438).

After the lovers' long separation occasioned by Van's discovery of Ada's affairs, Lucette brings to Van a last, desparate letter from Ada. For a long time the letter, in a blue envelope, is left protruding from Lucette's open handbag. "Chows, too, have blue tongues," thinks Van (369). Talking with Lucette, Van keeps staring at the blue envelope, and he mentions "a kennel girl who brings a letter" (381). When at last he reads the letter, Van agrees to see Ada, and the lovers are joyfully reunited.

Fateful hounds in *Ada* are variously associated with death. As mentioned above, the description of Aqua's insanity prior to her suicide includes the Russian phrase *k chertyam sobachim,* translated as "to the devil" (23)—later translated as "to hell's hounds" (151) and "to the hell curs" (438). All these meanings seem reflected in the signature to Aqua's suicide note, which plays upon Ada's name and the Russian phrase *iz ada,* "out of hell" (29).

The association of hounds with Lucette's tragic fate is exceedingly complex. To begin with, an intimate episode under "the great weeping cedar" (204) intensifies the girl's love for Van. Ada, we are told, "seemed to enjoy" making "her innocent sister notice and register what Van could not control." Lucette then becomes an impossible pest: the "frolic under the sealyham cedar proved to be a mistake" (211). The tree thus changes its name from "great weeping" to "sealyham" (on Terra, a kind of terrier) as we learn of the ultimately fatal passion promoted below it. Especially in a view of the supernatural episode involving a "terrier" or "weeping-willow dog" in *Pale Fire* (discussed below in connection with Hazel Shade, also a water suicide), one may be tempted to suspect some sort of fateful supernatural influence in Lucette's life. A dog provides a clue. When Van had helped little Lucette "to plough" (by holding her ankles as she walked on her hands), we were told: "Dack barked in strident protest" (91). As Bobbie Ann Mason has noted,[26] Lucette's suicidal dive into the ocean is prefigured by her "ploughing" with Van. Mary McCarthy has observed that "a hazel wand" is "a divining rod."[27] To all this we may add that in holding Lucette up by the ankles, Van turns her into a sort of human diving rod, or stick used to find water, held by the forked end. Thus Lucette seems still further related to Hazel, which reinforces the possible supernatural parallel, especially in view of Dack's "strident protest."

Early in Part Three of the novel, Van meets Greg, who tells him that seeing Ada on the screen would be: "Like a drowning man seeing his whole past, and the trees, and the flowers, and the wreathed dachshund" (455). Later, as Lucette drowns: "She saw...a girl with long black hair quickly bend in passing to clap her hands over a dackel in a half-torn wreath" (494). Presumably, all this was fatefully anticipated by the fact that when Ada, as seen above, fashioned a wreath for Dack, "Lucette looked on."

In *Look at the Harlequins!* (which contains so many echoes of other Nabokov works) Vadim's first wife Iris is murdered near the end of Part One. Dying, she cries out "something loud and brave, as if she were driving away a fierce hound" (69). This may be related to Martha's moribund vision of Tom, Lucette's moribund vision of Dack, and perhaps to Chernyshevski's moribund notion in *The Gift*: "One effort—and I'll understand all. The search for God: the longing of any hound for a master; give me a boss and I shall kneel at his enormous feet" (322).

Late in *Look at the Harlequins!* Vadim's daughter Isabel shows him a poem she has written:

> In the dark basement, I stroked
> the silky head of a wolf.
> When the light returned
> and all cried "Ah!,"
> it turned out to be only
> Médor, a dead dog.

Vadim says he found the poem "rather obscure" at that time. Now, however, he sees through its "starry crystal" a "tremendous commentary" he could write (172). Given Vadim's special brand of madness (he suspects that he may be a copy of someone else, but of course cannot identify that someone as Nabokov), we may be reminded of Nabokov's own "tremendous commentary" to *Eugene Onegin*, wherein one finds a note about the difficulty of distinguishing a dog from a wolf (II:484-485), which seems to "recall" Isabel's poem about Médor. Within Vadim's own book, Médor figures in an experiment designed to demonstrate Vadim's peculiar mental illness (41).

Lydia Nikolaevna, whose *pension* is the stage for most of *Mary*, shares the armchair in her room with her old dachshund (6). "The only other person to go into her room was Podtyagin, who would stroke her affectionate black dachshund, tickle its ears and the wart on its hoary muzzle, and try to make the dog sit up and proffer its crooked paw."[28]

Podtyagin, who "really had no luck" (51), seems "doomed" (85) not to go to Paris as he hopes. In fact, as the novel ends, he appears to be dying in result of a series of heart seizures. He thus resembles Pnin, who also befriends a dog and has heart seizures; also like Pnin, Podtyagin appears in another novel—though not by name and not alive.[29]

When Podtyagin has his last attack, he is carried to his room, whereupon: "In the passage, the dachshund began yelping in a high-pitched, excited voice" (104). Alfyorov, who is drunkenly counting the time until Mary's arrival, says: "Lousy little dog. Ought to be run over." After this, Podtyagin does not die, and Alfyorov is tricked by Ganin into missing Mary at the train station.

When Ganin (who is leaving on the same day as Mary is arriving) goes to settle up with Lydia Nikolaevna: "Her dachshund slithered off the bed and began thrashing about in a little fit of hysterical devotion at Ganin's feet" (87). Early in the novel, Ganin had dreamed of leaving Berlin, watching trains from his window: "olive-drab carriages with a row of dark dog-nipples along their roofs and a stubby little locomotive"(10). This strangely dog-related dream proves prophetic at the end of the novel. Ganin is planning to meet Mary himself, whereupon we read of "a large red-haired dog" pulling a flower-seller's cart: "Its tongue hanging out, the dog was straining forward, exerting every one of its sinewy muscles devoted to man" (112). Soon after this, Ganin decides not to meet Mary after all—and finally leaves

Berlin by train in the last sentence of the novel.

In *Laughter in The Dark* we read, of amorous Albinus: "fate seemed to be urging him to come to his senses" (97). At this point (Irma has just died), he painfully decides to return to his wife. Albinus then walks to the window and looks out: "an adventurous Alsatian was insistenly [*sic*] following a tiny Pikinese, which snarled, turned and slithered at the end of its leash" (98-9). Margot awakes and asks Albinus where he is going. " 'Nowhere,' he said, without turning around." (Similarly, Ganin's decision not to meet Mary was attended by a dog, as was Dreyer's fateful decision to invite Franz to Berlin. [30]) Here, Albinus may be seen as the "adventurous Alsatian" who "insistently follows " Margot, "the tiny Pikinese" who is held by the "leash" of his money but "snarls, turns, and slithers" away to Rex. "Slithers" seems especially apt because Margot is constantly associated with snakes.

Rex becomes interested in Margot upon seeing a snapshot of her "with the sun in her eyes and a dog in her arms" (18). She first hears of him with a "fat yellow dachshund in her lap" (18). While "kissing the wart on the dog's cheek," she wrongly assumes that Rex is an "old dodderer." Learning that he is young and "distinguished," she decides to take the dachshund for a walk. After this, the two first meet alone when Margot walks the dachshund (20). Late in the novel, Rex plans with Margot to acquire all of Albinus' money and then leave him: "...and before we go we'll buy him a dog—as a small token of our gratitude" (144). Finally, it seems faintly patterned that Margot is said to be "going to the dogs" (110). She kills Albinus at the end of the novel; Hermann, also said to be "going to the dogs," kills Felix near the end of *Despair*.

When Martin, the hero of *Glory*, "...was about eight, he had attempted to shear the hair off a shaggy little dog, and had inadvertently cut its ear" (12). Martin later lives in a chalet and sees sheep herded by a shepherd and "a shaggy dog" (44). He develops an unrequited interest in Marie, who prefers a shepherd (46). Later, just before Martin's long-anticipated return to Russia, he walks with his mother and the Gruzinovs: "...a sheepdog dashed out of a farmyard and stood, growling, in their path...Martin took his mother's cane out of her hand, while she tried to pacify the dog by emitting in its direction sounds used in Russia to urge on the horses" (173). At this point Gruzinov chases the dog away: "A trifle, of course, but Martin cherished that kind of trifle." We then learn that on another walk, Gruzinov carved a walking stick for Martin: "Another trifle, but somehow that stick seemed to smell of Russia." This "trifle" more obviously reveals that Martin is intent upon his secret return. And the "smell of Russia" adds a touch of irony to his mother's attempt to pacify the sheepdog by "sounds used in Russia"—she has already laughingly declared, when Martin says he must go to Berlin but will soon return: "You won't, I know you" (167).

Several other dogs (performing, pursuing, artificial, and even hypothetical) seem fatefully associated with Martin's doomed love (for Sonia Zilanov) and with his "exploit" of returning to Russia ("They'll kill him, oh God, they'll kill him," says Mr. Zilanov at the end). Martin visits Sonia Zilanov just before she moves to Berlin: "When Martin arrived, the Zilanovs' house was in that dreary state of havoc that is so hateful to elderly, homey dogs—fat dachshunds, for instance" (115). Martin suggests "hopelessly" that she'll get married in Berlin. Sonia smiles, kisses him on the nose, and whispers: "I don't know—maybe" (118). Then. "wriggling out of Martin's violent embrace," she says: *Tout beau,* doggy." In the Russian original, this is simply *"Tubo"* (137).

Besides the dog used to describe the "havoc" at the Zilanovs', two other hypothetical dogs appear in the novel. These are a "brown dachshund," in Martin's "prophetic daydreams" of leaving Russia (135-6), and "a mad dog," when he "forgot his usual reserve" and spoke of Horace to Sonia—after which she allowed him to kiss her" (144).

The next day after this kiss, Martin: "...bought a large crimson-ribboned plush dog and was approaching her house with the thing under his arm when he met the whole returning party on the street; Sonia had Kallistratov's jacket over her shoulders, and between him and her there flashed repeatedly a chance jest, whose meaning nobody bothered to explain to Martin"(145).

Just before he sees Sonia for the last time, Martin feels that the air of Berlin is "saturated" with "memories of her. Over there, at the zoo, they had stared together...at the yellow dog dingo that could jump so high" (186). Finally, as Martin makes final arrangements for his return to Russia:

> A poodle ran past in pursuit of a black whippet; the latter
> stopped and looked back in fear, raising one bent front paw and
> quivering. "What's the matter, for goodness' sake," thought
> Martin. "What's all this to me? I know I'm going to return.
> I must return." (196)

In his Foreword to *The Defense,* Nabokov mentions that he "greatly enjoyed taking advantage of this or that image and scene to introduce a fatal pattern into Luzhin's life" (6). In context, this refers to Luzhin's life becoming a chess game with its defense of suicide, but the novel contains other patterns. Luzhin's therapeutic drawings form a Nabokovian cluster of prophetic details.[31] Fateful dogs are also carefully patterned.

In school, little Luzhin is viciously teased by his classmates, who have been admonished by the teacher to read a children's book by Luzhin's father. Luzhin is dubbed "Tony " (the book's hero) and a picture torn from the book is tacked to the underside of his desk lid. The picture shows "a bright-eyed schoolboy on a streetcorner feeding his luncheon to a scruffy dog" (26). Much later, when Luzhin is desperately trying not to remember his past, he meets an old schoolmate who calls him "Tony" (197) and utters the recollection "chess!" (198). After this, Luzhin is mysteriously bothered by "a riddle, a splinter"—the old schoolmate had "referred obliquely to a certain torn book about little Tony" (200). Luzhin decides that meeting his schoolmate was "the continuation of something" and that he must "replay all the moves of his life."

This "something" is not only the theme of chess but of fateful dogs, as a review of key episodes in Luzhin's life reveals. Besides the dog picture in the "Tony" book, there is the wallpaper in little Luzhin's room: "...white, and higher up was a blue band on which were drawn gray geese and ginger puppies. A goose advanced on a pup and so on thirty-eight times around the entire room" (28). The "pup" in this Nabokovian prophetic childhood bedroom wallpaper[32] appears late in the novel, when Valentinov tracks down Luzhin and fatally submerges the latter in chess. Valentinov, whom Luzhin's wife has been frantically attempting to keep away, arrives at Luzhin's place and says:

> They told me you were in bed, ill, dear boy. But that was some
> kind of slipup..." and in stressing the "pup" Valentinov pursed

Valentinov immediately rekindles Luzhin's love of chess: "And this love was fatal" (244).

As young Luzhin becomes a prodigy at chess, Valentinov moves in to exploit him: "He was interested in Luzhin only inasmuch as he remained a freak, an odd phenomenon, somewhat deformed but enchanting, like a dachshund's crooked legs" (90). Successful and famous, Luzhin meets his future wife: "it was said of her that she adored dogs" (103).

Luzhin becomes engaged, breaks down in a chess match with Turati, and goes to a sanitorium where:

> ...beside him walked his fiancée and thought for some reason of a book she had read in childhood in which all the difficulties in the life of a schoolboy, who had run away fom home together with a dog he had saved, were resolved by a convenient (for the author) fever... (162)

Presumably, this is the "Tony" book (written by Luzhin's father) from which a picture of boy and dog was tacked to Luzhin's desk. And it now seems clear that Luzhin's later meeting with the old schoolmate (which "referred obliquely to a certain torn book about little Tony") was "a continuation" of this dog book in particular and the fateful dog motif in general. This then is the "riddle" or "splinter" bothering Luzhin.

When Luzhin recovers enough to leave the sanitorium, his fiancée rents an apartment in which someone had left "a fat-faced toy dog with broad pink soles and a black spot over one eye" (173). Just married, Luzhin walks sleepily through the new apartment : "He was already on his way into the dining room when he noticed he was carrying in his arms a large, plush dog with pink soles. He put it on the table and a fluffy imp hanging from the lamp immediately came down like a spider" (181). This figure was earlier termed "a lone, fluffy, little toy dev-il " (173). In the Russian original, both references are *"pushistyi chortik"* (184, 192). After Luzhin puts down the dog and the devil-imp falls, he goes to the bathroom (where he will commit suicide by falling from its window) and locks the door (which he also does prior to suicide).

Trying to divert Luzhin's mind from chess, his wife takes him to the museum, where: "...she directed his attention to two dogs domestically looking for crumbs beneath the narrow, poorly spread table of 'The Last Supper'"(191). Much earlier, Luzhin's father's affair with a young aunt was signalled by her playful action as he spoke at the table: "...the young aunt landed a crumb right in Father's mouth" (40). Since she "never again came to visit them" (43), the crumb was thrown at a sort of "last supper." After this, Luzhin's father has a crumb on his beard, and the crumb "jumps off' in the middle of his proposal to teach Luzhin chess (59). At least in retrospect, the dogs seeking crumbs at The Last Supper, the crumb at Luzhin's father's "last supper," and the "chess crumb" all seem fatefully related.

In the Russian original, all the above references to pictures of dogs (on wallpaper, in storybook, in painting), toy dogs, and live dogs are present. And, as seen above, the "devil-imp" (activated by the plush dog) is more accurately echoed. But Valentinov's stressed "pup" in "slipup" was simply a "stress" (udarenie) on "mixup" (putanitsa), although in both versions Valentinov dons a "bowler" (kotelok), which could render him the sort of "executioner in his top hat" related to fateful dogs by Hermann in Despair. In Look at the Harlequins! the novel Invitation to a Beheading becomes The Red Top Hat.

In Pale Fire, Gradus is briefly associated with Pnin's dog prior to killing John Shade. Pnin himself pays no attention to Gradus who, we read, "stepped over a fat little dog without awakening it" (199). Then, after the shooting, Kinbote tells us that "the gunman gave his name as Jack Grey, no fixed abode, except the Institute for the Criminal Insane, ici, good dog" (208). At least as imagined by Kinbote, Gradus seems Nabokov's most repulsive killer, and his, Kinbote's, ironic epithet "good dog" aptly fits the overall pattern of Nabokovian "executioners."

A fateful dog also seems part of the setting for Shade's death. Having noted "the ecstatic barking of the boxer dog whom most of the neighbors disliked (he overturned garbage cans)," Kinbote declares: "It was the medley of metallic melodies which surrounded me on that fateful, much too luminous evening..." (202). This boxer dog is also involved in a series of details that may suggest a strange twist of the dog theme in Ada and Lolita.

As seen above, Van and Humbert unwittingly emulate dogs—or at least repeat their actions, recreating similar situations. With Kinbote, it seems to be the mirror-like reverse: dogs emulate him. Early in his Commentary, Kinbote sneaks over to the Shades' and spies on them through the window of their back parlor: "As I strained to see better, standing up to my knees in a horribly elastic box hedge, I dislodged the sonorous lid of a garbage can" (65). The slip proves fatal to Kinbote: Sybil closes the window and pulls down its blind. Kinbote thus performs an act later associated with the fateful boxer dog ("he overturned garbage cans"). Moreover, the "boxer" echo may even be confirmed: Kinbote dislodges the garbage can lid while standing in a "box" hedge. Soon after this, Kinbote is terrified that someone is coming to kill him at night: "Stealthy rustles, the footsteps of yesteryear leaves, an idle breeze, a dog touring the garbage cans—everything sounded to me like a bloodthirsty prowler" (69). Since this is in the context of feared "regicide," Kinbote is twice emulated by dogs—here in a hypothetical, and later in a problematical, attempt to kill the Zemblan King.

Kinbote also seems emulated by a dog when he, the King of Zembla, escapes into the Bera Mountains. Fleeing at night, in a storm, he is about to give up and sleep in the undergrowth when: "A dog barked" (101). The King then finds "welcome shelter" at a farmer's house. The next morning, homosexual Kinbote is helped by the farmer's daughter and "a happy sheepdog"to find his way again. Oriented, he decides to rest: "He sank down on the grass near a patch of matted elfinwood and inhaled the bright air. The panting dog lay down at his feet" (102). Thinking Kinbote wishes to have sex, the farmer's daughter strips to the waist and "floods" him "with all the acridity of ungroomed womanhood." Kinbote, we read, "patted the innocent dog" (103). He then resumes his journey, "chuckling over the wench's discomfiture." The dog thus follows Kinbote both in lying down on the grass and in receiving unsexual caresses. The second of these was anticipated earlier by "...Charles Xavier's chaste romance with Fleur, who was pretty yet not repellent (as some cats are less repugnant than others to the good-natured dog told to endure the bitter effluvium of an alien genus)" (81). Note the interplay of "effluvium" and the farmer's daughter's "acridity". Similarly, Kinbote's patting of the "innocent" dog, following the farmer's daughter's ironically innocent advances, humorously echoes the "alien genus" notion.

When Shade's daughter Hazel drowns, we read:

Out of his lakeside shack
A Watchman, Father Time, all gray and bent,
Emerged with his uneasy dog and went
Along the reedy bank. He came too late. (poem, 474-77)

As Kinbote tells us (156), these lines echo Hazel's earlier appearance as "Mother Time" (line 312), but his helpful note tends to
obscure the fateful dog, just as the italics of *ici* tend to distract
the reader's attention from Kinbote's killer epithet "good dog."
    Immediately after Hazel drowns (line 500), we read of:
"L'if, lifeless tree" (501) and "I.P.H." (502). The three letters
represent "Institute of Preparation for the Hereafter," the discussion of which mentions various details hopefully "found in Heav-
en by the newly dead" (535), one of which is: "the way/ You
smile at dogs" (530-31).[33] And as Kinbote tells us regarding *L'if*
"It is curious that the Zemblan word for weeping willow is also
'if' " (158).[34]
    This is more than "curious." As we learned earlier:

> ...sixteen-year-old Hazel was involved in some appalling 'psycho-
> kinetic' manifestations that lasted for nearly a month. Initially,
> one gathers, the poltergeist meant to impregnate the disturbance
> with the identity of Aunt Maud who had just died; the first
> object to perform was the basket in which she had once kept
> her half-paralyzed Skye terrier (the breed called in our country
> "weeping-willow dog"). (118)

The interconnection with Hazel's suicide has now become: *"if"*
and "I.P.H." (in the poem); *"if"* (Zemblan for "weeping-willow")
and the "psychokinetic manifestation " (of the "weeping-willow
dog's basket"); "I.P.H." and "the way you smile at dogs" ("found
in Heaven by the newly dead").
    Another psychokinetic manifestation mentioned in connec-
tion with Hazel Shade is that "lamps kept lighting up in various
parts of the house" (119). A short poem by John Shade contains:

> The dead, the gentle dead—who knows?—
> In tungsten filaments abide,
> And on my bedside table glows
> Another man's departed bride. (138)

Hazel is also involved with an apparently supernatural "round-let of pale light" (134) in a barn, but the more direct connection with the poem seems to be the eerie lamp. In *The Eye* there is a character named Weinstock who believes in "the jinx and the hex, in magic numbers and the Devil" (48). He has a lady friend who

> ...encouraged Weinstock in his experiments with the hereafter and used to tell...how once her bedside lamp had hopped down from its table and begun to imitate a dog impatiently tugging at its leash; the plug had finally shot out, there was the sound of a scampering off in the dark, and the lamp was later found in the hall, right by the front door. (51)

In Turgenev's story "The Dog," there is much ado about the sounds made by a possibly supernatural dog on a bedroom floor in the dark. Here, Nabokov's parody of that story seems confirmed by the fact that Weinstock has just called Turgenev's voice in a seance (50).

Nabokov's short stories contain numerous fateful hounds. In "That in Aleppo Once..." the narrator describes his "insane" wife, revealing by degrees that it is probably he, rather than she, who is mad. A foremost clue involves the couple's dog.

The narrator relates his honeymoon with his wife: she once began to sob in a railway carriage.

> "The dog," she said, "the dog we left. I cannot forget the poor dog." The honesty of her grief shocked me, as we had never had any dog. "I know," she said, "But I tried to imagine we had actually bought that setter. And just think, he would be now whining behind a locked door." There had never been any talk of buying a setter. (105)

110

The apparently non-existent dog seems quite appropriate as a figment of the wife's imagination because the narrator twice declares that she herself "never existed" (103,111). He also terms her "a phantom" (104) and "ghostly" (110). Moreover, she briefly disappears, later confesses that she had a brief affair, and finally insists that she did not: perhaps she wanted to "test" her husband (109). Soon after this, she disappears again.

Questioning acquaintances, the narrator is finally told by an old woman that he is "a bully and a cad" and that his wife has gone with another man to a château in Lozère. The reader may be wondering whether it is safe to believe all this—the narrator has termed one of the old lady's insults "quite unjustified" —when she concludes: "But one thing I shall never forgive you— her dog, that poor beast which you hanged with your own hands before leaving Paris" (111). This suddenly real dog, abruptly revealed as a key element in what the narrator terms the "pattern of our fates" (109), seems to fix as also real both the ghostly wife and her ghostly affair.

Erwin, the hero of "A Nursery Tale," is permitted by the Devil to choose his own harem, provided he does so between noon and midnight and picks an odd number of girls. He is told that his desire is enough to effect selection, whereupon he will receive a signal, such as: "a smile, not necessarily addressed to you, a chance word in the crowd" (46).

Just past noon, Erwin notices "a girl in a white dress who had squatted down to tousle with two fingers a fat shaggy pup with warts on its belly" (48). He looks for the promised signal: "At that moment the girl turned her head as she ran and flashed a smile at the plump little creature that could barely keep up with her."

Girls two, three, and four are confirmed by the word "yes"— in casual conversation and in a billboard advertisement. Erwin then hurries to avoid the even number by selecting a girl he has seen working in a cheap restaurant.

> His table was next to the telephone. A man in a bowler called a number and started to jabber as ardently as a hound that has picked up the scent of a hare. Erwin's glance wandered toward the bar—and there was the girl he had seen three or four times before. She was beautiful in a drab, freckled way, if beauty can be drabbly russet. As she raised her bare arms to place her washed

111

beer steins he saw the red tufts of her armpits.

"All right, all right!" barked the man into the mouth-piece. (50)

Girl five is thus confirmed, and Erwin heaves a sigh of relief that his total is once again an odd number. Less obviously, the man who confirms is first likened to "a hound" and then "barks" the Devil's signal. We may therefore recall the dog-like man in *The Real Life of Sebastian Knight* who seems to influence V.'s luck in telephoning. Note also that the man here wears a bowler, which Nabokov sometimes associates with fateful dogs.

Erwin has accumulated a potential harem of twelve when he notices that only a half hour remains. He catches sight of a girl and rapturously stalks her for a long time. Finally he overtakes her, whereupon: "he recognized the girl who had been playing that morning with a woolly black pup on a graveled path, and immediately remembered" (57). Girl thirteen was thus girl one; and since it is now too late, Erwin's harem is foiled by the even number twelve. And of course it was the girl with the dog who proved his undoing.

In "Ultima Thule," the narrator frequently addresses his dead wife. Before her death, he recalls, they were invited by Falter to lunch. She then "petted the wonderful nervous dog that feared its master, and after a minute of silence, in the midst of which Falter suddenly uttered a distinct 'Yes,' as if concluding a diagnostic deliberation, we parted" (155). Not long after this, she dies. The Russian original contains all of this (280).

In his Foreword to the English version, Nabokov observes: "Perhaps, had I finished my book, readers would not have been left wondering about a few things: was Falter a quack? Was he a true seer?" (147). From the perspective of the present study, it seems likely that Falter is indeed a seer, and that he sees the narrator's wife's death as she pets his "wonderful nervous" dog who "fears" him.

Somewhat like Falter in "Ultima Thule," the narrator of "Terror" sees " the actual essence of things" (119). He has

...but one desire: not to go mad. I am convinced that nobody ever saw the world in the way I saw it in those moments, in all its terrifying nakedness and terrifying absurdity. Near me a dog

112

> **was sniffing the snow. I was tortured by my efforts to recog-
> nize what "dog" might mean, and *because* I had been
> staring at it hard, it crept up to me *trustingly,* and I felt
> so nauseated that I got up from the bench and walked
> away. It was then that my terror reached its highest
> point. (120)**

After this, he "finds himself" at his hotel, where he is handed
a telegram saying that the woman he loves is dying. "Her death
saved me from insanity" (121), he concludes, unaware of the
fateful dog's role in his own life experience. Nor can he, may
he, recognize the agent of his creator ("recognize what 'dog'
might mean") without total madness—or perhaps death. (I have
italicized his therefore necessarily incorrect presumptions about
the dog's behavior.) Indeed, to recognize the author's agent would
presumably be tantamount to entering a different dimension—
to raising one's head out of the very painting in which one is
pictured by the artist. Pnin seems to attempt this but fortunately
sees only darkness (in a doorway) and remains sane. Krug, who
sees his horribly murdered little son and thereupon strikes a toy
dog, does indeed go mad—does perhaps become aware of the
author's dimension. Nabokov himself has referred to "...Krug's
blessed madness when he suddenly perceives the simple reality of
things and knows but cannot express in the words of his world
that he and his son and his wife and everybody else are merely
my whims and megrims" (xiv).

In "Cloud, Castle, Lake," the unhappy hero walks to an inn:
"A dog still quite young greeted him; it crept on its belly, its
jaws laughing, its tail fervently beating the ground. Vasili Ivano-
vich accompanied the dog into the house..." (88). Enchanted
by a view (from the window) of lake, cloud, and castle, he decides
to live at the inn for the rest of his life.

The fateful dog who laughingly greets the hero and leads
him into the inn is anticipated earlier by the description: "Whispy
clouds—greyhounds of heaven" (84). This is followed by mention
of a distant "spot so enchanting" that one wishes to go there
"forever" and the words "my love." Later, we read of "a very
long, very pink cloud...my love" (86). Finally, as Vasili Ivano-
vich first glimpses the "unique harmoniousness" of cloud, castle,
and lake, his enchantment is attended by the expression "my
love!" (87). The Russian original contains all these details, in-

cluding the three uses of "my love" to link dog clouds, pink cloud, and the title scene (239-44).

The narrator of "The Visit to the Museum" enters a museum in Montisert and mysteriously emerges in Soviet Russia, whence he departs only after "incredible patience and effort" (104). Before his fateful entrance, he visits the museum's director, "one M. Godard." This man has: "a face very much resembling a Russian wolf-hound; as if that were not enough, he was licking his chops in a most doglike manner" (96). Together they enter the museum, where Godard tears up a document "which fell like snow-flakes" (99). When the narrator leaves, he emerges in Soviet Russia covered with "newly fallen snow" (102). Stunned, he declares: "Everything was real—the air that seemed to mingle with scattered snowflakes..." (103). Also to be noted are the reversable first three letters of doglike Godard's name. In the Russian original, his name is *Godar,* and he resembles "a white borzoi" (106).

In "An Affair of Honor," the hero's fate seems persistently altered for the worse by "a Russified German with the strange name of Gnushke" (17). This person, we learn, is "a very long-faced man in a very tall collar, who resembled a dachshund" (18). Although he has not met the hero before, Gnushke delivers his challenge note (25) and advises him to take shooting lessons before the duel (27). He also encourages the hero to have a drink (18), which presumably contributes to his rash decision to chal-lenge Berg, an alleged marksman. Gnushke then praises the hero's decision, adding: "By a strange coincidence, I am not unfamiliar with these matters. A cousin of mine was also killed in a duel" (20). "Why 'also'?" the hero wonders in terror. "Can this be a portent?"

Olga, the heroine of "A Russian Beauty," leads a dull, un-eventful life to age thirty. One day, she meets her former friend Vera "...with a shaggy-eyed terrier, whose leash immediately be-came wound twice around her skirt. She pounced upon Olga, imploring her to come and stay at their summer villa, saying that it was Fate itself..." (6-7). Olga declines, but: "Vera con-tinued coaxing her, pulling at the terrier, turning this way and that." Vera then takes up "arranging Olga's fate." Soon after Olga arrives at the villa, a suitor also comes for a week. He marries Olga, and she dies the next summer in childbirth.

Nabokovian hounds of fate even seem to appear in *Speak,*

Memory. Besides the association of Chekhov's *Lady and Dog* with executions (mentioned above), two episodes may be noted. Together, they may be considered Mr. Nabokov's two foiled childhood getaways.

The first involves Colette, whose dog is "...a female fox terrier with bells on her collar and a most waggly behind. From sheer exuberance, she would lap up salt water out of Colette's toy pail.... I cannot recall the dog's name, and this bothers me" (150). Intending to elope, the two children enter a pitch-dark movie house: "There we sat, holding hands across the dog, which now and then gently jingled in Colette's lap..." (151). After this, the elopement is foiled, but the memoirist has a final triumph. "I try again to recall the name of Colette's dog...here it comes, echoing and vibrating: Floss, Floss, Floss!"[35]

In the section about Mademoiselle, Nabokov writes: "Another dog, the sweet-tempered sire of a ferocious family, a Great Dane not allowed in the house, played a pleasant part in an adventure..." (102). Deceiving Mademoiselle, Nabokov and his brother go off into the snow with Turka (the Great Dane), but evening falls "with uncanny suddenness" (103-104). The two boys grow cold and tired—especially Nabokov's brother, whom he forces to "ride the dog (the only member of the party to be still enjoying himself)." Finally led home by a servant, little Nabokov attempts to preserve his dignity, but his brother tearfully surrenders.

Also in *Speak, Memory* Nabokov suggests that "the bright mental image (as, for instance, the face of a beloved parent long dead) conjured up by a wing-stroke of the will" is "one of the bravest movements a human spirit can make" (33). Nabokov's father died in 1922. A poem called "Evening on a Vacant Lot, In memory of V.D.N." (dated 1932) opens:

> Inspiration, rosy sky,
> black house, with a single window,
> fiery. Oh, that sky,
> drunk up by the fiery window!
> Trash of solitary outskirts,
> weedy little stalk with teardrop,
> skull of happiness, long, slender,
> like the skull of a borzoi.
> What's the matter with me?[36]

The speaker then likens his present feeling to his past desires to create poetry (note the "teardrop" interconnection with *Speak, Memory*, 217). Now however his desire seems still more intense, and the poem concludes as follows:

> I glimpse a slender hound with snow-white coat.
> Lost, I presume. But in the distance sounds
> insistently and tenderly a whistling,
> And in the twilight toward me a man
> comes, calls. I recognize
> your energetic stride. You haven't
> changed much since you died.

As the speaker's intense, mysterious feeling finally conjures up a living figure from the dead, the initial borzoi skull seems, in parallel transformation, to become a living hound.[37]

As seen above, Nabokov's fateful hounds sometimes extend rather whimsically beyond live dogs to toys, carved figures, pictures, hypothetical dogs, doglike people, metaphorical dogs, and even occasional puns. Particularly when word play is involved, such hounds may seem both ominous and comic. For example, "going to the dogs" (said of both Hermann and Margot) and Krug's calling death "a dog and an abomination" seem to suggest an unwitting accuracy characteristic of Gogolian remarks about the devil. One may also be reminded of Gogol *(nos-son)* by the reverse spellings of "dog" and "god" in *Despair* and *Ada*.[38]

Nabokovian associations of dogs with the supernatural and religion sometimes acquire a comic tinge. Ada, for instance, cocks her head at Dack and asks him how a complex religious discussion got started (91). A comic tinge may also result from associations of dogs with furtive sex, most notably in *Lolita* and *Ada*. And in *The Gift*, a woman is accused of "...consorting with a great Dane; the chief witness was the janitress, who through the door had allegedly heard the wife talking to the hound and expressing delight concerning certain details of its organism" (203). "Great Dane" was *"dog"* in the Russian original (215). And Chernyshevski's plot for a novel (which as Proffer has noted, remarkably anticipates *Lolita*[39]) begins: "An old dog—but still in his prime, fiery, thirsting for happiness—gets to know a widow, and she has a daughter" (198). Here, "old dog" was *"staryi pyos"* (209).

Generally, there seems to be a pattern as to the fateful

associations of certain types of Nabokovian dogs. Alsatians and poodles tend to signal love affairs; dachshunds, lust. Setters often signify death; fox terriers, danger and disappointment. Pugs, boxers and especially bulldogs attend people's "executions" (either by killing or by means of a vicious practical joke). Sheep-dogs are involved with journeys and escape. Dogs unnamed as to breed frequently attend fateful meetings and catch the attention of a person who is making a fateful decision.[40] In such cases, phrases like "for some reason" and "for no reason at all" typically qualify the people's noticing the dogs. Occasionally, people seem *almost* to sense the presence of some fateful influence, whereupon they ask something like "What is the matter with me?" Moreover, the dogs' behavior (straining at a leash, high-pitched yelps, stri-dent barks, etc.) may be quite pertinent to the human context.

Clarence Brown has observed that Nabokov is "extremely repetitious" and that Fate is really one of the "guises" of his muse.[41] Barbara Monter has suggested that the Nabokovian nar-rator typically "strives to grasp the full pattern of the mosaic in which he himself is depicted."[42] But presumably even the most haunted narrator cannot be permitted to detect the exact nature of the author's fateful forces. When a Nabokov character seems on the point of understanding that a dog functions as an agent of fate, the character apparently must either become insane (like Krug in *Bend Sinister*) or die (like Martha in *King, Queen, Knave*) or both (like Chernyshevski in *The Gift*). The narrator of "Ter-ror," who remains alive and barely remains sane, seems to come very close (to "recognizing" what " 'dog' might mean"), but he does not quite understand. If he had, his nausea and terror would presumably have turned into madness.

Nabokovian dogs have been very briefly related here to uses of dogs by James Joyce, T.S. Eliot, Anton Chekhov, Ivan Tur-genev, Nikolai Gogol, and Kurt Vonnegut, Jr. It cannot be over-emphasized however that Nabokov's fateful hounds are uniquely and complexly his own. Uses of dogs by other writers typically pale by comparison, both as to scope and role. Even some of Dostoevsky's dogs, which may seem to suggest parallels, are gener-ally so different in use and effect from Nabokov's as to render invidious the comparisons now footnoted.[43] Simon Karlinsky has aptly observed the "vastly different" treatment of "similar themes" by these two writers.[44]

Nabokovian fateful hounds are associated with human

destiny in several ways. Dogs frequently attend important encounters and fateful decisions. They are often associated, playfully and/or eerily, with death, life after death, and supernatural phenomena. Nabokov has even created a series of executioner-like people with "bulldog" faces. References to Chekhov's "The Lady with the Dog" seem related to executions, and the appearance of a lady with a dog often portends disaster and death. People who abuse dogs typically die or go mad. Humbert Humbert and Van Veen, who intensely dislike dogs, may be seen to imitate their behavior without realizing it. Kinbote, who indirectly likens himself to a dog, is emulated by dogs. Pnin, whose adventures seem related to three dogs, befriends a dog who accompanies him to success in another book. As part of the overall pattern, all such dogs may be seen as the author's fateful agents—inconspicuously prefiguring, promoting, or presiding over, key episodes in Nabokovian "reality."

NOTES

1. All references to Nabokov's works, unless otherwise noted, will be to the following editions:

Ada (New York, 1969)
Bend Sinister (New York, 1964)
The Defense (New York, 1964)
Zashchita Luzhina (Paris, 1930)
Despair (New York, 1966)
Otchayanie (Berlin, 1936)
Details of a Sunset and Other Stories (New York, 1976)
      "A Bad Day"
      "A Busy Man"
      "The Return of Chorb"
      "The Reunion"
      "The Thunderstorm"
Eugene Onegin (Princeton, 1975)
The Eye (New York, 1965)
The Gift (New York, 1970)
Dar (Ann Arbor, 1975)
Glory (New York, 1971)
Podvig (Ann Arbor, 1974)
Invitation to a Beheading (New York, 1965)
Priglashenie na kazn (Paris, 1938)
King, Queen, Knave (New York, 1968)
Korol, dama valet (New York, 1969)

Laughter in The Dark (New York, 1966)
Lolita (New York, 1955)
Look at the Harlequins! (New York, 1974)
Mary (New York, 1970)
Mashenka (Ann Arbor, 1974)
Nabokov's Dozen (New York, 1958)
    "Cloud, Castle, Lake"
    "That in Aleppo Once..."
Nabokov's Quartet (New York, 1966)
    "An Affair of Honor"
    "'Lik"
    "The Visit to the Museum"
Nikolai Gogol (New York, 1961)
Pale Fire (New York, 1966)
Pnin (New York, 1965)
The Real Life of Sebastian Knight (Norfolk, Conn., 1959)
A Russian Beauty and Other Stories (New York, 1973)
    "The Circle"
    "The Potato Elf"
    "A Russian Beauty"
    "Solus Rex"
    "Ultima Thule"
Speak, Memory (New York, 1966)
Drugie berega (New York, 1954)
Transparent Things (New York, 1972)
Tyrants Destroyed and Other Stories (New York, 1975)
    "A Nursery Tale"
    "Terror"
    "Vasiliy Shishkov"
Vesna v Fial'te (New York, 1956)
    "Krug"
    "Oblako, ozero, bashnya"
    "Poseshchenie muzeya"
    "Vasilij Shishkov"
    "Ultima Thule"

2. See also p. 220. It even seems possible that an apparently frivolous notion of Lydia's ("Is the hidden sense worth disclosing?", p. 48) about dogs relates to Hermann's ominous dogs, just as her silly notion about "mystic" previews his fatal "stick" mistake (see Carl R. Proffer, "From *Otchaianie* to *Despair*," *Slavic Review*, June, 1968, p. 266).

3. Joseph Campbell, *The Masks of God: Creative Mythology* (New York, 1968), pp. 273-6.

4. Campbell (pp. 276-7) finds that the same reversal "is suggested" in T.S. Eliot's *The Waste Land*.

5. *Strong Opinions* (New York, 1973), p. 57.

6. As in *Despair*, fateful hounds in *Bend Sinister* may extend even to word play. We are told that when Krug's parents both died in a train accident, he had "Managed to alleviate the pain and the panic" by writing his *'Mirokonzepsia'* wherein "he looked straight into the eyesockets of death and called him a dog and an abomination" (p. 122).

7. Also rather eerily, Tom had seemed to sense the danger of his own impending death. Just before trapping Martha in Franz's room, Tom stubbornly stops at two different times. First, Dreyer almost falls over him (p. 219); second, he says "March-march," and: "with his knee pushed the *intelligent* hound" (p. 220, my emphasis). In the Russian

original, Martha ironically echoes her earlier opinion that Tom is a "fool" (p. 32) when he detects her presence behind Franz's door (p. 212).

8. Carl R. Proffer, *Keys to Lolita* (Bloomington, 1968), p. 6.

9. Alfred Appel, Jr., *The Annotated Lolita* (New York, 1970), p. 410.

10. As in other works, the pattern may even extend to word play: early in the novel, when Humbert's wife Valeria is about to inform him of her affair with Taxovich, she begins "to shake her poodle head vigorously" (p. 29).

11. See *Encounter,* March, 1973, pp. 78-9.

12. Word play may be involved when Humbert fixes drinks concurrently with Charlotte's dog-related death: "Bark and bang went the icebox" (p. 98).

13. As Pnin and his little white dog leave, they are watched by the narrator (presumably Nabokov himself) and a dog called Sobakevich ("son of a dog," like Gogol's character—see Proffer, *Keys,* p. 139). This punning includes the fact that Sobakevich, a cocker, is let in by Jack Cockerell.

14. Anthony Olcott, "The Author's Special Intention: A Study of *The Real Life of Sebastian Knight,*" in: Carl R. Proffer, ed., *A Book of Things About Vladimir Nabokov* (Ann Arbor, 1974), pp. 105-6.

15. In "The Potato Elf," Fred tries to get over his impossible love for Norma: he "grew fond of" his surroundings, including a picture of "a St. Bernard dog, complete with barrelet, *reviving* a mountaineer on his bleak rock" (p. 243, my emphasis). At the end, Fred runs after Norma: "All the dogs of the town woke up." Then, against a background of "barking" and "inciting halloos," Fred collapses and dies.

16. The word "remember" refers to p. 202. We have also been told that "Dr. Anton Chekhov's Quina and Brom" were the grandparents of the Nabokovs' Box II (p. 48).

As John Updike has noted, a comparison with the 1951 edition *(Conclusive Evidence,* New York, p. 27) reveals that Nabokov "has smoothly stricken an irreverent reference" to this dog as being "one of my few connections with the main current of Russian literature" *(Picked-Up Pieces,* New York, 1975, p. 193).

17. In "A Busy Man," Grafitski has a prophetic dream of his own death date, but at the last minute the forces of Fate seem to arrange for an "extension." At this point in the story, Grafitski looks out his window and sees an apparently irrelevant occurence: "a bare-calved housemaid was walking a pinkish toy poodle" (p. 178).

In "A Bad Day," Peter visits the Kozlovs' estate, where he seems to win a hiding game, only to discover that everyone has stopped playing. His participation in the game is interrupted by a "corpulent brown dachshund" followed by a "little old woman" who forcefully shows him a supposedly better hiding place (p. 39). When Peter finally rushes back to the garden, apparently to win, he is met by the same dog (p. 41).

18. In "The Return of Chorb," as the hero arrives in town to finish recreating the image of his dead bride, he encounters a familiar scene in the station square including "the same black poodle with apathetic eyes" (p. 62).

19. *Strong Opinions,* p. 196.

20. In "Solus Rex," the king tries to give Adulph "that fine little riding whip with the doggie's head." (197). Adulph does not accept it however, and he is still alive as the story ends. Nabokov has explained that he had planned to have Adulph killed in a subsequent chapter "in some horrible, clumsy manner" (p. 148).

21. In *Lolita,* Humbert tells us of a woman who was fatally stabbed, presumably by a former lover, "soon after her marriage." Her husband, "a small bulldog of a man, hung onto the murderer's arm. By a miraculous and beautiful coincidence, right at the moment when the operator was in the act of loosening the angry little husband's jaws" (p. 86), a nearby explosion knocked out the husband, allowing the murderer to escape. Humbert's point is that perfect murders are more easily committed by accident than by design, but in the present context we may note that the woman is murdered soon

after her marriage to a bulldog-like person.

22. Anna Maria Salehar, "Nabokov's *Gift*: An Apprenticeship in Creativity," in: Proffer, ed., *A Book of Things...*, p. 81.

23. See especially pp. 39, 346, 376 in English and also the Nabokov-specified cover of the Ardis Russian edition.

24. Carl R. Proffer, "*Ada* as Wonderland: A Glossary of Allusions to Russian Literature," *Russian Literature Triquarterly*, No. 3, p. 426.

25. Of course, "log" seems to have replaced "god" in *Ada*; but "log" and "dog" are combined there in an apparently casual but rather complex sentence (p. 199). For that matter, there are at least three appearances of *"Bozhe moy"* (pp. 438,454,463).

26. Bobbie Ann Mason, *Nabokov's Garden: A Guide to Ada* (Ann Arbor, 1974), p. 106.

27. Mary McCarthy, "A Bolt from the Blue," *The New Republic*, June 4, 1962, p. 24.

28. In the Russian version, this sentence goes on to mention Podtyagin's difficulties in obtaining a visa for Paris (p. 16).

29. In *The Defense*, we learn that Alfyorov "liked to relate how an old poet had once died in his arms" (p. 226; in Russian, p. 238).

30. Dreyer visits his cousin Lina: "An old pug dozed on an embroidered cushion" (p. 8). In the next sentence, Dreyer invites Franz to Berlin, whereupon the latter cuckholds him and plots to kill him. In the original version, the "old pug" was "an evil decrepit dog" (*zlaya obvetshalaia sobachka*, p. 11).

31. The drawings depict a cube, a train on a bridge spanning an abyss, a skull on a telephone directory, oranges, and "a confidential conversation between a cone and pyramid" (p. 207). The cube drawing is hung in the bathroom where Luzhin commits suicide and is mentioned then (p. 251). It may also suggest the shape of the window whence he fatally defenestrates. The train and abyss are mentioned twice (pp. 215, 245) —both at times when Luzhin is disastrously returning to chess contemplation. The skull and telephone directory suggest Valentinov's mortally successful attempts to reach Luzhin at the end. As Luzhin becomes less and less sane, he eats oranges (pp. 203,229); and the last picture may be seen to suggest the referential-mania-like nature of his madness.

32. See my "Pnin's Uncanny Looking Glass," below, p. 126.

33. As seen above, Nabokov has declared that "newly-dead Hugh" is greeted by a "discarnate" (dog-faced) Mr. R. in *Transparent Things.*

34. He goes on to explain a French interplay, which tends to obscure the Russian one ("willow" is *iva,* genitive plural *iv,* pronounced "eef").

35. In "The Reunion," there is also great effort, and final success, in remembering a dog's name. The problem is suggested by a picture of "a girl in red with a soot-black poodle" (pp. 134,136), and its solution is presented through a delicate evocation of the strange workings of memory—of one's need to focus alongside, or even away from, the subject that eludes one's mnemonic grasp (pp. 137-138). In the story, the joint effort to recall the dog's name rather ironically unites two brothers who have otherwise grown quite apart.

36. *Poems and Problems* (New York, 1970), p. 69.

37. In "The Thunderstorm," the narrator is joined by an "old, shaggy dog" to witness a supernatural occurrence. The dog is first to look up: "like a person, with frightened hazed eyes" (p. 122). Both narrator and dog then see Elijah (who has fallen from his chariot) ascend a fiery sky and disappear.

38. Still another dimension of Nabokovian word play may involve apparently innocent uses of dog in expressions such as "dog Latin" and "doggerel." In two strikingly similar passages ("Lik," p. 53 and *Nikolai Gogol*, p. 2), "dog Latin" is linked

121

with death. "Doggerel" seems gratuitously insterted at a key point in Nabokov's English translation of his very fateful story "Vasiliy Shishkov" (p. 210, in Russian, p. 209).

39. *Keys*, pp. 3-4.

40. I have tried, I fear unsuccessfully, to detect a pattern in Nabokovian uses of fateful "pups"—to attend or signal a child's dangerous exposure to knowledge. Examples are Lolita's introduction to male sex by Charlie and to perversion by Quilty (both "pups" noted above) and the "pups" on little Luzhin's wallpaper, which may be seen to preview his fatal re-exposure to chess (also discussed above). There is also the juxtaposition of a child and "pup" with execution in Sebastian Knight's study (mentioned above); and in *Pale Fire*, Kinbote calls Gerald Emerald, whom he presumes to make sexual advances to his students, "a four-mouthed pup" (p. 189). Finally, the word "pup" appears in a simile associated with the supernatural phenomena to which young Hazel Shade is exposed (p. 133).

Yet another faintly possible pattern is that cloth toy dogs may signal death (Krug's son's, Luzhin's, and—if Mr. Zilanov is correct—Martin's).

41. Clarence Brown, "Nabokov's Pushkin and Nabokov's Nabokov, " in: L.S. Dembo, ed., *Nabokov: The Man and His Work* (Milwaukee, Wisconsin, 1967), pp. 200, 201.

42. Barbara Heldt Monter, " 'Spring in Fialta': the choice that mimics chance," *TriQuarterly,* No. 17, p. 132.

43. At the beginning of *The Injured and The Insulted*, the narrator has a strange feeling that "something unusual" is about to happen: at that moment, he catches sight of old man Smit and his dog Azorka (F.M. Dostoevsky, *Sobranie sochinenii v desyati tomakh*, Moscow, 1956-1958, III:8). He soon notices that this dog

> ...is an unusual dog; that there had to be something fantastic, enchanted in it; that perhaps it was some sort of Mephistopheles in a dog's form and that its fate was united in some mysterious, unknown way with the fate of its owner. (9)

Old man Smit dies almost immediately after the death of Azorka.

A few days later, the narrator moves into Smit's apartment. In the evening he experiences what he terms a *"mystical terror"* (p. 60). He imagines that "every night in every corner I would see Smit." And "...at his feet would be Azorka. And at that very instant I had an experience which struck me strongly." Here, the little girl Nelli appears and asks a "strange question" (did Azorka also die) "as if she was certain that Azorka had to die together with the old man" (p. 62). The *"mystical terror"* experienced by Dostoevsky's narrator may recall Nabokov's story "Terror," especially since the same Russian word is used *(uzhas)* and since fateful dogs seem involved with both "terrors."

In *The Idiot*, Ippolit discribes a nightmare in which he sees "some king of monster" (VI:441). It resembles a "scorpion," but is "more vile and more terrible." The creature terrifies Ippolit until Norma ("our dog," who "died five years ago") appears.

> Animals, if I am not mistaken, cannot feel mystical fright; but at that minute it seemed to me that in Norma's fright there was something very unusual, also almost mystical, and that she, then, also forefelt, as did I, that the beast contained something fateful and some kind of mystery. (442)

Despite her fright, Norma seizes the creature in her teeth. Just before awakening, Ippolit notices that the creature's "half-crushed body" has released onto Norma's tongue "a quantity of white fluid, resembling the fluid of a crushed cockroach" (p. 443). This unpleasant dream may recall Hermann's dream of the terrifying white dog: "No, not flesh, but rather grease or jelly" (p. 106)—*Despair* does seem to parody *The Double* (which Nabokov considers Dostoevsky's best work) in several places. Incidentally, Mr. Golyadkin is strangely upset by a little dog when his replica first appears (I:255).

44. See his "Dostoevsky as Rorshach Test," *New York Times Book Review,* June 13, 1971 and his "Nabokov and Chekhov: the lesser Russian tradition," *TriQuarterly,* No. 17, p. 13.

Chapter Eight

PNIN'S UNCANNY LOOKING GLASS

Vladimir Nabokov's ingeniously hidden predictions[1] have lurked in some rather unlikely places. In *Despair,* it is an apparently ridiculous definition of a word: Lydia's vague notion that "mystic" somehow connects "mistake" and "stick" prefigures Hermann's fatal "stick mistake" when he murders Felix (as Carl Proffer has observed).[2] In *Laughter in the Dark,* it is two movie scenes watched by Albinus. (These subtly preview two crucial episodes much later, as Dabney Stuart has shown).[3] In *Lolita,* it is a book in Humbert's prison library entitled *Who's Who In the Limelight.* (The quotation he offers us from it foreshadows much of the ensuing novel, as Alfred Appel, Jr. has demonstrated).[4]

The walls and furnishings of Nabokovian bedrooms seem to be the area richest in such hidden prophecies. For instance, two pictures posted on Lolita's bedroom wall (one labeled "H.H."; the other, of Quilty) aptly foreshadow her two most important affairs.[5] In *The Gift,* the wallpaper of Fyodor's newly rented room ("pale yellow, with bluish tulips") soon reappears with his landlady, who is wearing a "pale yellow dress with bluish tulips."[6] Franz's newly rented room *(King, Queen, Knave)* displays above the bed a picture of "a bare-bosomed slave girl on sale," being "leered at" by "hesitant lechers."[7] Not only does this suggest the lustful sessions soon enjoyed there by Martha and initially hesitant Franz; the picture almost seems to participate in the action: "For the last time in the shabby room...The lewd bidders were appraising the big-nippled bronze-bangled slave girl for the last time" (225).

Focusing more closely, we may note that Nabokovian childhood bedrooms seem especially rich in hidden predictions. As Mr. Nabokov explains in his Foreword to *Glory:* "The perilous path that Martin finally follows into forbidden Zoorland...only continues to its illogical end the fairy-tale trail winding through the painted woods of a nursery-wall picture."[8] In *Speak, Memory* Mr. Nabokov describes the wall of his own childhood bedroom: " . . . a framed acquarelle showed a dusky path winding through one of those eerily dense European beechwoods...."[9] He goes on, quite revealingly, to connect this same picture with the events of his later life. "In an English fairy tale my mother had once read to me, a small boy stepped out of his bed into a picture and rode his hobbyhorse along a painted path between silent trees. While I knelt on my pillow...rapidly going through my prayer, I imagined the motion of climbing into the picture above my bed and plunging into that enchanted beechwood—which I did visit in due time." This characteristic passage[10] seems to explain Mr. Nabokov's interest in the fairy-tale-like prophetic potential of childhood bedrooms, as noted in *Glory,* above. It may also help to explain why he chose to translate *Alice in Wonderland* into Russian. The present paper views *Pnin* as an elusive synthesis of "Cinderella" and Lewis Carroll's *Alice*— seen through the Nabokovian looking glass of Timofey Pnin's childhood bedroom. It also seeks to pinpoint a few hidden interconnections between *Pnin* and other Nabokov works, including the preview of Timofey Pnin's migration to *Pale Fire.*

In Chapter One we follow fifty-two-year-old Pnin, precariously en route to the Cremona Women's Club. After various troubles, he has a strange heart seizure and sits down on a park bench. "Familiar shapes," we read, "became the breeding places of evil delusions."[11] Pnin recalls his childhood bedroom, when he was eleven and quite ill with a similar heart seizure. He remembers a four-section screen of polished wood that pictured "an old man hunched up on a bench, and a squirrel holding a reddish object in its front paws." As Pnin's recollection ends, we are told that a gray squirrel was "sampling a peach stone" in front of his park bench (25). Our narrator points up the parallel between Pnin's past and present by referring to "the twofold nature of his surroundings" (24). Yet the childhood bedroom also seems uncannily prophetic. For when little Pnin had attempted to discover what system of recurrence governed his wallpaper pattern: "he forthwith lost himself in a meaningless tangle of rhododendron and oak" (23). The older Pnin is now quite literally "lost" in the "rhododendrons" and "oak" (19, 20) of his park. "Probing one's childhood," Mr. Nabokov suggests in *Speak, Memory,* "is the next best to probing one's eternity" (20-21).

Eleven-year-old Pnin contemplates his wallpaper: "It stood to reason that if the evil designer—the destroyer of minds, the friend of fever—had concealed the key of the pattern with such monstrous care, that key must be as precious as life itself..." The pattern comprises "three different clusters of purple flowers and seven different oak leaves"(23). It is, in a very real sense, "as precious as life itself, because the theme of "threes" and "sevens" has luminous extension throughout the novel. In fact, the "system of recurrence" of fatidic threes and sevens is almost diabolically complex.

Pnin was born on February 3 in St. Petersburg (67). He is very fond of a fatidical Pushkin poem dated "3:03 p.m. St. Petersburg" (67). He has three key birthdays: the heart-seizure one (21); the one he fails to recognize (67); and the one on which the novel ends (186). These last two are connected by Charles Nicol, who incisively suggests (referring to Pnin's interest in the Pushkin poem) that Pnin is unknowingly preparing, in Chapter Three, "for a Pushkinian 'future anniversary,' the birthday...when he will leave Waindell College"[12] in Chapter Seven. And the Pushkinian anniversary to which Pnin refers but is prevented from naming (68) is of course '37.

Pnin is composed of seven chapters. Pnin has seven mysterious heart seizures (five are listed, 21); the sixth is in the park (19-24); the seventh is at The Pines (131).

Pnin has variously unsuccessful relationships with three women: Mira Belochkin, Liza Bogolepov, and Betty Bliss. The narrator's third meeting with Pnin occurs at "the Three Fountains" (179). There are also the "three papers" that Pnin stuffs into his coat in a desperate attempt to thwart mischance (26). And at times the hidden pattern seems to comprise an almost impossibly complex interrelation of detail.[13]

Of greater importance to what the present paper will focus upon is the fact that there are three artificial squirrels in the novel and three people who are either termed, or likened to, squirrels. The artificial squirrels are: on Pnin's childhood bedroom screen (23), on Pnin's postcard to Victor (88), and the stuffed one in the Pnin apartment (177). The people are Dr. Belochkin ("squirrel" is belka in Russian; more on this later), Mira Belochkin, and Pnin himself. Researching "squirrels" in the library, Pnin takes a card-catalogue drawer "like a big nut" to a corner (76); he gives to Joan Clements his past history "in a nutshell" (33); he frequently sits "cracking nuts" with Joan at the kitchen table (40); he quite mysteriously "understands" the squirrel who wants a drink (58); and he even seems habitually squirrel-like: "At noon, as usual, Pnin washed his hands and head" (70).

Returning to Pnin's recollection in the park, we find: "He could still make out...certain parts of the nursery more tenacious of life than the rest, such as the lacquered screen, the gleam of a tumbler, the brass knobs of his bedstead..." (24). In context, these are simply the most vivid objects that Pnin recalls. However, he will soon be "holding aloft" (at the Clementses') "a tumbler" (36). The screen and bedstead knobs may be seen to reappear as the "large folding screen" and "fourposter bed" (164) in Pnin's bedroom of the house he later inhabits. The phrase "more tenacious of life" thus seems uncannily true. Similarly, the "wardrobe" of his childhood bedroom (23) may be seen to reappear as the "stuffy wardrobe in the maid's chamber" (147), where little Pnin remains hidden after his playmates have already gone home.

The cryptographic character of Pnin's childhood bedroom extends to his experience in the park. "During one melting moment, he had the sensation of holding at last the key he had sought; but, coming from very far, a rustling wind, its soft volume increasing as it ruffled the rhododendrons—now blossomless, blind—confused whatever rational pattern Timofey Pnin's surroundings had once had." As we learn later, Pnin's wife leaves him for a Dr. "Wind" (43), who "comes from very far." Pnin's wife Liza may thus be associated with the "blind" rhododendrons, which are "stirred" (25) by the "wind." Later, when Pnin recalls Liza's eyes, he pictures a "blind moist aquamarine blaze" (44).

As Pnin's recollection in the park ends, we read: "The back of the bench against which he still sprawled felt as real as his clothes, or his wallet, or the date of the Great Moscow Fire—

1812." Pnin had just experienced a "Pninian quandary" involving his "clothes" and his "wallet" (16). He will soon frequently mis-pronounce Mrs. Thayer's name as "Mrs. Fire." The ultimate reali-zation of this "real" feeling, however, is when Pnin repeatedly realizes that he is being "fired" from his job (169,170). Note also that "his wallet" is mentioned alongside the (almost archly ironic) "Great Fire."

Fire seems to suggest special trouble for Pnin, which possibly relates to the "Cinderella" theme discussed below. Besides his being "fired" from his job,[14] "Mrs. Fire" points out his blunder of requesting a library book he already has (74); he slips near a fire "to crash into the poker and tongs" (43); and his bedroom at the Clementses's is cluttered with various books (which Pnin moves out) including a dictionary "('With more than 600 illustra-tions depicting zoos, the human body, farms, *fires—all scienti-fically chosen')*" (35; my italics).

When Pnin first sees this new bedroom, it is snowing outside, and this is "...refelected in the silent looking glass. Methodically Pnin inspected Hoecker's 'Girl with a Cat' above the bed, and Hunt's 'The Belated Kid' above the bookshelf" (34). Typically, "The Belated Kid" anticipates Liza's son Victor by Dr. Wind while she is still childless as Pnin's wife. The other cryptographic bedroom picture, in conjunction with the words "looking glass," may be seen to suggest Lewis Carroll's Alice and Cheshire Cat. It also echoes Pnin's childhood-bedroom recollection in the park, which vision is significantly associated with "the reflection of an inside object in a windowpane" plus "the outside scenery per-ceived through the same glass" (24). Thus, Pnin's prophetic bed-room surroundings traced above may be seen as a mysterious "looking glass" that he never quite understands. In the final chapter of the novel, the narrator (who seems to be Mr. Nabokov himself) talks with Timofey Pnin, noting in a somewhat different context "how reluctant he was to recognize his own past" (180).

Other illusions in *Pnin* to the world of Lewis Carroll's Alice teasingly recur. There is Pnin's "Duchess of Wonderland chin" (65), plus an apparently casual (more of this later) reference to "meeting a duchess" (155). We may also note the winking rabbit that Pnin can shadowgraph (13), a "live" playing card (a king, 84), plus a "Bachelor of Hearts" (151) and the repeti-tious "tarts" at Pnin's party (152,171).[15] Perhaps most important is Pnin's triumphant croquet game at The Pines (which may be seen as his "Wonderland," the preserved secluded fragment of his Russian childhood past). When Pnin is "transfigured" (130), there are repeated mentions of "tea" and "chess" (132, 136). Quite ironically, the children at The Pines are rather indifferent to its "Wonderland" pleasures, only occasionally appreciating it "through a kind of interdimensional shimmer" (118). This Russian "Wonderland," it seems, is primarily for adults.

In his intriguing article on *Pnin* and "Cinderella," Charles Nicol has ably demonstrated that Pnin and Victor represent two versions of the children's story. In the earlier one (Pnin's version), "...Cinderella is befriended not by a fairy godmother but by a helpful animal, which has to be killed for its magic to take effect" (201). As Nicol observes, Pnin is befriended by a series of uncanny squirrels. This seems especially appropriate, he suggests, since Pnin's research has revealed that Cinderella's slippers were made of Russian squirrel fur in the older version.

Mr. Nicol's convincing argument may be considerably strengthened by the fact that the Russian word for squirrel is "belka." In the flashback to his childhood bedroom, sick Pnin is visited by the pediatrician Dr. Belochkin. He is the father of Mira Belochkin, Pnin's sweetheart who was "cremated" in Buchenwald (135) after marrying "a fur dealer of Russian extraction" (134). More important than these further manifestations of the "Russian squirrel fur" and "ashes" themes traced by Nicol in relation to "Cinderella," however, is the eerie possibility that Mira "Squirrel" reappears throughout the novel. Since "the exact form of her death had not been recorded," we read, "Mira kept dying a great number of deaths in one's mind, and undergoing a great number of resurrections, only to die again and again" (135). In context, this refers only to Pnin's vision-like memory of Mira, yet he is sitting on "a bench under the pines" (131) at The Pines, once again resembling the old man on his childhood bedroom screen. And it seems difficult to ignore the notion that the "Cinderella" animal must be killed for its magic to take effect. Here, unlike the park-bench scene, there is no live reappearance of the screen-painted squirrel, but Pnin does recall Mira "Squirrel." Can it be that she "undergoes a great number of resurrections," eerily reappearing as the series (noted by Nicol) of uncanny squirrels that befriend Pnin throughout the novel? For one thing, these uncanny squirrels not only befriend, but even seem to help Pnin out of trouble (as did Mira's father Dr. Belochkin).

Immediately after Pnin sees the first squirrel in the park, he recovers from his heart seizure, recovers his unobtainable suitcase, and manages to board a Cremona-bound truck (25). Similarly, when Pnin is once again "hopelessly lost," the sudden appearance of a squirrel (shot at in the forest[16]) seems almost supernaturally beneficial: "...then everything happened at once: the ant found an upright beam leading to the roof of the tower and started to ascend it with renewed zest; the sun appeared; and Pnin at the height of hopelessness, found himself on a paved road with a rusty but still glistening sign directing wayfarers 'To the Pines' " (115). En route to the library, Pnin slips twice on the path but regains his balance (73), over which recovery "a skimpy squirrel" seems to preside. Also, "a stuffed squirrel" attends the account of little Pnin's receiving an A-plus on an Algebra exam (177). There is one unhelpful squirrel, who seems to demand a drink from Pnin and who, after he has obligingly worked a water fountain, leaves "without the least sign of gratitude" (58). The gratitude, we may infer, recurs in forms Pnin fails to discern, just as he remains so "reluctant" to "recognize his own past."

We may note yet another factor suggesting that the uncanny squirrels are perhaps the fairy-tale-like reincarnations of Mira Belochkin: the theme of curious heart disorder, associated with a feeling of death-like dissociation, which Pnin tends to experience at such times. This peculiar heart condition is carefully explained by the narrator as a departure from the "discreteness" of our normal state (20), and it attends the following key scenes: Pnin's childhood sickness (when Dr. Belochkin comes, and young Pnin's bedroom is described), his recollections thereof in the park, his vision at the Cremona women's Club of (as we realize only much later) Mira Belochkin (27), and his vision-like memory of Mira at The Pines (131). Ambrose Gordon, Jr. has termed Pnin's cardiograph "the signature" of the novel.[17]

A last addition to Charles Nicol's "Cinderella" findings may be seen in the first sentence of Chapter Seven: "My first recollection of Timofey Pnin is connected with a speck of coal dust that entered my left eye on a spring Sunday in 1911." As we soon learn, the narrator then visited Pnin's father, an opthamologist, and met little Pnin. But if the "speck of coal dust" is considered a "cinder," then the words "first recollection" may also subtly allude to the genesis of Nabokov's novel.

After describing his successful treatment, the narrator

remarks: "I wonder where that speck is now? The dull, mad fact is that it *does* exist somewhere" (176). Perhaps only because this is the world of Vladimir Nabokov, one is tempted to speculate that the narrator's left-eye speck may be the same "speck" removed by Humbert from Lolita's "left eye" (45).

If this is so, the teasing cross-reference is hardly atypical. Indeed, *Pnin* contains several hidden interconnections with Mr. Nabokov's other works. In *Transparent Things,* for example, Hugh Person finds himself in "a jumble of boulders and a jungle of rhododendrons... No wonder he soon lost his way."[18] In *Pnin,* we encounter the apparently innocent sentence: "Hermann found his cane" (164). This cane, five lines later termed a "walking stick," may be seen to evoke the "stick mistake" (in *Despair*, mentioned above), wherein "Hermann" did not "find" the "stick." Similarly, there is casual mention in *Pnin* of a facial expression conveying "...a respectful, congratulatory, and slightly awed recognition of such things as dining with one's boss, being in *Who's Who,* or meeting a duchess" (155). Here, it is the "being in *Who's Who*" (from *Lolita,* also mentioned above) which, in conjunction with meeting a duchess," subtly serves to confirm the allusions to Lewis Carroll's *Alice* (traced above, including Pnin's own "Duchess of Wonderland chin."

There are others; but for present purposes, the most important such Nabokovian interconnection involves Timofey Pnin's final departure and his reappearance in *Pale Fire* as Head of the Russian Department at Wordsmith College. This involves the highly unusual relationship between Pnin and the narrator. For when it becomes apparent that the narrator, presumably Mr. Nabokov himself, is coming to Waindell College, Pnin remarks: "I will never work under him" (170). As Nicol had observed, Pnin has a remarkable confrontation[19] with his narrator soon after this, and Pnin's punchbowl, apparently broken in the soapy dishwater, remains intact (173). This Pninian victory over his own narrator seems somewhat odd, since Mr. Nabokov has declared that his characters are "galley slaves."[20] However, it is possible (with regard to the "squirrel" and "nut" themes traced above) that within Pnin's Nabokov-imposed pattern, a "nutcracker" (dropped by Pnin into the soapy water) could not break a Cinderella-colored (158) bowl anyway. And as Mr. Nabokov has arranged it, the squirrels' help is only temporary. Helped to arrive in time at the Cremona Women's Club, for example, Pnin still brought the wrong lecture with him, as we learn from the last sentence of the novel. Mr. Nabokov's characters are indeed "galley slaves."

And this is partly why Pnin fails to detect the hidden prediction of his migration to *Pale Fire*. As both Nicol and Gordon have noted, Pnin's dream at the end of Chapter Four uncannily continues Victor's fantasy about "The King, his father" as the chapter begins.[21] Pnin's strange dream also predicts his escape to *Pale Fire:* "...Pnin saw himself fantastically cloaked, fleeing... from a chimerical palace, and then pacing a desolate strand with his dead friend Ilya Isidorovich Polyanski as they waited for some mysterious deliverance to arrive in a throbbing boat from beyond the hopeless sea" (109-110). In *Pale Fire,* the King of Zembla flees from the palace in fantastic garb and escapes in a "powerful motorboat" that awaits him "in a coastal cave" (87). Both Kings, after their escapes, will teach together at Wordsmith College in *Pale Fire.* And when Gradus finally arrives at Wordsmith, he visits both Kings but kills neither (first, Pnin in the library, 199; then Kinbote, 207). There is even a brief confusion about whether Gradus seeks Kinbote or Pnin (200). The parallel is striking, but it is the words "mysterious deliverance" in Pnin's dream that suggest how tantalizingly close Pnin is permitted to come to understanding the signficance of his dream. But Pnin does not suspect, in fact, cannot be allowed to suspect his impending escape from one Nabokov book to another.[22]

To explain this fully, we must take a final look at the wallpaper pattern of Pnin's childhood bedroom. "He had always been able to see that in the vertical plane a combination made up of three different clusters of purple flowers and seven different oak leaves was repeated a number of times with soothing exactitude, but...he could not find what system of inclusion and circumspection governed the horizontal recurrence of the pattern..." (23). As seen above, the pattern in *Pnin* of fatidical "threes" and "sevens" is almost diabolically complex, but the crucial "wallpaper" elements relating to Pnin's life are its "vertical" and "horizontal" components. For within the strangely expanding confines of Mr. Nabokov's world, his individual works may be seen as separate vertical planes, intersected by horizontal ones (therefore) composed of haunting interconnections. And while a particular character may vaguely sense that some sort of controlled pattern informs his vertical (intrabook) existence, he must remain unaware of his (interbook) horizontal potential. (Presumably, a character could only achieve such a perspective through either madness[23] or death.) Thus, Pnin can be "soothed" by the fairy-tale-like exactitude of his vertical pattern; he may even confront and defy, as Nicol suggests, its author. Yet Pnin must be limited to the "wonderment," as Barbara Monter has put it, of a Nabokov character who "strives to grasp the full pattern of the mosaic in which he himself is depicted."[24] Like any other Nabokovian "galley slave," he must remain unable to discover the authorial "system of inclusion and circumspection" that governs "the horizontal recurrence of the pattern." Pnin is finally released, but only for "further use," to quote John Shade, in Kinbote's "Pale Fire" Commentary. The escape to *Pale Fire* must remain, as glimpsed from within *Pnin,* an enigmatic, hopeful dream—or a triumphant, but unclear horizon.

NOTES

1. See my *Nabokov's Deceptive World* (New York, 1972), pp. ii, 79, 84, 99, 126, 131, 143, 147, 156.

2. Carl R. Proffer, "From *Otchaianie* to *Despair*," *Slavic Review,* June, 1968, p. 266.

3. Dabney Stuart, *"Laughter in the Dark:* dimensions of parody," *Triquarterly,* Winter, 1970, pp. 77-78.

4. Alfred Appel, Jr., ed., *The Annotated Lolita* (New York, 1970), pp. 347-352.

5. Vladimir Nabokov, *Lolita* (New York, 1955), p. 71. Subsequent references will be to this edition.

6. Vladimir Nabokov, *The Gift* (New York,1970), p. 20.

7. Vladimir Nabokov, *King, Queen, Knave* (New York, 1968), p. 53. Subsequent references will be to this edition.

8. Vladimir Nabokov, *Glory* (New York, 1970), p.xii.

9. Vladimir Nabokov, *Speak, Memory* (New York, 1966), p. 86. Subsequent references will be to this edition.

10. Also in *Speak, Memory,* Mr. Nabokov describes the "fabulous lights" he saw (as a child in "the window of a sleeping car" on a train) as "diamonds" that he later "gave away" to his characters (24). A complex variation of Nabokovian prophetic childhood-bedroom furnishings occurs in *Pale Fire.* Captured by revolutionaries, the King sleeps in a room with an old photograph "in a frame of black velvet" (88) on the wall. Later we learn that thirty years earlier, as a boy of thirteen, the King (then Prince) had discovered a secret passage in the closet of this same room while trying to dislodge a piece of "black velvet" (90) that was caught behind a closet shelf. Finally (95) the captured King goes to bed in this room and then escapes through the passage he had discovered as a boy.

11. Vladimir Nabokov, *Pnin* (New York, 1965), p. 23. Subsequent references will be made to this edition.

12. Charles Nicol, "Pnin's History," *Novel,* Spring, 1971, p. 207. Subsequent page references to this article will be in the text, in parentheses.

13. For example, human anatomy seems grotesquely altered to produce a "third hand" (16) and a "third side" (21). And by a strange coincidence, Pnin's "February 3" birthday and the "3:03" Pushkin poem are mentioned in section "3" of Chapter Three; the narrator's third meeting with Pnin (at the Three Fountains) occurs in section "3" of Chapter Seven. Yet, as Alfred Appel, Jr. has suggested, Nabokovian coincidence is often not a coincidence. (*The Annotated Lolita,* p. xxviii.)

   Given the almost endless complexity of such coincidences, it seems little wonder, as Mr. Nabokov once told me, that he produces only about two hundred pages of fiction per year.

14. Nabokov even makes two puns in this regard: "Boom-boom-boom" (171) and "shot" (188).

15. Since the author of this work is Vladimir Nabokov, it may not be too far-fetched to connect the following two details with Alice's abrupt alterations in size. In Pnin's bedroom at the Clementses' (which had been their daughter's) there are "height-level marks penciled on the doorjamb, beginning from a four-foot altitude" (65). Later Pnin looks "up, up, up at tall, tall, tall Victor," who is so much more grown up than Pnin had anticipated (103).

16. The hunter is apparently Praskovia's husband (119). Strangely enough, the appearances both of this squirrel and of the squirrel in the park seem to stop the "wind" (25, 115).

17. Ambrose Gordon, Jr., "The Double Pnin," in *Nabokov: The Man and His Work,* ed. L. S. Dembo (Madison, Wisconsin, 1967), p. 147.

18. Vladimir Nabokov, *Transparent Things* (New York, 1972), p. 89.

19. Poor Pnin has just learned that he will be fired, and hence, will lose the house he had proudly hoped to buy. The apparently broken bowl (a present from Victor) thus seems almost more than any fictional character should be forced to take from his author. Outraged, Pnin stares at the "blackness" beyond an open door (172) and a "quiet, lacy-winged little green insect" circles his head. Nicol terms this insect "an emblem of entomologist Nabokov... the evidence of Nabokov's presence in the scene" (208).

20. Vladimir Nabokov, "The Art of Fiction," *The Paris Review,* Summer-Fall, 1967, p. 96.

21. Nicol, p. 204; Gordon, p. 153.

22. Not the least fantastic aspect of Pnin's migration to *Pale Fire* is the haunting possibility that some trucks and even their "thunder" (190) follow him there. On the last page of *Pnin* we see them: "truck one, Pnin, truck two" (191). "Then the little sedan," we read, "boldly swung past the front truck and...there was simply no saying *what miracle might happen.*" (my italics) This happens on Tuesday. In *Pale Fire,* there is much suspicious ado about trucks: a "groaning truck" (70), Kinbote's footnote on trucks (192) and the "damned Tuesday night trucks" (206), which seem to echo, almost impossibly, Pnin's truck-filled Tuesday departure.

23. Madness for Pnin, it seems, could easily ensue from an "alas, too lucid" (24) deciphering of the referential-mania-like "evil delusions" (23) of his prophetic childhood bedroom established by the "evil designer" (23).

24. Barbara Heldt Monter, " 'Spring in Fialta': the choice that mimics chance," *Triquarterly,* Winter, 1970, p. 132.

Chapter Nine

RUSSIAN OAKS AND NABOKOV'S "BALLAD"

In Vladimir Nabokov's "The Ballad of Longwood Glen"[1] (reproduced below) a man climbs up into a leafy oak tree and disappears. This poem characteristically reflects other areas of Nabokov's written world. It also seems related to a tradition of what may be termed fateful oak tree episodes in Russian literature.

Oaks were worshiped by European peoples as embodiments of the life-spirit, as Sir James George Frazer has observed.[2] In Russian literature, oaks have been frequently personified, and perhaps still more often, they seem associated with human destiny and death. In an ancient folk tale, Ivan the Warrior, sent to kill Miron the Hermit, allows him a last prayer beneath a sapling oak. Miron prays until the oak grows "to the sky." An entire forest springs up from the acorns, and so it is to this day: Ivan stands waiting and powerless to move.[3]

In Karamzin's "Poor Liza" (1792), the heroine meets her lover near a pond in the shade of hundred-year-old oaks. When he later bids her farewell beneath a tall oak tree, she drowns herself in the pond "...in the shade of the ancient oak trees which several weeks before had been silent witnesses to her raptures." She is buried "near the pond under a somber oak."[4]

In Pushkin's play *The Water Nymph* (1826-32), a prince loves and abandons a miller's daughter who drowns herself in the Dnepr River. The prince later returns to the Dnepr and recognizes "the cherished oak" where she had embraced him.[5] He then (in Pushkin's stage direction) *goes to the trees; the leaves pour down.* "What does this mean?" says the prince. Declaring that the leaves are showering down on him like ashes, he compares the dark, naked oak to "a tree of damnation."

In Lermontov's famous poem "I walk out alone..." (1841), the poet concludes with a desire to fall asleep forever. But he does not wish "the cold sleep of the grave." Rather, Lermontov longs to hear a sweet voice sing of love while, above him, "...eternally showing green, / A dark oak rustles and bends down."

In Tolstoi's *War and Peace* (1869), a bare old oak seems to accost Prince Andrew with several pessimistic pronouncements. Soon after, Andrew is struck by the oak's transfiguration. Abruptly and effusively green, it seems to renew his faith in life. Frazer explains an ancient belief that the life of an oak resides in mistletoe growing thereon, noting that in winter the mistletoe "remains green while the oak itself is leafless" (347). In *Anna Karenina* (1877), Levin watches lightning strike the green crown of a large oak. His relief that his wife and son are still alive then seems to contribute positively to his personal search for a meaning in life. Frazer suggests that the reverence accorded the oak in ancient Europe probably derived from its being struck by lightning more often than other trees (348).[6]

In Andrei Bely's novel *The Silver Dove* (1910), the hero Daryalsky sits for a long time in the hollow of a large five-hundred-year-old oak thinking "about his fate, and about the oak."[7] "It is still not known," we are told, "what this oak knew, and about what past events its leaves were whispering now...."

In Solzhenitsyn's *The First Circle* (1968), Kondrashev-Ivanov has produced "a six-foot-tall painting entitled 'The Maimed Oak'": "It showed a solitary oak which grew with mysterious power on the naked face of a cliff...What hurricanes had blown here! How they had bent that oak!...This stubborn, angular tree...refused to quit the battle and perilously clung to its place over the abyss."[8] Before Solzhenitsyn's banishment, one critic compared this brave, tenacious oak to the author himself: "Like the tree, Solzhenitsyn has refused to be uprooted, to risk the danger of exile by going to Sweden to receive the Nobel Prize."[9]

To this Russian tradition of fateful oaks, one may be tempted to relate the famous "green oak" under which Pushkin's "Ruslan and Liudmila" is magically told. As described by Pushkin, this oak seems an appropriate setting for all sorts of "miracles" including a wood-goblin, a mermaid who sits on the oak's branches, and a talking tomcat (IV:11). Some other Pushkinian oaks, however, seem quite closely related to the mysterious oak tree in Nabokov's "Ballad."

In Pushkin's short poem "The Water Nymph" (1819), a monk retires to a remote grove of oaks. He plans, Pushkin suggests, to spend his last years in heaven-assuring austerity. He seems to be succeeding, but the oaks suddenly grow dark, and a naked woman emerges from a nearby lake. The next day, the oaks darken again: the beauty reappears. This time, she alluringly invites the monk to follow her beneath the waters. Again he somehow resists. On the third day, the monk sits perched upon the shore, and the oaks wax dark once more. After this, he cannot be found, but some little boys catch sight of a grey beard floating in the water (I:364).

In Nabokov's poem, the oak tree also seems to conspire in a man's mysterious disappearance.

The Ballad of Longwood Glen

That Sunday morning, at half past ten,
Two cars crossed the creek and entered the glen.

In the first was Art Longwood, a local florist,
With his children and wife (now Mrs. Deforest).

In the one that followed, a ranger saw
Art's father, stepfather and father-in-law.

The three old men walked off to the cove.
Through tinkling weeds Art slowly drove.

Fair was the morning, with bright clouds afar.
Children and comics emerged from the car.

Silent Art, who could stare at a thing all day,
Watched a bug climb a stalk and fly away.

Pauline had asthma, Paul used a crutch.
They were cute little rascals but could not run much.

"I wish," said his mother to crippled Paul,
"Some man would teach you to pitch that ball."

Silent Art took the ball and tossed it high.
It stuck in a tree that was passing by.

And the grave green pilgrim turned and stopped.
The children waited, but no ball dropped.

"I never climbed trees in my timid prime,"
Thought Art; and forthwith started to climb.

Now and then his elbow or knee could be seen
In a jigsaw puzzle of blue and green.

Up and up Art Longwood swarmed and shinned,
And the leaves said *yes* to the questioning wind.

What tiaras of gardens! What torrents of light!
How accessible ether! How easy flight!

His family circled the tree all day.
Pauline concluded: "Dad climbed away."

None saw the delirious celestial crowds
Greet the hero from earth in the snow of the clouds.

Mrs. Longwood was getting a little concerned.
He never came down. He never returned.

She found some change at the foot of the tree.
The children grew bored. Paul was stung by a bee.

The old men walked over and stood looking up,
Each holding five cards and a paper cup.

Cars on the highway stopped, backed, and then
Up a rutted road waddled into the glen.

And the tree was suddenly full of noise,
Conventioners, fishermen, freckled boys.

Anacondas and pumas were mentioned by some,
And all kinds of humans continued to come:

Tree surgeons, detectives, the fire brigade.
An ambulance parked in the dancing shade.

A drunken rogue with a rope and a gun
Arrived on the scene to see justice done.

Explorers, dendrologists—all were there;
And a strange pale girl with gypsy hair.

And from Cape Fear to Cape Flattery
Every paper had: Man Lost in Tree.

And the sky-bound oak (where owls had perched
And the moon dripped gold) was felled and searched.

They discovered some inchworms, a red-cheeked gall,
And an ancient nest with a new-laid ball.

They varnished the stump, put up railings and signs.
Restrooms nestled in roses and vines.

Mrs. Longwood, retouched, when the children died,
Became a photographer's dreamy bride.

And now the Deforests, with *four* old men,
Like regular tourists visit the glen;

Munch their lunches, look up and down,
Wash their hands, and drive back to town.

The "celestial crowds" greet Art Longwood at mid-poem (couplet 16 of 32). In retrospect, the sixth couplet seems to contain a Nabokovian hidden preview of Art's disappearance: "Watched a bug climb a stalk and fly away." Also typically, the hero is allowed to observe the pattern of his own future.

Pushkin's oaks apparently signal (or promote) mysterious occurrences by turning dark. Nabokov's oak seems more specifically to arrange for Art's departure when its leaves say "yes to the questioning wind." In Nabokov's *Pnin,* a cryptographic wind repeatedly stirs the foliage while the hero sits in an oak grove.

Pnin is trying to discover the "key" to his life's "pattern," yet he cannot quite do so despite the presence of various clues (the wind signifies Dr. Eric Wind[10]).

The three oak episodes are strangely similar. Pushkin's oaks seem involved in promoting an after-life quite unlike the one for which the monk had so assiduously prepared. The oak scene in *Pnin* contains as a clue the presence of a possible animal reincarnation of Pnin's former sweetheart.[11] And of course Art Longwood seems to begin a quite unexpected "after-life."

The mysterious colloquy between leaves and wind in the "Ballad" highlights a conspiratorial atmosphere which is partially promoted by an odd twisting of perspective. The future shows through the present: when we first see Mrs. Longwood, she is termed "now Mrs. Deforest." The perspective even expands beyond human perception: "None saw the delirious celestial crowds/ Greet the hero from earth in the snow of the clouds." At this point, the apparently casual opening ("with bright clouds afar") may seem faintly anticipatory, like the bug's prophetic climb and flight. And what unusual perspective, we may wonder, has produced the matter-of-fact designation "all kinds of humans" (phonetically linked with "pumas")? Yet the faint eeriness of this poem seems quite natural: man follows bug's example; tree walks and talks like man.

Individual words contain conspiratorial shimmers of meaning. "Longwood," as Art climbs "up and up," acquires an appropriate suggestiveness. "Sky-bound oak" can be read not only as "bordered by the sky" but also as "headed for the sky." And of course "Mrs. Longwood" adds to the play of meaning by becoming "Mrs. Deforest." Whereupon: "Mrs. Longwood, retouched, when the children died,/ Became a photographer's dreamy bride." "Retouched" can signify 1) fresh make-up, 2) aptly photo-like, 3) her emotional reaction to her children's deaths and/or to her hew husband, and 4) refondled.

The two children's matter-of-fact early deaths seem uneasily patterned by the pun-like similarity of their names: Pauline and Paul. In *Pnin,* we read of a psychological test called "...the Doll Play, in which Patrick or Patricia is given two identical rubber dolls and a cute little bit of clay which Pat must fix on one of them before he or she starts playing...."[12] In the "Ballad," there may even be a play on "Art." Unappreciated, perhaps, Art escapes upwards, in symmetry with the earth-bound *poshlost*[13] dominating the poem's second half. And this *poshlost* (complete with rest-rooms nestling in roses and vines) may seem echoed by the final line if one realizes that Russians say euphemistically, "going to wash one's hands" instead of "going to the bathroom."

The poem takes place on Sunday. In Russian, the word Sunday *(voskresenie)* also means "resurrection," which could be seen to hint at Art's upward flight. Perhaps of greater relevance is the fact that in Celtic tradition, as Robert Graves has observed, the Druid, or poet, was an "oak-seer."[14] An early Cornish poem, Graves notes, describes how "the Druid Merddin, or Merlin," went to seek the "magical snake's egg" and "cut the highest twig from the top of the oak." Nabokov's oak, of course, contains "an ancient nest with a new-laid ball"—the ostensible object of Art's quest.

Several Nabokovian techniques promote the reader's vivifying participation. The "jigsaw puzzle of blue and green" must be actively interpreted as jagged patches of foliage and sky. The "change at the foot of the tree" evokes Art, upside down, scrambling upwards. "Each holding five cards and a paper cup" graphically fills us in on what has happened since the three old men repaired to the cove. In the line, "Through tinkling weeds Art slowly drove," the word "tinkling" gradually expands in meaning. Later, as other cars arrive, "rutted road" and "waddled" vividly interact. "The dancing shade" (in which the ambulance parks) is a favorite device for focusing the reader's attention. In *Speak, Memory,* for example, two stuffed bears are pictured "in the mobile shade of the trees," and a "green butterfly net" stands out against "the shady, tremulous trail."[15] In such flickering light, it seems, the reader must more actively, and vividly, picture whatever is mentioned. Beneath an oak tree in Nabokov's *Invitation to a Beheading,* we see "a corpse, still quivering with the throb of the leafy shadows."[16]

The "Ballad's" eerie feeling of conspiracy is amplified by its uneasy humor. "Some change" (found by Mrs. Longwood below the oak just after Art vanishes) playfully echoes the real, and quite undetected, change. "Anacondas and pumas were mentioned by some" also points up the absurd futility of human perspective. The "drunken rogue" ridiculously chases "justice." And when the oak is finally searched, the "discovery" of worms, plant tissue, and ball seems comically removed from the unseen "celestial crowds." Such humor is increased by the limited truth of the ubiquitous headline: Man Lost *in* Tree.

The meter also effectively contributes. As Art vanishes, a sudden scud ("celestial") interrupts the general flow of iambs and anapests. And after Art's disappearance, the dim dawning of Mrs. Longwood's concern is paralleled by a redundancy in the wording: "He never came down. He never returned."

In Nabokov's *Invitation to a Beheading,* little Emmie's face is "retouched" on a photograph to show her as a bride. This may suggest Mrs. Longwood, who, retouched, becomes a photographer's dreamy bride. The retouching gives Emmie "...wrinkles, drawn in...without knowledge of their true significance, but conveying something very bizarre to the expert, as a chance stirring of a tree's branches may coincide with a sign gesture comprehensible to a deaf-mute." (170-1) In a purely Nabokovian reality, Art Longwood may thus be seen as a "deaf-mute" (he never speaks, and he is repeatedly called "Silent Art") who "comprehends" the *yes* of his rustling oak branches. Graves has traced an ancient meaning of poetic inspiration to "the act of listening to the wind" in an oak grove (440).

Nabokov's Foreword to his English version of *Invitation to a Beheading* (ends with the signature: "Oak Creek Canyon, Arizona/ June 25,1959." The hero of this novel is reading *Quercus,* a 3,000-page biography of an oak. The oak is said to be "growing lone and mighty at the edge of a canyon at whose bottom the waters never ceased to din" (122). Somewhat eerily, the details of this description return us to the location of the author twenty-five years later: Oak Creek Canyon. (In his Foreword, Nabokov writes that he "composed the Russian original exactly a quarter of a century ago" (5); the Russian version contains all the lines quoted here except, of course, those from the 1959 "oak" Foreword.[17]) In his introduction to the Russian version, Julian Moynahan suggests that "the mysterious beings" approached by Cincinnatus at the end resemble "a heavenly throng, gathered to meet a saved Christian soul after death."[18] This description seems also to fit Art Longwood, greeted in the heavens by "delirious celestial crowds." Within Nabokov's world, the interconnections may thus include: retouched brides, strange stirrings of branches, a deaf-mute's comprehension, and silent celestial observers.[19]

Generally the oak in Nabokov's "Ballad" evinces a personification characteristic of various oak trees associated with human

destiny and death in Russian literature. More specifically, Nabokov's oak may be deemed an extension of the fateful oak grove
in Pushkin's poem "The Water Nymph." As we have seen, the
"Ballad" echoes and reflects other Nabokov works, especially
Pnin and *Invitation to a Beheading.* Also typical are its vivid,
glittering language, its scorn for the *poshlost* of most "humans,"
and its subtly conspiratorial atmosphere. Tinged with a Gogolian
blending of humor, irony and eeriness, the action of the poem
seems faintly anticipated. It almost seems staged, in Nabokov's
words, "with the feigned naiveté of Fate, when meaning business."[20] Consequently, the reader tends to share the experience of
a Nabokovian narrator who (as Barbara Monter has put it) appre-
hends "the details of his world" as "clues to the mystery that
can be solved only by his own memory."[21] For "the eidetic
reader" (Carl Proffer's term[22]) of at least the rereader, Nabokov
frequently prepares the uneasy pleasure of what he has called
"a forbidden foray into the future."[23]

NOTES

1. This poem has appeared in *The New Yorker,* July 6, 1957; *Nabokov's Con-
geries* (1968); and *Poems and Problems* (1970).
2. *The New Golden Bough* (New York, 1961), p. 41, *passim.* Subsequent references will be to this edition.
3. This tale is reproduced in Maxim Gorky's *Autobiography* (New York, 1962),
pp. 106-8.
    In *The Song of Igor's Campaign* (which Nabokov has translated and dated
1187), Prince Igor leads his warriors out to a disastrous battle: "His misfortunes already/
are forefelt by the birds in the/ oakscrub" (New York, 1960, p. 36.)
4. Quotations are from Carl R. Proffer, Trans. and ed., *From Karamzin to
Bunin* (Bloomington, 1969), pp. 60-67.
5. A.S. Pushkin, *Polnoe sobranie sochinenii v desayti tomakh* (Moscow, 1962-
66), V, 445. Subsequent references to Pushkin's works will be to this edition.
6. Nabokov's translation of Tyutchev's poem "Appeasement" (1830) begins:
"The storm withdrew, but Thor had found his oak,/ and there it lay magnificently
slain" (*Three Russian Poets,* New York, 1944, p. 36).
7. Andrei Belyi, *Serebrianyi golub'* (Munich, 1967), p. 266.
8. Alexander I. Solzhenitsyn, *The First Circle,* Trans. Thomas P. Whitney (New
York, 1969), p. 290.
9. Rosette C. Lamont, "Solzhenitsyn's 'Maimed Oak,' " *Review of National Lit-
eratures,* Spring, 1972, p. 178.
10. See my "Pnin's Uncanny Looking Glass," above, p. 128.

11. See above, pp. 130-31.

12. Vladimir Nabokov, *Pnin* (New York, 1965), p. 91.

13. For a discussion of this puffy Russian word (which suggests a sort of smug, blind pretentiousness, especially as regards cultural or aesthetic values) see Vladimir Nabokov, *Nikolai Gogol* (New York, 1961), pp. 63-74.

14. Robert Graves, *The White Goddess: A historical grammar of poetic myth* (New York, 1966), p. 39. Subsequent references will be to this edition.

15. Vladimir Nabokov, *Speak, Memory* (New York, 1966), pp. 67, 72.

16. Vladimir Nabokov, *Invitation to a Beheading* (New York, 1965), p. 123. Subsequent references will be to this edition.

17. In *Speak, Memory* an "alley of slender oaks" on the Nabokov estate is frequently mentioned. This "avenue of oaklings," Nabokov writes, "seems to have been the main artery of my infancy" (103).

18. *Priglashenie na kazn'* (Paris, 1938), p. 16.

19. Peter Lubin has found that one pun, "planted" in *Ada,* connects three of Nabokov's past epigraphs—the oak from *The Gift,* the cat from *Pale Fire,* and Pushkin from *Mary: Quercus ruslan chat* (see his "Kickshaws and motley," *TriQuarterly,* Winter, 1970, p. 204). The 3,000-page oak biography *(Quercus)* in *Invitation to a Beheading* seems to provide yet another interconnection. As Clarence Brown has noted, "Nabokov has an extraordinary capacity for simultaneously dispersed and concentrated attention" ("Nabokov's Pushkin and Nabokov's Nabokov," in: L.S. Dembo, ed., *Nabokov: The Man and His Work,* Milwaukee, Wisconsin, 1967, p. 199).

20. *Speak, Memory,* p. 229.

21. Barbara Heldt Monter, " 'Spring in Fialta': the choice that mimics chance," *TriQuarterly,* Winter, 1970, p.133.

22. Carl R. Proffer, *Keys to Lolita* (Bloomington, 1968), p. 52.

23. See his *King, Queen, Knave* (New York, 1968), p.85.

Chapter Ten

**NABOKOV'S
BONUS EFFECTS**

Vladimir Nabokov's readers routinely encounter multiple meanings. In one effect, an image rather unexpectedly enriches a description with what may be termed "bonus" associations. For example, in *Lolita* Humbert attempts to drug Charlotte at night, but she awakens "as fresh and strong as an octopus."[1] Clearly, the connotations of "octopus" go far beyond freshness and strength. We vividly picture Charlotte's fleshy arms and Humbert's horrified retreat even before he adds: "I barely escaped." Similarly, when we are told that "indefatigable" Charlie Holmes, who copulates "by turns" with Barbara and Lolita, has "as much sex appeal as a raw carrot" (139), the selected image seems appropriate well beyond its lack of sex appeal.

A closer look suggests two dictinctions. The bonus effect of "raw carrot" derives from its physical properties; "octopus" evokes both physical properties (including shape and action) and also (Humbert's, our) emotional reaction. A second difference is that while "octopus" suggests action, the pun "raw" (especially since it directly follows "indefatigable" and "by turns") suggests "result of action." Carl Proffer has aptly used this term to describe some of Gogol's similes, for instance: "He (Chichikov) began to feel awkward, out of sorts, exactly as if he had unexpectedly set a beautifully polished boot into a filthy, stinking puddle."[2]

A property common to these examples, albeit in varying degrees, is the unexpectedness of the image selected. We do not expect Charlotte to be likened to an octopus, nor Charlie to a carrot, nor Chichikov to a hypothetical boot. John Donne's famous conceit of "stiff twin compasses" (suggesting lovers' legs) is especially effective by dint of unexpected similarity. Both shape and action combine to outweigh the unamorous associations of a compass. However, an image may be unexpectedly apt in both physical and emotional association. Nabokov's Pnin, when everything seems to be going wrong, drops a nutcracker into a sinkfull of soapy water. An excruciating crack of broken glass then suggests that his precious punch bowl has been smashed. We see the nutcracker fall: "...the leggy thing somehow slipped out of the towel and fell like a man from a roof."[3] Though the bowl remains intact, Pnin's initial feelings are eloquently suggested by the imaginary man's fall. In addition to the unexpected similarity of shape and action, we feel an emotional parallel.

In Pushkin's *Eugene Onegin,* Lensky falls, shot by the hero:

> Thus, slowly, down the slope of hills,
> shining with sparkles in the sun,
> a lump of snow descends.
> Deluged with instant cold,
> Onegin hastens to the youth,[4]

Here, the appropriately falling "lump of snow" seems almost explicitly to promote Onegin's cold fright. Nabokov's Commentary on these lines refers to Tolstoi's story "Haji-Murad" and its elaborate comparison involving the crushing of a vigorous thistle and the death of a Caucasian" (III:52). But whereas Pushkin's snow evokes both action and emotion, Tolstoi's thistle mainly suggests a situation: in its resistance to being cut down, the plant resembles Haji's own death. The fact that Haji is a strong, wiry natural man richly justifies his comparison to a thistle but renders the comparison less surprising. Tolstoi's famous likening of Anna Karenina's fall beneath a train to a swimmer's dive is also vivid but not startling—even if one does not know that Tolstoi formerly planned to have Anna drown herself. We feel horror at Anna's death, but her swimmer's dive may even add suggestions of escape, freedom, relief. The only appropriate emotional associations accrue from the fact that divers fall and may possibly drown—just as we may slightly admire, or at least pity, a stubborn thistle.

Yet the images of some bonus effects seem chosen precisely because of their abrupt emotional relevance. In Pushkin's story "Mistress into Maid," the neighboring landowners Muromsky and Berestov are hostile to one another. Out riding, Muromsky encounters Berestov quite unexpectedly "at the distance of a pistol shot."[5] In Tolstoi's *War and Peace,* old Bolkonsky says good-bye to his son Andrei, who is leaving to fight the French. Then, from Bolkonsky's study: "...could be heard, like shots, the often repeated angry sounds of the old man's nose-blowing."[6] In Nabokov's *Despair* Hermann, about to murder Felix, slams the door of his car "with a bang that was louder than any shot."[7] In each of these cases, the rather unexpected physical comparison is enhanced by a sudden emotional relevance.

Nabokov frequently employs unexpected images with appropriate emotional associations. In *Despair,* Hermann twice suggests that he and his murder victim resemble each other "like two drops of blood" (151,28). In *King, Queen, Knave,* when it first occurs to Martha that drowning is a convenient way to kill her husband, we read: "Two sickle-shaped dimples appeared on her flaming cheeks."[8] Here, the appropriate physical shape and emotional associations of "sickle" are especially successful because of its unexpected use to modify (normally pleasant) dimples.

In *Glory,* Martin jealously fears that Sonia has dressed up and gone to a dance with Darwin. Rushing into her room, he finds "a cloudlet of powder, like the smoke following a shot."[9] In Nabokov's poem "The Execution," the speaker dreams of being led to a ravine to be killed. Awakening, he sees the glowing dial of his watch staring at him "like a gun's steadfast muzzle."[10] After this, a focusing on the watch's ticking and then on the speaker's heart subtly develops the notion of how much time remains for him to live. In *Mary,* as Podtyagin is dying of a heart seizure, Ganin's "heavy footfalls" make "a noise on the stairs like a slow heart beat."[11]

Nabokovian bonus effects sometimes include a Gogolian

faint eeriness, which may be seen by comparing the following two descriptions. In *Glory,* Archibald Moon removes "his prince-nez as carefully as if it were a dragonfly" (65)—a comparison suggesting delicate substance, with a bonus effect of shape. In *Lolita,* Humbert and Annabel passionately caress each other on the beach "with somebody's lost pair of sunglasses for only witness" (15). In this context, an emotional bonus effect eerily enlivens the "sunglasses": Humbert and Annabel are continually haunted by "witnesses" of their furtive intimacies.

Such effects may suggest the presence of hidden forces, especially where fate and chance are concerned. In *Bend Sinister* Dr. Hammecke, who fears that at any moment the authorities may somewhat arbitrarily decide upon his execution, is seen with "his false teeth rattling in his head like dice."[12] In *Glory,* when Rose tells Martin that she is pregnant: "...it seemed to him as if that meteorite which ordinarily lands somewhere in the Gobi desert had fallen straight upon him" (103). Here, the subtly eerie bonus effect involves a suggested metaphor of fertilization. In *The Defense,* Luzhin's wife tarries on her wedding night: "Suddenly she realized that she was dawdling on purpose, standing in her pajamas before the mirror—and a shiver went through her breast, as when you are leafing through last year's magazine, knowing that in a second, in just a second, the door will open and the dentist will appear on the threshold."[13] Here, a bonus effect derives from the notion of an unavoidable, and rather painful, invading of a person's body. Moreover the door, threshold, and an (implied) unpleasant drilling may be seen as metaphorically suggestive. In *King, Queen, Knave,* amorous Franz approaches Martha: "Because he wore glasses even for love-making, he reminded her of a handsome, hairy young pearl diver ready to pry the live pearl out of its rosy shell..." (166). The comparison of Franz's exposed body and glasses to a diver's body and goggles unexpectedly blends with an elaborate sexual metaphor involving Martha. Nabokov's term "spontaneous generation" (used to describe Gogol's writing[14]) seems also appropriate for his own.

The additional life that abruptly materializes in such bonus effects seems to derive from a playful, faintly magical quality. In *The Gift:* "On occasion, having camped in a completely deserted spot, I would suddenly see in the morning that around us during the night a wide circle of brigands' tents had grown up like black toadstools—which, however, very quickly disappeared."[15]

Here the similarity of shape between toadstools and tents becomes almost secondary, so striking is the parallel of sudden appearance as if by magic. This magic seems to draw upon our sense of adventure in exotic lands, a child's fascination for transformations, and sudden glimpses of toadstools in a silent forest. Even the abrupt disappearance develops the furtive magic at work throughout the passage. In "The Vane Sisters" a less suggestive passage focuses on "glasses that grew like mushrooms in the shade of chairs."[16] The comparison of (presumably stemmed) glasses to mushrooms may seem more physically apt than that of toad-stools to brigands' tents, just as a dragonfly pince-nez is physically more appropriate than "sunglasses" for "witness." Yet the more disquieting, and more magical, bonus effects seem to lurk in the watchful eyes of those invisible brigands, and in the inquisitive stare of those almost human sunglasses.

Nabokov's bonus effects may entail a relationship between two or more passages. Early in his short story "The Aurelian," we learn that Pilgrim once had a nearly fatal stroke: "like a mountain falling upon him from behind just as he had bent towards his shoestrings."[17] Later, this butterfly dealer prepares to abandon his wife and take a long journey: "In the twilight of the strangely still shop, eyed wings stared at him from all sides, and Pilgrim perceived something almost appalling in the richness of the huge happiness that was leaning toward him like a mountain" (79). Despite the ensuing description of Pilgrim's long, successful journey, the reader who connects these two passages will have suspected, when Pilgrim's wife finds him dead on the floor at the end of the story, that he was actually killed by a fatal stroke. The "mountain" of "happiness," recalling the earlier "mountain" of a "stroke," signals the entrance to a strange twilight world of moribund delirium.

In *Glory,* we are told: "The day promised to be lovely; the cloudless sky still had a hazy cast, as a sheet of gauze paper sometimes covers an exceptionally vivid frontispiece in an expensive edition of fairy tales" (36). Martin, we read, "carefully removed this translucent sheet," whereupon he sees Alla, with whom he soon has an affair. They are then separated. "Upon her, upon that frontispiece, which , after the removal of the gauze paper, had proved to be a little coarse, a little too gaudy, Martin replaced the haze and through it the colors reassumed their mysterious charm" (40). The original gauze paper, which vaguely separated adolescent dreams from reality, has now more specifically evolved to suggest a woman's clothing. The full bonus effect thus involves an association of these two passages.

Early in *Mary,* we are told that "Occasionally...something would happen which no one walking in a city ever notices: a star, faster than thought and with less sound than a tear, would fall" (26). In context the tear, compared for silence, shares a bonus gleam of brightness with the star as both fall. Much later, Ganin recalls the first letter he received from Mary, whereupon he had walked out at night and seen that "...the new moon glistened like a translucent nail clipping, and beside it, by the lower horn, trembled a drop of brightness—the first star" (89). That night, he had written to Mary about this star. The word "drop" recalls the earlier blending of star and tear, appropriately evoking Ganin's emotions. Even the earlier bonus effect of implied brightness has now become explicit. All this is especially effective because Ganin now expects to meet Mary (now Alfyorov's wife) again. After this, we read a description of trains at night: "The clattering roar and mass of smoke seemed to pass right through the house as it quivered between the chasm where the rail tracks lay like lines drawn by a moonlit fingernail and the street where it was crossed by the flat bridge waiting for the next regular thunder of railway carriages" (95). The novel ends as Ganin decides not to meet Mary at the railway station, but rather to leave town from "a different station at the other end of the city" (114). The image of a moonlit fingernail drawing the rail tracks thus seems fatefully related to the moon which had resembled a translucent nail clipping, which, through conjunction with the tear-like star, recalls Ganin's separation from Mary, his isolation, and their togetherness whch apparently must now exist only in the realm of memory.

Such associations may seem to extend from book to book. The narrator of Nabokov's short story "Lance" declares: "Only by a heroic effort can I make myself unscrew a bulb that has died an inexplicable death and screw in another, which will light up in my face with the hideous instancy of a dragon's egg hatching in one's bare hand" [18] In *Pale Fire,* a poem by John Shade begins:

> The dead, the gentle dead—who knows?—
> In tungsten filaments abide,
> And on my bedside table glows
> Another man's departed bride. [19]

In retrospect (''Lance was written in 1952), these lines remarkably justify the rather squeamish image of a suddenly hatching dragon's egg.

It even seems possible that Nabokovian bonus effects may involve allusions to other authors. In *Glory* Martin, ''as if pressing upon an aching tooth'' (98), jealously pictures Sonia and Darwin together. Sydney Schultze has traced the ''toothache motif'' in Tolstoi's *Anna Karenina*,[20] a work to which Nabokov often refers. Most pertinent here are the two time that Karenin, told of his wife's adultery, is likened to a man with an aching tooth removed.

Why does Nabokov favor bonus effects? They facilitate economical, suggestive description. Readers, feeling the additional force of what is implied but unsaid, tend to participate creatively as their perceptions are channeled and expanded by the author. In Clarence Brown's words: ''Reading Nabokov is using, for a time, his central nervous system. We cease to be ourselves and become the person whom he supplies''[21] And although Nabokovian bonus effects have been related here to effects by Pushkin, Tolstoi and Gogol, with Nabokov the descriptive image seems especially rich in appropriate emotional connotations. Another factor is undoubtedly Nabokov's capacity for multilevel thinking. His mind resists single links and associations.[22] Through bonus effects, he abruptly multiplies what John Updike has termed ''the little ecstasy of extracting resemblances from different things.''[23] Finally, Nabokov's bonus effects contain an element of unexpectedness that seems, though often quite playful or faintly eerie, to derive from the magic of all serious art.

NOTES

1. Vladimir Nabokov, *Lolita* (New York, 1955), p. 96. Subsequent references will be to this edition.

2. Carl R. Proffer, *The Simile and Gogol's Dead Souls* (The Hague, 1967), p. 25.

3. Vladimir Nabokov, *Pnin* (New York, 1965), p. 172.

4. Vladimir Nabokov, *Eugene Onegin by Aleksandr Pushkin* (New York, 1964), I, 250. Subsequent references will be to this edition.

5. A.S. Pushkin, *Polnoe sobranie sochinenii v desyati tomakh* (Moscow, 1962-1965), VI, 159.

6. L.N. Tolstoi, *Sobranie sochinenii v dvenadtsati tomakh* (Moscow, 1958-1959), IV, 144.

7. Vladimir Nabokov, *Despair* (New York, 1966), p. 173. Subsequent references will be to this edition.

8. Vladimir Nabokov, *King, Queen, Knave* (New York, 1968), p. 212. Subsequent references will be to this edition.

9. Vladimir Nabokov, *Glory* (New York, 1971), p. 82. Subsequent references will be to this edition.

10. Vladimir Nabokov, *Poems and Problems* (New York, 1970), p. 47.

11. Vladimir Nabokov, *Mary* (New York, 1970), p. 111. Subsequent references will be to this edition.

12. Vladimir Nabokov, *Bend Sinister* (London, 1960), p. 193.

13. Vladimir Nabokov, *The Defense* (New York, 1964), pp. 182-183.

14. Vladimir Nabokov, *Nikolai Gogol* (New York, 1961), p. 83.

15. Vladimir Nabokov, *The Gift* (New York, 1970), p. 136.

16. Vladimir Nabokov, *Nabokov's Quartet* (New York, 1966), p. 87.

17. Vladimir Nabokov, *Nabokov's Dozen* (New York, 1958), p. 71. Subsequent references will be to this edition.

18. *Ibid.,* p. 146.

19. Vladimir Nabokov, *Pale Fire* (New York, 1966), p. 138.

20. Sydney Schultze, "Notes on Imagery and Motifs in *Anna Karenina,*" *Russian Literature Triquarterly* No. 1 (Fall, 1971), p. 367.

21. Clarence Brown, "Nabokov's Pushkin and Nabokov's Nabokov," in: L.S. Dembo, ed., *Nabokov: The Man and His Work* (Milwaukee, Wisconsin, 1967), p. 207.

22. In *Nikolai Gogol* Nabokov threatened, if required to include a bibliography, to allay his boredom "by inserting here and there fictitious titles and imaginary authors" (154).

23. John Updike, *Picked-Up Pieces* (New York, 1975), p. 34.

Chapter Eleven

NABOKOVIAN SHIMMERS OF MEANING

Ronald Hingley has related the "masterly" quality of Vladimir Nabokov's English to "twists" which "would never occur to a native user."[1] In one type of twist, Mr. Nabokov creates an additional shimmer of meaning between two parts of a word or between two adjacent words. The present essay discusses such shimmerings. Several, it will be argued, serve as remarkably complex connections between key episodes in a given work.

Perhaps partly because of the importance of root meanings in Russian, and partly because of his aptitude for "multi-level thinking,"[2] Mr. Nabokov notices hidden shimmers in English words. In his book *Nikolai Gogol,* we find: "beautiful word, stratagem—a treasure in a cave."[3] Separated as strata-gem, the word reveals an additional shimmer of meaning. A stratagem is indeed a precious idea, secretly hidden away.

Nabokovian shimmers redound from a literal construction of two syllables or words. For example, happily sniffing dogs are said to be "beside themselves" with new scents.[4] The reader of *Hamlet* is likened to a "mongrel," in awe of a "Great Dane."[5]

The device often promotes a Gogolian uneasy humor. "Nobody," says Hermann of corpses, wants to be disinhumed.[6] Kinbote acquires his house "sight unseen" (59). Hugh Person has a last "interview" with the mirror.[7] Of Gogol himself, Nabokov reports: "In Switzerland, he had quite a field-day knocking the life out of the lizards all along the sunny mountain paths"(7). In context, "field-day" is enhanced by the "mixture of nausea and ecstasy which results from "squashing" a little Russian devil. In *Ada,* the casual combination "never mind" subtly but disturbingly suggests insanity.[8] Later, Van invites us to realize the futility of trying to grasp the concept of Time, since this process itself "takes time"(538).

The effect may include neighboring words, and perhaps one recalls Nabokov's notion that a word may be used so as to "come alive" and "share its neighbor's sheen, heat, shadow, while reflecting itself in its neighbor."[9] In *Speak, Memory* he describes his affair with Tamara: "The rain pipe at one side of the porch, a small busybody of water, could be heard steadily bubbling."[10] Here, the shimmer "busybody" reflects still another play, "body of water." In *Ada* the term "relief map" suggests the topography of Van's erect penis: a vein is "the blue Nile" leading to "its jungle" (119). Then, as Ada's exploration causes Van to dissolve in a "puddle of pleasure, " the shimmer "relief" seems aptly prophetic.

Nabokovian shimmers also utilize other languages. Kinbote informs us that the name "irondell" comes "not from a little valley yielding iron ore but from the French for 'swallow' "(123). He also refers to three conjoined lakes with garbled Indian names: "Omega, Ozero, and Zero"(66-7). Among the shades of meaning here, *Ozero* (which reduces to O-O) means "lake" in Russian. One of Kinbote's most ingenious such shimmers involves Fleur, whom he pictures wearing only a sleeveless pajama top which exposes her "three mousepits"(80). Armpit in Russian is *podmyshka*, which suggestively combines *pod* ("under") and *mysh'* ("mouse") in this context.

Early in his Commentary, Kinbote remarks that "Parachuting had become a popular sport"(54). Later, dilating on suicide techniques, he suggests casting off one's parachute: "farewell, *shootka* (little chute)!"(158) The resulting shimmers of meaning include "farewell, joke of life!" (*shutka* in Russian is "joke"), recalling Axel Rex ("Death is often the point of life's joke."[11]) and "parashoot" (echoed in *Ada*: "The silly girl had not rehearsed the technique of suicide as, say, free-fall parachutists do every day in the element of another chapter"[494]).

Discussing the Russian concept *poshlost*, Mr. Nabokov alters the English transliteration *poshlost* to *poshlust* in his book on Gogol (63). Both pairs of syllables help to suggest the complex associations of this puffy Russian word. In *Despair,* one compound shimmer derives from a customary Russian manual signal. Hermann tells Ardalion he has heard that the latter has "stopped..." He does not say what, but by "a succession of fillips" under his jaw produces "the sound of a gurgling bottleneck"(137). Ardalion correctly interprets the colloquial Russian signal as "drinking." In English, the vivid shimmer "bottleneck" helps to preserve this meaning.

In another type of shimmer, Mr. Nabokov plays upon proper names. In *The Real Life of Sebastan Knight,* the hero, a writer, is accused of being "Conradish" with the suggestion that he leave out the "con" and cultivate the "radish."[12] (Of his own writing, Mr. Nabokov has declared: "I differ from Joseph Conradically."[13]) In *Ada*, one finds Vaniada (226, 373, 409), Aquamarina (19), and Adalucindas (375). The first and last of these combinations suggest sexual unions.

Another type of shimmer derives from improper colloquial puns. In *Ada*, Van's sexual initiation by a prostitute causes him to spill "...on the welcome mat what she would have gladly helped him to take indoors"(33). The door metaphor (with perhaps even a faint suggestion of "matted" hair) seems ingeniously enlivened by the two syllables of "welcome." Later, after *her* sexual initiation, Ada appears at breakfast, where Uncle Dan, we read, acknowledged "the newcomer"(126).

Other such shimmers also seem reinforced by dual appearances. In *King, Queen, Knave*: "It was especially hard on lanky Franz"(115). "She rose, leaning hard on him as she did so"(157). In the first example, Martha is pressing her knee against Franz's leg; in the second, she has been sitting on his lap. In Nabokov's play *The Waltz Invention*, the Minister says of the Colonel: "He's always mislaying women, I mean, things."[14] In *Lolita*, Valeria is said to have "mislaid her virginity under circumstances that changed with her reminiscent moods."[15]

Of Pnin, we read: "The zipper a gentleman depends on most would come loose in his puzzled hand at some nightmare moment of haste and despair."[16] Part of the dark humor here derives from the ambiguity of "the gentleman's" need. And to at least one need, the shimmer "gentleman" seems quite pertinent. Discussing fits of insanity, Kinbote mentions a trustworthy old college porter who one day suddenly exhibited himself to a squeamish coed in the "Projection Room"(168).

Humbert Humbert admits scheming to "blackmail—no, that is too strong a word—mauvemail big Haze into letting me consort with little Haze"(73). In context, "mauvemail" playfully evokes a sort of muted blackmail. Yet Humbert later mentions various shades of bathing suits including "glans mauve"(109). As Alfred Appel has noted, "glans" is an "anatomical word; the conical vascular body which forms the extremity of the penis."[17] But is it possible, even in Nabokov's world, that "mauvemail" contains the shimmer "mauvemale"? In "A Note about Symbols and Colors re 'Annotated Lolita'," Mr. Nabokov urges readers "to discriminate between visual shades as the author does, and not to lump them under such arbitrary labels as 'red' (using it, moreover, as a sexual symbol, though actually the dominant shades in males are mauve— to bright blue in certain monkeys)"(362).

There is much ado in Lolita about "Our Glass Lake" (45ff) before Humbert realizes that the real name is Hourglass Lake. It is at this lake that Charlotte's time nearly runs out. The shimmer "Hourglass" becomes subtly ominous—especially in association with Humbert's wrist watch, which innocently inspires the following shimmer connecting key episodes across the novel.

In his essay "On a Book Entitled Lolita," Mr. Nabokov singles out several images for special delectation (318). These include "Charlotte saying 'waterproof.' " She says it to Jean Farlow about Humbert's wristwatch (91) just after he has vividly decided not to drown her in Hourglass Lake: "Emphatically, no killers are we." She then tells Jean (who has been hiding nearby) "You could see anything that way." Charlotte of course unwittingly refers to her own drowning, and her pronouncement "waterproof" seems to acquire a playful shimmer of meaning anent her own body. As Humbert has just concluded: "...thank God, not water, not water!" Yet it is on a "freshly watered" pavement that Charlotte slips and plunges forward to her death (104).

When Lolita reveals Quilty's name to Humbert, he tells us: "Waterproof. Why did a flash from Hourglass Lake cross my consciousness?"(274). As Appel has observed (lxvii), Jean Farlow had almost mentioned Quilty's name just after Charlotte said "waterproof." But perhaps this is not merely a "teasing exercise in ratiocination," as Appel suggests. For we are returned via "waterproof"

158

to Humbert's lengthy statement that he could not drown Charlotte (89-90).. "Water" becomes a kind of "proof" that Humbert is not entirely evil, especially because of the trial atmosphere established as the novel opens ("Ladies and gentlemen of the jury"). Although Humbert is presumably a murderer (in proportion as Quilty may be considered human), he could not kill Charlotte, even though this seemed the only way to obtain what he desired above all else. Charlotte's "waterproof" statement, echoed by Humbert, may thus be seen to have two hidden references: to her own body (ironically undermined by the "freshly watered" pavement) and to Humbert's tortured (but at least partially relieved) conscience. Little wonder that Nabokov calls Charlotte saying "waterproof" one of "the nerves of the novel... the secret points, the subliminal coordinates by means of which the book is plotted" (318).

In Mr. Nabokov's translation of *Lolita* into Russian, he has Charlotte say *"Uoterpruf"* ("waterproof" transliterated) and adds the Russian translation *nepromokaemye* in parentheses.[18] The crucial shimmer "water [as a] proof" is thus preserved at least for the Russian reader who knows English.[19]

Early in *King, Queen, Knave* Martha helps Franz to look for an apartment: "...how splendid it was to stroll along with this red-lipped beauty.... Add a new suit and a flaming tie—and his happiness would be complete"(51). As I have suggested elsewhere,[20] the prophetic submeaning of "flaming tie" is reinforced by a later definition of "happiness" as sexual intercourse (104). Also aptly, the "new suit" seems to materialize as the prophylactic in which Martha soon dresses Franz.

The novel contains a wide pattern of shimmering references to Franz's "tie" with Martha. Still earlier, Dreyer asks Franz if he plays tennis. Receiving an affirmative, Dreyer continues:

"Fine. So we can play on Sundays. Then you will need a decent suit, shirts, soft collars, ties, all kinds of things. How did you get on with my wife?"
Franz grinned, not knowing the answer (34).

It is on a Sunday (93) that Franz begins his affair with Dreyer's wife.[21] They first make love in a standing position (97). The question, how did Franz "get on" with Martha thus becomes a typical[22] ironic shimmer. Franz's fatuous grin, "not [yet] knowing the answer," also becomes quite ironic, as does Dreyer's suggestion that Franz will need a decent suit and ties.

The pattern becomes more complex when Dreyer, suspected by Martha of going out to "fix up" Franz "with some dirty slut" (64), gives him a four-page lesson in how to sell ties. Doing so, Dreyer demonstrates "...not the way ties should be sold in real life, but the way they might be sold if the salesman were both artist and clairvoyant"(70). (Franz's "flaming tie" has not yet begun). Dreyer repeatedly shows how to "tempt" the customer, even proposing to "squeeze out of him 'an extra throb and an extra bob,' as they say in London"(71). He also impersonates various customers, including "the brute who objected to his being told the price before he asked for it," "the saint to whom price was no object," and "a Russian who pleads gently for a *galstook*." In the Russian version of the novel, this same word is used to articulate Franz's desire for a "flaming tie."[23]

Later, when Franz and Martha make love: "In the rickety wardrobe a blue black-spotted tie slithered off its twig like a snake"(98). Finally, just before Martha catches her fatal chill, she remarks "...that it looked like rain and the tie would be ruined" (239). In context, her reference is to Dreyer's necktie, but the water (as it becomes "the solution" after all) seems quite appropriate for ruining her flaming tie with Franz.

Not long before Martha catches her fatal chill in the rain, a barometer engages Dreyer's "awed attention"(234). The instrument has "different sexes emerging according to differences in the weather," which also fatidically suggests the precarious triangle King, Queen, and Knave. Dreyer of course does not realize this, although "for no particular reason" he suddenly feels "very sad."

In the poem "Pale Fire," Shade experiences "a sudden sunburst" in his head when, as an eleven-year-old boy, he "...lay/ Prone on the floor and watched a clockwork toy/ A tin wheelbarrow pushed by a tin boy—"(ll. 142-44). Like Dreyer's barometer, this intently observed preview of a death remains undeciphered. The last lines Shade writes before he dies depict Kinbote's gardener pushing his wheelbarrow. Kinbote's note to "a clockwork toy" confirms the correspondence by describing the toy: the tin boy pushing the wheelbarrow was a "Negro" (as was the gardener). Concludes Kinbote: "...now the rustic clockwork shall work again, for I have the key"(99).

The "key" thus refers both to the mechanism of the tin toy and to the mechanism of the novel. Indeed, the "clockwork toy" is the "mysterious truth" that Shade stumbles upon "in the fainting fits of his boyhood"(85). Kinbote's Commentary is laced with attempts to *synchronize* Shade's approaching death (in the form of Gradus) with the development of the poem. Moreover, Kinbote terms Gradus "our clockwork man"(109) and employs the word "clockwork"(211), though negatively, in describing Shade's death. Perhaps the "clock" that "works" in Shade's murder is related to "Infinite foretime and/ Infinite aftertime: above your head/ They close like giant wings, and you are dead"(ll. 122-24). The sudden sunburst in Shade's head, then, may result from his almost deciphering the "mysterious truth" of the "clockwork" preview. "It is forbidden," Nabokov has written, "to ransack the future."[24]

Kinbote's play on "clockwork" ("the rustic clockwork shall work again") may even lead one to find shimmers of meaning in the Zemblan "Glass Works"(108), where Gradus was "designated" to kill the King on the "fatidic" date "upon which an innocent poet penned the first lines of his last poem"(109). Indeed, "glass works" rather ominously throughout the entire book—the lethal "false azure in the windowpane"(ll. 1-2), the numerous windows through which Kinbote spies (14, 15, 17, etc.), and perhaps even the "really fantastic mirror, signed with a diamond by its maker, Sudarg of Bokay"(81). For as the "glass works," killing the waxwing, this palindromic signature (Yakob Gradus) may be seen to anticipate the final (unwritten) echo of the "shadow slain" (in line 1,000)—Shade himself. As Kinbote puts it: When the feigned remoteness of the windowpane performs its dreadful duty, "we cannot help reading into these lines something more than mirrorplay and mirage shimmer"(98).

In *Despair*, as Carl Proffer has observed, Lydia's notion that the word "mystic" somehow combines "mistake" and "stick" prefigures Hermann's fatal stick mistake in the murder scene.[25] Stephen Suagee has further developed "the stick theme," including Hermann's dream of a walking stick.[26]

In the present context, "mystic" may be seen as the combination "miss stick"—a precise definition of Hermann's mistake. "The stick theme" is thus reinforced still more specifically.

With yet another shimmer of meaning, "mystic" also fits into a pattern of allusions to, and parodies of, Dostoevsky. These include, besides what is discussed below, other allusions to Dostoevsky, the pun Rascalnikov, puns on dust and dusty—for instance, Hermann both literally (179) and figuratively (149) puts himself in Felix's dusty shoes—and even Golyadkin's habit of writing letters to himself (201). Asked about *The Double*, which Hermann considers as a possible title for his manuscript, Mr. Nabokov replied that it is Dostoevsky's "best work." "Felix in *Despair*," he added, "is really a *false* double."[27] Nabokov has also observed that Russians who love Dostoevsky "venerate him as a mystic."[28]

The word "mist," which Lydia also associates with "mystic" (33), also relates to the Dostoevsky pattern. According to Hermann, "Mist, vapor...in the mist a chord that quivers" comes from "Dusty's great book, *Crime and Slime*"(187). Hermann even envisions himself and Felix as reflected by a "misty and, to all appearances, sick mirror"(99). The first three titles considered by Hermann for his book are: The Double, Crime and Pun, and The Mirror (211). As Suagee has observed, "it is obvious that Dostoevsky, as novelist and as mystic, is parodied rather than emulated."[29]

Elsewhere I have noted that fire seems to suggest special trouble for Pnin, including a mention of "the Great Moscow Fire," which cryptographically signifies the great to-do (including puns) about Pnin's being fired from his job.[30] Within *Pnin*, the notion "Great Fire" seems almost archly ironic. Yet considering Pnin's quite triumphant appearance in *Pale Fire*, the "Great Fire" acquires rather unexpected justification—at least in a broader Nabokovian reality.

In a Foreword to his play *The Waltz Invention*, Mr. Nabokov notes that the original Russian title is ambiguous: *Izobretenie Valsa* "means not only 'the invention of Vals (or Valse)', but also 'the invention of the waltz' "(1). In both languages however, there are two other vital shimmers of meaning. First, in addition to Waltz's invention of a doomsday machine, there are constant, haunting suggestions that he (as a madman) invents the entire reality of the play. As the Colonel puts it, "We are all only participants in your delirium, and everything that is taking place is the ringing and throbbing inside your sick brain"(77). Moreover, the title may suggest not only "the invention of the waltz," in Nabokov's words, but his own invention "of Waltz"—an apt reminder that a Creator's multilevel brain has arranged the entire stage, be it a subordinate madman's fabrication or not.

In *Ada*, Van Veen constantly attempts to justify his incestuous love, as Bobbie Ann Mason has thoroughly demonstrated.[31] At one point, the question is asked: "What, then, was it that raised the animal act to a level higher than even that of the most exact arts or the wildest flights of pure science?"(219). The answer, after some meandering, focuses upon "the rapture of her identity." This, we read, "...placed under the microscope of reality.(which is the only reality), shows a complex system of those subtle bridges which the senses traverse—laughing, embraced, throwing flowers in the air—between membrane and brain, and which always was and is a form of memory, even at the moment of its perception"(221). The word "membrane" thus becomes an eloquent attempt to justify the brain's memory of incest at Ardis. But as Mason has also thoroughly shown, Van's attempts fail for many reasons. There may even be (given the relationship between gymnastics and sex in the novel: for example, Van's handstands and Lucette's admission, "We interweaved like serpents and sobbed like pumas. We were Mongolian tumblers..."[375]) a Nabokovian derisive shimmer, above, in the words "animal act."

As seen above, Nabokovian shimmers range from local sub-meanings ("stratagem") to complex interconnections with similar references across many pages ("flaming tie"). Some shimmers enliven neighboring words ("busybody of water"). Others play on two or more languages ("Ozero") and on proper names ("Conradish"). And though only one pun may be involved ("proof" in "waterproof"), the shimmer may serve to connect vital episodes across one or more novels (water and death in *Lolita*; fire from *Pnin* to *Pale Fire*, where Pnin reappears). A cautious conclusion: shimmers of meaning which help to connect vital episodes tend to feature basic substances and elements, especially fire and water. (In both *Lolita* and *King, Queen, Knave*, water becomes "the solution" after all.) If another category may be noted, it is perhaps mind, memory, imagination. Presumably, these are far from all:

Fire and Water
> flaming tie (*King, Queen, Knave*; also water)
> waterproof (*Lolita*—Charlotte's lake)
> Great Fire (*Pnin*—including *Pale Fire*)
> Ozero (*Pale Fire*—Hazel's lake?)

Other Substances
> mystic (*Despair*—miss stick: wood)
> clockwork (*Pale Fire*—toy: tin)
> Glass Works (*Pale Fire*—windows, mirrors: glass)
> Our Glass Lake (*Lolita*—Hourglass: glass, sand)

163

Mind, Memory, Imagination
membrane (*Ada*—sex, memory, brain)
Waltz Invention (Waltz's reality; Nabokov's)
mystic (*Despair*—Dostoevsky parody)

NOTES

1. Ronald Hingley, "An Aggressively Private Person," *The New York Times Book Review,* January 15, 1967, p. 16.

2. The term is Mr. Nabokov's; see his *The Gift* (New York, 1963), p. 186.

3. Vladimir Nabokov, *Nikolai Gogol* (New York, 1961). p. 59.

4. Vladimir Nabokov, *King, Queen, Knave* (New York, 1968), p. 171.

5. Vladimir Nabokov, *Pale Fire* (New York, 1966), p. 112.

6. Vladimir Nabokov, *Despair* (New York, 1966), p. 157.

7. Vladimir Nabokov, *Transparent Things* (New York, 1972), p. 49.

8. Vladimir Nabokov, *Ada* (New York, 1969), p. 25.

9. Vladimir Nabokov, *Invitation to a Beheading* (New York, 1959), p. 93.

10. Vladimir Nabokov, *Speak, Memory* (New York, 1966), p. 233.

11. Vladimir Nabokov, *Laughter in the Dark* (New York, 1961), p. 100.

12. Vladimir Nabokov, *The Real Life of Sebastian Knight* (Norfolk, Conn., 1959), p. 42.

13. Vladimir Nabokov, *Strong Opinions* (New York, 1973), p. 57.

14. Vladimir Nabokov, *The Waltz Invention* (New York, 1966), p. 12.

15. Vladimir Nabokov, *Lolita* (New York, 1955), p. 27. "Circumstances" (even in this context) may be better left untouched, although triple shimmers are not entirely rare in Nabokov's works (e.g. "Picador"—*Lolita*, 253).

Three other pairs are: "*Qu'il t'y*—what a tongue-twister!" (*Lolita*, 225) and "tongue-in-cheek delights" (*Ada*, 436); "peter out" and "petering out" (*Lolita*, 25, 156); "crack-up" (*King, Queen, Knave*, 137) and "crack players" (*Lolita*, 235).

16. Vladimir Nabokov, *Pnin* (New York, 1965), p. 14.

17. Alfred Appel, Jr., *The Annotated Lolita* (New York, 1970), p. 370.

18. Vladimir Nabokov, *Lolita* [in Russian] (New York, 1967), p. 77.

19. In this connection, it should perhaps be noted that two of the complex shimmers discussed below (in *King, Queen, Knave* and *Despair*) are presumably not present in the Russian originals. Even for Nabokov, prophetic Englishings of the Russian words *galstuk* and *mistik* (as "gals took" and "miss stick") seem quite unlikely.

20. *Nabokov's Deceptive World* (New York, 1971), pp. 99-100.

21. In bed, Dreyer suggests to Martha that they go riding on Sunday (76), and though she is "no Emma," Martha is already dreaming of Franz's bedroom. In Mr. Nabokov's world, sex sometimes seems to have been created on a Sunday (e.g. Humbert's lap climax).

22. In *Pale Fire*, the homosexual King is urged to take a "night off" and lawfully engender an heir (124). In *Look at the Harlequins!* the hero is asked by his wife: "Did that girl get in touch with you at your office?" (New York, 1974, p. 140). He has just had sexual intercourse on his office desk.

23. Vladimir Nabokov, *Korol', dama, valet* (New York, 1968), p. 52. See also footnote 19 above.

24. *King, Queen, Knave*, p. 85.

25. Carl R. Proffer, "From *Otchaianie* to *Despair*," *Slavic Review*, June 1968, p. 266.

26. Stephen Suagee, "An Artist's Memory Beats All Other Kinds: An Essay on *Despair*," in: Carl R. Proffer, ed., *A Book of Things about Vladimir Nabokov* (Ann Arbor, 1974), pp. 55-6.

27. *Strong Opinions*, p. 84.

28. Ibid., p. 42.

29. Suagee, p. 61.

30. "Pnin's Uncanny Looking Glass," above, p. 129.

31. Bobbie Ann Mason, *Nabokov's Garden: A Guide to Ada* (Ann Arbor, 1974), p. 13 *passim.*

Chapter Twelve

**NABOKOVIAN
SUPERIMPOSED AND
ALTERNATIVE REALITIES**

The problem of depicting separate scenes simultaneously is discussed by Joseph Frank in his well-known essay on spacial form in literature. Flaubert, he notes, shifts the descriptive focus back and forth with increasing frequency, finally promoting the desired impression of simultaneity.[1] Different events seem superimposed upon a single moment of time.

The present essay illustrates how Vladimir Nabokov has achieved what could be termed the converse of this effect: different moments of time superimposed upon a single event. It also discusses methods whereby Nabokov and others have promoted the impression that time splits or forks, permitting glimpses of alternative realities.

"I confess I do not believe in time," Mr. Nabokov has written.[2] Characteristically sensitive to the edges of sanity, he seems to sense a possibility of seeing through, or across, temporal barriers: "Whenever I did manage to go to Prague, there was always that initial pang one feels just before time, caught unawares, again dons its familiar mask"(49). The prospect is faintly disturbing. With a broad enough temporal perspective, perhaps, the visits to Prague could be viewed simultaneously.

From his authorial vantage point, Mr. Nabokov frequently

suggests, or reveals, such temporal perspectives to his readers. In *Speak, Memory* he mentions an ocean liner which "left Greece on May 18, 1919 (twenty-one years too soon as far as I was concerned) for New York"(253-4). To Nabokov, the present departure from Greece suggests a future one. His description of the liner thus superimposes the future upon the present.

About to begin her affair with Humbert, Lolita stops to pet a dog. Then: "Lo, leaving the dog as she would leave me some day, rose from her haunches...."[3] Once again, the future and the present are superimposed upon a single event—Lolita leaving. The effect seems slightly self-conscious, yet it abruptly enlarges the reader's perspective.

No doubt some find the device distracting, even irritating. In *Transparent Things* Nabokov focuses on a "dark-tousled traveler" who is "...deciding what to take out of the valise (which he will send by mail coach ahead) and transfer to the knapsack (which he will carry himself across the mountains to the Italian frontier)."[4] Here, the future is twice superimposed upon the present in a single sentence. Yet the two parenthetical interruptions typically, vividly expand our temporal perspective.

Some readers also object to Mr. Nabokov's propensity for grim humor. In *Lolita*, Jean Farlow, age thirty-one, is insouciantly described as "already nursing the cancer that was to kill her at thirty-three"(106). Humbert soon adds: "(Jean, whatever, wherever you are, in minus time-space or plus soul-time, forgive me all this, parenthesis included)." Thus, a dead man (as Humbert informs us on the last page, neither he nor Lolita "is alive when the reader opens this book") apologizes to a dead person for superimposing her death upon her life as he describes it. Nabokov's disbelief in time acquires a shade of arch disdain. In *Speak, Memory* he declares: "I like to fold my magic carpet, after use, in such a way as to superimpose one part of the pattern upon another. Let visitors trip"(139). But the redeeming feature of such temporal superimposings is that our "tripping" jolts us into awareness, makes us notice, elicits our vivifying participation. Just as Flaubert cuts across space, Nabokov "folds over" time.

Thus far, we have examined superimposings of future upon present. For past events, the ghostly emissary is favored. In *Speak, Memory* Nabokov recalls some peasant girls swimming "...stark naked in shallow water...heeding me as little as if I were the discarnate carrier of my present reminiscences"(138). Also typically, he recalls Mademoiselle: "...vainly my ghostly envoy offers her an arm that she cannot see"(98). This technique superimposes the present and a past memory upon the rememberer-observer. In each case, the remembered reality gains substance by dint of imperviousness to the present. In fact, the past tends to become more real than the present, displaying what Nabokov has termed his "almost pathological keenness of the retrospective faculty'" (75).

Also in *Speak, Memory,* he recalls a Russian winter landscape. Then: "Somehow, the two sleighs have slipped away, leaving behind a passportless spy standing on the blue-white road in his New England snowboots and stormcoat. The vibration in my ears is no longer their receding bells but only my own blood singing"(99-100). In result of this strange disenchantment, the rememberer-observer is left stranded in a comparatively unreal present. Garbed as the past, his surroundings had magically seemed more real.

With an unreliable, or warily insane narrator, it is imagination which tends to acquire disarming verisimilitude. Kinbote, whose presumably fabricated recollections lace the Commentary in *Pale Fire*, describes Gradus, en route to kill the King: "We can even make out (as, head-on but quite safely, phantom-like, we pass through him, through the shimmering propeller of his flying machine, through the delegates waving and grinning at us) his magenta and mulberry insides, and the strange, not so good sea swell undulating in his entrails."[5] Here, we ourselves must join Kinbote in becoming ghostly emissaries to the past—a past, however, which seems to exist only in Kinbote's mind. Imagination, Mr. Nabokov has claimed, is a form of memory.[6] After experiencing a climax with Lolita in his lap, Humbert declares: "...and still Lolita was safe—and I was safe. What I had madly possessed was not she, but my own creation, another, fanciful Lolita—perhaps, more real than Lolita...."(64). It was "quite safely" that we, phantom-like, passed through the shimmering propeller of Gradus' airplane.

The warily insane Nabokovian narrator may seem (feign?) not to understand that his memory has outstripped itself. As Stephen Suagee has noted, Hermann (*Despair*) "inadvertently" superimposes winter upon a summer scene, thus foreglimpsing the day of the murder.[7] Mentioning a "bare birch," Hermann wonders: "(now, why did I write 'bare'? It was not winter yet, winter was still remote)."[8] Somewhat similarly, in *Ada*: "A pair of candlesticks, mere phantoms of metal and tallow stood, or seemed to stand, on the broad window ledge."[9] Here, we are allowed to foreglimpse a detail from the "scene of the Burning Barn"(117), when Ada and Van first make love. Unlike Hermann however, the narrators of *Ada* seem rather smug in their mnemonic impatience.

Thus far we have focused upon temporal superimposings within a single continuous reality. Unfolded, Nabokov's "magic carpet" is still of a piece. Yet he and other writers have managed to promote the impression that alternative events occur.

Intense moments of choice wherein a person anticipates diverse, far-reaching consequences often come teasingly close to a suggestion of other realities. We recall Dunya's perplexed hesitation as Pushkin's Stationmaster urges her to drive away with Minsky, Kitty's unexpected rapture before refusing the first proposal of marriage by Tolstoi's Levin. Yet the choice is usually made. Usually, a writer proceeds to dispel the tension. (An exception is Stockton's "The Lady or the Tiger?" which leaves us the uneasy luxury of imagining alternative dénouements.)

Yet writers occasionally anticipate events so that they seem to have occurred—even after we later realize that they did not. Our reactions vividly linger. Mitya Karamazov conveys to the proud Katerina that only if she visits his apartment will he cover her father's embezzlement. We then encounter a graphic description of his overpowering desires when she arrived. This is followed by his decision to insult her, saying that she might perhaps be worth a small portion of the required sum. Finally, we learn that Mitya graciously, selflessly gave her the money.[10] Each of these three alternatives has a powerful effect upon the reader, as Robert Belknap has noted.[11]

In a somewhat similar effect Captain Snegiryov, offered money by Alyosha, rapturously enumerates the uses to which it can be put. Convinced that Snegiryov will accept the money, Alyosha enthusiastically supplements these daydreams. Finally, Snegiryov violently refuses the money, declaring that his honor is not for sale (IX, 263-6).

Despite the technical similarities between the presentation of these episodes and some in Nabokov, one should note their vastly different emotional tone. As Simon Karlinsky has put it, Dostoevsky lacks the "restraint in evaluation" characteristic of Pushkin, Chekhov and Nabokov.[12]

Closer to Nabokovian narration is Yury Olesha's *Envy,* wherein Ivan Kavalerov informs us that he will "now fall on his knees" before Andrei Babichev. The next paragraph contains a desperate, humble plea for forgiveness. After this, we learn that Kavelerov did not fall on his knees; rather, he insulted Babichev.[13] In Mr. Nabokov's "An Affair of Honor," what seems a triumphant, happy ending is abruptly undercut by: "Such things don't happen in real life."[14] Unlike Dostoevsky, whose passionate anticipations play upon the reader's emotions even after they fail to be realized, Nabokov and Olesha seem almost to scorn a reader whose heartstrings are so readily plucked. Indeed, one senses a disappointment in any reader who would expect, and accept, such unrestrained sentiment from the author. The deception assumes a tinge of vengeance. Humbert, repulsed by Lolita, provides a rather extreme example: "Then I pulled out my automatic—I mean, this is the kind of a fool thing a reader might suppose I did. It never even occurred to me to do it."(282)

Perhaps one reason why expectations are so ruthlessly demolished by Nabokov is because the future is perceived as alien in substance to both present and past. In Van Veen's words, the future is "a fantasm" belonging to a "category of thought essentially different from that of the Past"(544). (He describes the present as a "constant building up of the Past, its smoothly and relentlessly rising level"[551]). Van also wonders: "Has there ever been a 'primitive' form of Time in which, say, the Past was not yet clearly differentiated from the Present, so that past shadows and shapes showed through the still soft, long, larval 'now'?"(539). In Apukhtin's "A Fantastic Story," it is proposed that future events, already existing, cast faint shadows back into the present.

Even when a Nabokovian future is quite accurately anticipated, it may retain its fantasmic uncertainty through syllogistic narration. In *The Real Life of Sebastian Knight*, the narrator vehemently informs Madame Lecerf that he has seen through her deception. He then tells us that in reality, he left her without saying "a word of all this." Finally we read: "She will be sent a copy of this book and will understand."[15] Our anticipation of Madame Lecerf's reaction to the narrator's speech is ultimately recreated and even reinforced.

Syllogistic narration thus facilitates not only the depiction of a vivid alternative reality but also an intensification of the initial one. In Olesha's *Envy*, Kavalerov writes a long, hostile letter to Andrei Babichev and leaves it on Babichev's desk. Then, changing his mind, Kavalerov repossesses it. As we learn only later, he has

171

retrieved the wrong letter (49-58). In Solzhenitsyn's *The First Circle*, Klimentiev considers allowing Nerzhin's wife to visit him in prison. Then he remembers having exhibited "stupid softness" in the past: the prisoners had blabbed about it. "It was impossible to show any leniency now!"[16] Soon after this, he allows her the visit after all.

Ultimately the question arises: Can alternative realities be presented with equal verisimilitude? Can a writer enable the readder, in Robert Frost's phrase, to travel both roads and be one traveler? Joseph Frank deems Flaubert's "cutting back and forth between various levels of action" a necessary approach to "simultaneity of perception" because "language proceeds in time"(322). Mr. Nabokov, who disbelieves in time, has sought to transcend its limitations.

Hermann, the insane narrator of *Despair*, opens Chapter Three as follows: "How shall we begin this chapter? I offer several variations to choose from"(53). All three ensuing beginnings, and especially Hermann's interlaced remarks, contribute to the narrational mainstream. Despite their sequence upon the printed page, they ultimately blend as a co-existent triple alternative. John Barth's narrator Todd Andrews had gone still further in *The Floating Opera* by offering two parallel columns designed to be read simultaneously. As with Nabokov, each alternative instructively contributes.[17]

In *Ada* (the setting of which is itself a sort of alternative reality to our own) time seems to divide or split as Van Veen places an automatic to his head and presses the trigger. "Nothing happened—or perhaps everything happened, and his destiny simply forked at that instant..."(445). A few lines later, we discover that "...what he held in his right hand was no longer a pistol but a pocket comb which he passed through his hair at the temples." This casual shift from one reality to another evinces what Mr. Nabokov has termed "the special logic of dreams."[18] Van's vividly imagined suicide renders the surviving reality quite dull by contrast. Similarly, his imagined duel with Ada's husband (which also seems in context to occur) splits and lapses into mundane reality. "Van got his adversary plunk in the underbelly—a serious wound from which he recovered in due time, if at all [here the forking swims in the mist]. Actually it was all much duller"(531). Typically, the imagined reality vividly lingers—as did the remembered one, vainly invaded by ghostly emissaries.

172

Look at the Harlequins! may be deemed a refined culmination of Nabokovian hints at alternative realities. For whereas the characters in *Ada* inhabit a world whence our own world is "insanely" inferred, this later novel features a hero who "dreads" that he himself impersonates "a real being" in another reality.[19] And since Vadim is patently a variation on Vladimir Nabokov, the reader confirms both suspected alternatives: the person as well as the world. Indeed, he enjoys a faintly disturbing perspective upon Vadim's "...feeling of its all being a nightmare that I had had or would have in some other existence, some other bound sequence of numbered dreams"(174).

Vladimir Nabokov's superimposed and alternative realities may be seen as suggestive attempts to transcend the limitations of time and space. By asserting his powerful detachment, the writer stands out as creator, possibly an analogous one. Indeed, this relentless transcending of space and time in art promotes a glimmer of uneasy insight into life itself: the reader may begin to wonder just Who is writing his own story. He may even begin to suspect, "with relief, with humiliation, with terror," as Borges has put it, that "he too" is "a mere appearance, dreamt by another."[20] The Creator, in Sir James Jeans' words, is envisioned as "working outside time and space, which are part of his creation, just as the artist is outside his canvas."[21] Thus the "mind of such a Creator is dimly inferred to be a dimension wherein "the atoms out of which our individual minds have grown exist as thoughts"(181). And the exhilarating, but disturbing, aspect of such inferences is that we can imagine the existence, but not the essence, of alternative realities. We can fully visualize temporal superimposings only in one continuous reality. One "magic carpet," however folded, merely suggests another. Alternative realities may only be conjectured—as, in *Ada*: "...when we happen to die in our sleep, but continue our normal existence, with no perceptible break in the faked serialization, on the following, neatly prepared morning, with a spurious past discreetly but firmly attached behind"(445). Vadim (in *Look at the Harlequins!*) seems to have the last word: "...I was bothered that night, and the next and some time before, by a dream feeling that my life was the non-identical twin, a parody, an inferior variant of another man's life, somewhere on this or another earth"(89).

NOTES

1. Joseph Frank, "Spacial Form in Modern Literature," Robert Wooster Stallman, ed., *Critiques and Essays in Criticism: 1920-1940* (New York, 1949), p. 322. Subsequent references will be to this edition.

2. Vladimir Nabokov, *Speak, Memory* (New York, 1966), p. 139. Subsequent references will be to this edition.

3. Vladimir Nabokov, *Lolita* (New York, 1955), p. 120. Subsequent references will be to this edition.

4. Vladimir Nabokov, *Transparent Things* (New York, 1972), p. 18.

5. Vladimir Nabokov, *Pale Fire* (New York, 1966), p. 196.

6. Vladimir Nabokov Talks About Nabokov," *Vogue*, December 1969, p. 190.

7. Stephen Suagee, "An Artist's Memory Beats All Other Kinds: An Essay on *Despair*," Carl R. Proffer, ed., *A Book of Things about Vladimir Nabokov* (Ann Arbor, 1974), p. 55.

8. Vladimir Nabokov, *Despair* (New York, 1966), p. 46. Subsequent references will be to this edition.

9. Vladimir Nabokov, *Ada* (New York, 1969), p. 41. Subsequent references will be to this edition.

10. F.M. Dostoevskii, *Sobranie sochinenii* (Moscow, 1956-58), IX, 145-46. Subsequent references will be to this edition.

11. Robert Belknap, *The Structure of the Brothers Karamazov* (The Hague, 1967), pp. 99-100.

12. Simon Karlinsky, "Nabokov and Chekhov: the Lesser Russian Tradition," *Tri-Quarterly*, Winter 1970, p. 13. See also Karlinsky's "Dostoevsky as Rorschach Test," *The New York Times Book Review,* June 13, 1971.

13. Yurii Olesha, *Povesti i rasskazy* (Moscow, 1965), p. 61. Subsequent references to Olesha will be to this volume.

14. Vladimir Nabokov, *Nabokov's Quartet* (New York, 1966), p. 43.

15. Vladimir Nabokov, *The Real Life of Sebastian Knight* (Norfolk, Conn., 1959), p. 173.

16. Alexander Solzhenitsyn, *V kruge pervom* (New York, 1968), p. 138.

17. Mr. Nabokov has two people talking simultaneously in *King, Queen, Knave* "...so that their dialogue is hard to record. Music paper would be necessary with two clefs. As he was saying: 'You were the last person...' she was already continuing: '...ten seats away from you.' "(New York, 1968, p. 173). The "two clefs" seem similar to Barth's two columns of print, except that as recorded, Nabokov's dialogue still cuts back and forth, recalling Flaubert (who may be parodied here, as in other parts of the novel).

Another example of Flaubert's device occurs in *Pale Fire,* where time explicitly "forks" and the focus abruptly shifts back and forth between the Shades watching television and their daughter's suicide (33-6).

A slight variation appears in a stream of consciousness in *King, Queen, Knave* as frustrated Franz, walking down the street, imagines Martha undressing for bed: "Three or four houses more, and she will be naked"(120).

18. Vladimir Nabokov, *Nikolai Gogol* (New York, 1961), pp. 32-33.

19. Vladimir Nabokov, *Look at the Harlequins!* (New York, 1974), pp. 96-97. Subsequent references will be to this edition.

20. Jorge Luis Borges, *Labyrinths* (New York, 1964), p. 50.

21. Sir James Jeans, *The Mysterious Universe* (New York, 1958), p. 177. Subsequent references will be to this edition.

How not to panic when you're made a ghost:
Sidle and slide, choose a smooth
                               surd, and coast,
Meet solid bodies and glissade right through,
Or let a person circulate through you.
                               —*Pale Fire* (37-38)

He did believe, dimly, in a democracy of
ghosts. The souls of the dead, perhaps,
formed committees, and these, in continuous session, attended to the destinies
of the quick.
                               —*Pnin* (136)

Chapter Thirteen

**NABOKOV'S GHOSTS:
SOME NOTES ON**
TRANSPARENT THINGS

In 1972, John Updike can-
didly confessed: "I do not understand Vladimir Nabokov's new
novel, *Transparent Things*."[1]
Perhaps because of this and similar responses, Nabokov himself
chose in 1973 to publish some
clues about the novel.[2] Using
these clues, the present essay
seeks to work towards an understanding of *Transparent Things*.

Two other Nabokov works
may be seen as a helpful background. In *Pale Fire*, a roundlet
of pale light spells out, during an
"electric storm,"[3] a somewhat
garbled warning that could presumably have saved John Shade's
life. But the letters "not ogo old
wart," very possibly sent by
Shade's deceased sister Maud, are
never interpreted as "not to go
"Goldworth." This may remind
us of "The Vane Sisters," wherein the dead exert a faint, undetected influence. In Nabokov's
own words, the narrator " . . . is
supposed to be unaware that his
last paragraph has been used
acrostically by two dead girls to

assert their mysterious participation in the story."[4] We shall now attempt to trace the "mysterious participation" of the dead in *Transparent Things*, which participation has remained generally undetected despite the clues offered subsequently by Nabokov himself.

One reason for the difficulty of detecting the dead's influence in this novel is that readers tend automatically to attribute first person references to the author. As will be shown, however, such words (I, me, my, we, us, our) are sometimes not authorial but ghostly. In Nabokov's words: "Reviewers of my book made the mistake of assuming that seeing through things is the professional function of a novelist. . . . Unlike the mysterious observer or observers in *Transparent Things*, a novelist is, like all mortals, more fully at home on the surface of the present. . ." (*S.O.*, 195).

Given this clue, the first person references on page one of the novel may be seen to refer to its "mysterious observers."

> When *we* concentrate on a material object, whatever its situation, the very act of attention may lead to our involuntarily sinking into the history of that object. Novices must learn to skim over matter if they want to stay at the exact level of the moment. Transparent things, through which the past shines![5]

However eerie, it does seem quite possible to attribute this passage not to a novelist, who, as Nabokov suggests, "is, like all mortals, more fully at home on the surface of the present," but to a deceased observer. Thus, the words *"we"* and "our" refer to the dead in general; "novices," to the recently deceased.

Nabokov has partially admitted this. Asked about the identity of "I" (line 1) and the above *"we"* (line 14), he replied: "An incidental but curiously active component of my novel is Mr. R. . . . ." (*S.O.*, 195). Explaining that Mr. R. annoyingly inserts expressions such as "you know," Nabokov continues: "A good specimen is his intrusive, though well meant, admonition in the last line of my last chapter: 'Easy, you know, does it, son.'" As Nabokov himself concludes: " . . . it is no other than a discarnate, but still rather grotesque, Mr. R. who greets newly-dead Hugh in the last line of the book" (*S.O.*, 196). At this point, the hero Hugh Person has just died and is presumably becoming accustomed to a new state of being. The sentence immediately preceding

R.'s "admonition" reads: "This is, I believe, *it*: not the crude anguish of physical death but the incomparable pangs of mysterious mental maneuver needed to pass from one state of being to another." Very possibly, the "I" of this sentence is also the deceased Mr. R., who thus "intrudes as a component" (to use Nabokov's words) just before his final "admonition." Two clues are the rather "annoyingly inserted" (as Nabokov puts it) "I believe" and, as will be shown, the italics of *"it."*

We may also suppose that Chapter One of the novel occurs in another state of being, *after* the hero's death; the beginning of the story, in our dimension at least, is Chapter Two (Hugh's fourth visit to Switzerland), or, chronologically in our dimension, the second sentence of Chapter Four (Hugh's first visit).[6] Nabokov himself has also hinted at this:

> On the threshold of my novel Hugh Person is welcomed by a ghost or ghosts—by his dead father, perhaps, or dead wife; more probably, by the late Monsieur Kronig, former director of the Ascot Hotel; still more probably by Mr. R.'s phantom. This promises a thriller: whose ghost will keep intruding upon the plot? (*S.O.*, 196)

We shall now attempt to trace the intranovel clues suggesting "whose ghost intrudes upon" *Transparent Things.* Chapter One begins as follows: "Here's the person I want. Hullo, person! Doesn't hear me." The speaker is not, as it seems at first, the author,[7] but rather the deceased Mr. R., who, while both he and Person are still alive, greets Hugh in exactly the same way: "Hullo, Person!" (30). In Chapter One, Hugh has just died and is presumably still "passing from one state of being to another." The notion of "wanting a person" thus becomes rather disquieting. As will be shown, various ghosts "want" Hugh (though some more than others) to join them in their new state of being.

Perhaps because Hugh killed his wife Armande, her ghost seems to "want" him (and his prerequisite death) most of all. Late in the novel we are told that "something connected with spectral visitations had impelled him to come all the way from another continent" (94). This is immediately explained by the fact that after Armande's death, she frequently appeared to Hugh in a Swiss or Italian setting in his dreams. He is thus slightly influenced by these dreams to return to the setting where he will die: "The desideratum was a moment of contact with her essential image in exactly remembered surroundings" (95).

This spectral dream influence is explained by one of Mr. R.'s ghost's narrational intrusions. (He is easily recognized by choppy colloquial expressions, one of which echoes the title of his book: "O.K." and "on the other, tralatitiously speaking, hand."[8]) "Direct interference in a person's life," says R.'s ghost, "does not enter our scope of activity" (92). "The most we can do . . . is to act as a breath of wind and to apply the lightest, the most indirect pressure such as *trying* to induce a dream that we *hope* our favorite will recall as prophetic if a likely event does actually happen." R.'s ghost then explains that "we depend on italics"—which tends to reconfirm his spectral presence (noted above) both on page one (*"we,"* line 14) and in the penultimate sentence of the novel ("This is, I believe, *it*. . .").

Even outside of Hugh's dreams, Armande's ghost seems to "act as a breath of wind and to apply the lightest, the most indirect pressure." When Hugh arrives for his fourth, and fatal, visit, the hotel receptionist speaks "with his late wife's habitual intonation" (4). Ostensibly, the receptionist may seem to mimic Armande because Hugh is trying to recapture the memory of his dead wife. But when we later learn of Armande's spectral, and influential, dream appearances, and when the faintly Armande-like receptionist gives Hugh the "good news" (99) that he can have the room where he will die, Armande's "indirect pressure" seems quite probable even outside Hugh's dreams.

Just before this, Hugh enters the hotel lounge, where "there were only two people" (95). One is the occupant of the room in which he will die—deducible from the ham fat she wraps in a napkin (96), presumably for her dog, who is responsible for her departure (99) and thus, for Hugh's getting his death room. The other person is a Swiss businessman whose "English resembled in many ways that of Armande, both in grammar and intonation" (96). He speaks to Hugh about "a man who murdered his spouse," which apparent coincidence may be interpreted as further evidence of Armande's ghostly influence upon the web of fate now being spun about Hugh.

Yet another instance of Armande's spectral influence on Hugh's waking life occurs when he returns to the climbing trails where he first made love to Armande. Then, we were told of a "minor miracle" (55), a very special kiss after the lovemaking. "A shiver of tenderness rippled her features, as a breeze does a reflection

178

. . . she dissolved with the sun. . . . That kiss, and not anything preceding it, was the real beginning of their courtship." Now, as Hugh returns to these same climbing trails, it begins to rain: "He felt a first kiss on his bald spot and walked back to the woods and his widowhood" (91). This seems almost literally to be, in R.'s ghost's words, Armande's ghost "acting as a breath of wind," but Hugh of course never realizes the spectral influence. In fact, we are later told that he "had not even found" the location of the "unforgettable kiss" (94-95). The elemental echo of this "minor miracle" kiss, even though undetected by Hugh, may indicate that Armande's ghost "wants" his death not only vengefully but with an admixture of loneliness and even tenderness.

Just prior to Hugh's death, R.'s ghost intrudes upon the narration once again. The first clue is his statement that "Novices" (read "the recently deceased," as on page one re "transparent things") are fond of seeing through a person's head to his pillow. "Person, *this* person," R.'s ghost continues (further confirming his presence with italics), "was on the imagined brink of imagined bliss when Armande's footfalls approached. . . . This is where the orgasm of art courses through the whole spine with incomparably more force than sexual ecstasy or metaphysical panic" (102). At this point Armande's ghost enters *through* Hugh's (closed) door and apparently "induces," to use R.'s ghost's term, a prophetic dream: "At this moment of her now indelible dawning through the limpid door of his room he felt the elation a tourist feels when taking off. . . ." On this dream flight, the "air hostess" is Armande (this was previewed on p. 67). Finally, when the airplane "explodes" with a "cough," Hugh awakes "coughing" in the hotel fire which kills him. A final eerie touch is added as: " . . . he realized before choking to death that a storm outside was aiding the inside fire" (103). This seems considerably stronger than a "breath of wind" influence, and we may suspect here some manipulation by the "real" author, von Librikov, although the storm's force could be seen as a collective effort of several ghosts.[9]

Hugh's death also seems desired by his father's ghost. Hugh's father dies while trying on trousers in a clothing store "as if falling from some great height" (15). Soon after this, Hugh opens the window of his fourth-floor hotel room and: "our acrophobic Person felt the pull of gravity inviting him to join the night and his father" (19). This echo of Hugh's father's oddly described death renders the "invitation" faintly sinister. Hugh, a former sleepwalker, counters his father's spectral influence by sitting "in an armchair until dawn."

Just prior to Hugh's father's death, Hugh had become greatly annoyed with him. At one point, he had impatiently "wrenched" an umbrella from his father's fumbling hands, "fiercely" folding the thing himself (11). The umbrella is then focused in a clothing-store mirror as we read of Hugh's father's death (15). Eighteen years later, when Hugh arrives to die in Switzerland, he finds in his hotel room "a bulbless and shadeless lamp resembling the carcass of a broken umbrella" (6). This slightly ominous description may be seen to underscore Hugh's previous discourtesy to his father and to suggest that the latter's ghost, like Armande's, desires his death.

Kronig's ghost, also mentioned by Nabokov as probably greeting newly-dead Hugh on the threshold of the novel, makes no appearances that I have been able to detect. Of course, it seems quite possible that Kronig, the former director of the Ascot Hotel, still lurks there in spectral aspect, especially since Hugh is moved to ask about him when he arrives there to die. Also quite possibly, Hugh's unflattering recollection of Kronig—"fat face, false jovial-ity" (3)—induces the latter's ghost, like Hugh's father's, to "want" Hugh. Yet another factor is that Kronig committed suicide, as the faintly Armande-like receptionist tells Hugh (4). Hugh's unwitting "decision to die" (discussed below) can be seen as a form of suicide.

Mr. R.'s ghost, who sometimes intrudes to speak for all the ghosts ("we," "novices," etc.), also "wants" Hugh but seems in no hurry. After we are told the history of a pencil early in the novel, Mr. R.'s ghost declares: "Alas, the solid pencil itself as fin-gered briefly by Hugh Person still somehow eludes us! But *he* won't, oh no" (8). As usual, the italics and colloquial style signal R.'s ghost's intrusion into the narration.

What is perhaps the novel's most uncanny passage begins when the faintly Armande-like receptionist says *"Mais"* to Hugh. She is then interrupted by a narrational voice which explains that Hugh "was conscious of something or somebody warning him that he should leave" (98). But Hugh, we are told, does not "heed" this warning, whereupon the receptionist repeats her *Mais!* and gives him the "good news" that his (death) room is available.

Strangest of all, Hugh's warning seems to come from another sort of ghost. It is termed Hugh's "umbral companion" by the narrational voice, which declares: " . . . and had he been without that transparent shadow, we would not have bothered to speak about our dear Person." At first reading, it seems that Mr. R.'s ghost is speaking here. The term "umbral companion" is borrowed from Mr. R.'s writing, and the passage concludes (when Hugh ignores the warning): "We thought that he had in him a few years of animal pleasure; we were ready to waft that girl into his bed, but after all it was for him to decide, for him to die, if he wished." As a former lecher, R.'s spectral self would presumably allow Hugh some more sex—and perhaps even "enjoy" observing it. But this is not the choppy, colloquial style of R.'s ghost's intrusions, and the italics (of *Mais*) are the receptionist's. Moreover, this narrational voice ("we were ready to waft that girl") clearly does not speak for the two ghosts who seem impatient for Hugh's death. This, I think, is the voice of von Librikov, who was willing to spare Hugh temporarily. If so, the situation seems strangely symmetrical to an earlier one. Hugh, who "disliked insects," was about to "crush" a butterfly, but: "a mood of unusual kindliness made him surmount the impulse" (90). If the butterfly emblematically suggests von Librikov, the notion that Hugh could have spared *him* proves appropriately illusory: as Hugh tries to help the butterfly, it "vigorously" sails away. This however is pure speculation, and it still does not explain just who (or what) Hugh's "umbral companion" is—a being which, if my speculation is correct, von Librikov would have permitted to delay Hugh's death had Hugh only heeded its warning.

As traced above, various ghosts, in Nabokov's words, "intrude upon" *Transparent Things*. The last two sentences and first chapter of the novel both occur, in that order, in an unearthly, spectral dimension, after the hero's death. The ghosts are often identifiable as Mr. R.'s (which intrudes "verbally," posing as the real author) and Armande's and Hugh's father's (both of which intrude relatively "physically"). All three seem to "want" Hugh; Armande's, the most and R.'s, least. When R.'s ghost intrudes upon the narration, sometimes speaking for all the ghosts, his first person references deceptively seem authorial. Once one is aware of R.'s ghost's intrusions, however, expressions like "our person" become quite ominous as Hugh Person unwittingly encounters various spectral influences tending to lead him to his death. Strangest of all is Hugh's "umbral companion," who seems a different sort of spectral being and who intrudes only once, whereupon Hugh, failing to heed its warning, dies.

Two additional, and very tentative, conclusions may be suggested. First, the fact that newly-dead Hugh "doesn't hear" R.'s ghost's greeting in line one of the novel may indicate that Hugh has still not quite successfully "passed from one state of being to another." This contrasts with Cincinnatus's spectral self (after he dies at the end of *Invitation to a Beheading*), who makes "his way in that direction where, to judge by the voices, stood beings akin to him."[10] Hugh may thus still be at a precarious stage of transition, not yet able to "hear" kindred voices. Someone, or something, seems concerned about this. After Mr. R.'s ghost's second "Hullo, person!" (page one) he continues: "What's the matter, don't pull me. I'm *not* bothering him. Oh, all right." The apparently helpful being that "pulls" R.'s ghost (and which the latter apparently heeds) may possibly be Hugh's "umbral companion."

NOTES

1. John Updike, "The Translucing of Hugh Person," *The New Yorker*, November 18, 1972, p. 242.

2. Vladimir Nabokov, *Strong Opinions* (New York, 1973), pp. 194-96. Subsequent references will be indicated by *S.O.* in parentheses.

3. Vladimir Nabokov, *Pale Fire* (New York, 1966), p. 134. As Andrew Field has noted, there is a theme of fearing electricity in Nabokov's works (*Nabokov: His Life in Part*, New York, 1977, p. 11).

4. Vladimir Nabokov, *Nabokov's Quartet* (New York, 1966), p. 10.

5. Vladimir Nabokov, *Transparent Things* (New York, 1972), p. 1. Subsequent references will be to this edition.

6. A precedent for this circularly twisted chronology may be found in Nabokov's short story "The Circle," which opens: "In the second place . . ." and ends with a sentence beginning "In the first place." (*A Russian Beauty and Other Stories*, New York, 1973, pp. 255, 168.)

7. Nabokov has stated that the real, or main, author of *Transparent Things* is "an incomparably better artist than Mr. R."—"The infuriatingly smiling Adam von Librikov . . . an anagrammatic alias than any child can decode" (*S.O.*, pp. 195-96).

8. R.'s book is called *Tralatitions*, which, as we have been told, means "metaphor" (69).

9. Another eerie possibility is that Armande's ghost tries to promote Jacque's death. He was her lover before her marriage and probably after it, in Chute, Colorado (see pp. 66-67), where he eventually lies "buried under six feet of snow" (94).

10. Vladimir Nabokov, *Invitation to a Beheading* (New York, 1965), p. 223.

INDEX